SATYA P. AGARWAL,
URMILA AGARWAL,
in Collaboration with WILL TUTTLE

PRACTICAL VEDANTA MOVEMENT

Prasthanatraya widened to "Panch-Shastra"

New Age Books
New Delhi (India)

PRACTICAL VEDANTA MOVEMENT: Prasthanatraya widened to "Panch-Shastra"

Published by
NEW AGE BOOKS
A-44, Naraina Industrial Area, Phase-I
New Delhi–110 028 (INDIA)
E-mail: nab@newagebooksindia.com
Website: www.newagebooksindia.com

ISBN: 978-81-7822-477-0

First Edition: Delhi, **2016**

NAB Cataloging-in-Publication Data
PRACTICAL VEDANTA MOVEMENT
ISBN 978-81-7822-477-0
(Preface, Acknowledgement)

Printed and published by
RP Jain for New Age Books
A-44, Naraina Industrial Area
Phase-1, New Delhi 110 028. India

Dedicated To

Swami Vivekananda who started the Practical Vedanta Movement in 1896

Acknowledgement

1. Our special thanks go to Dr. Will Tuttle who accepted our request and wrote chapter 9, and also to his colleague, Susan Pitcairn, who interviewed him and prepared an excellent draft.
2. The drafting of the rest of the book was a family project. Valuable feedback at the time of finalization of the draft came informally from close friends, viz. Dr. Bhu Dev Sharma, Shri Gulab Khandelwal, Shri Himendra Thakur, Dr. M.M. Goel, Dr. Sham Narula, Dr. Rajan Narayanan, Dr. Satish Misra, Dr. R.S. Dwivedi, Dr. Anil and Babli Chopra, Drs. Sushil and Pratibha Sharma, Dr. Ashok and Mukta Shukla, Dr. Pooran and Kusum Shukla, Dr. Dinesh Sinha, Dr. Ramesh and Seema Godbole, Dr. Narendra and Chand Arora, Sharan Prasad, Santosh Aggarwal, Jaishriben and Ila Desai.
3. Technical and moral support came from all the members of the family, viz. Nishkam, Kokila, Seema, David, Isha, Kiran, Priya and Maya. Close relatives who rendered valuable help include Vinod Kashyap, Madan Mohan and Shashi Agarwal, Prabhat and Ambika Agarwal, Arun and Ritu Gupta, Veena and Anil Kumar, Manju and Dhanendra Kumar, Renu Mital, Dr. K.M. Mital, Rakesh and Alka Mital, Anil Narang, Savita and Anil Agarwal, and Abhay Bhushan. To all of them as well as to many others who rendered help but whose names are not specifically mentioned (in order to keep this list short), we express our sincere thankfulness.

Columbia, Maryland
October 2, 2015

Satya P. Agarwal
Urmila Agarwal

Preface

0.1 The year 1893 was a landmark in the modern history of Hinduism, when Swami Vivekananda was hailed as the outstanding delegate to the Parliament of World Religions held at Chicago (USA). The message that he gave, viz. that human beings are not sinners, rather, according to Vedanta, all of them have the Atman, and are therefore divine, captivated the audience. Through several presentations, the picture of Hinduism that he gave to the world, was not that of an orthodox religion, based on rituals perfomed by priests—rather it was a rational, scientific version which incorporated changes over time, so as to keep pace with advancement of knowledge.

0.2 Swami Vivekananda suggested that, in order to put an end to fanaticism and to make all religions serve the changing needs of the human society, the role of priests should be re-assessed, and if found unhelpful, should be redefined. So it was a happy coincidence that, at the same time, but in an unrelated setting, Max Muller, in the course of standardizing the text of Rigveda, discovered that some orthodox priest of Bengal had purposely distorted a Vedic mantra, to support the horrible practice of widow-burning.

0.3 Another Rishi-like presentation that Swami Vivekananda made in the West, in 1896, was on the subject of "Practical Vedanta"— a new expression coined by him. In this book, we focus our attention on this subject. Through a series of four lectures, he set in motion a process of updating "Traditional Vedanta". Why such updating was needed and how it could be done — this was briefly indicated by him in the following words —

> "Shankaracharya arose and revived the Vedanta philosophy. He worked out, rationalized, and placed before men the wonderful coherent system of Advaita. This was accomplished more than a thousand years ago. Today I feel that the practical aspect of Vedanta should be emphasized. For this purpose, along with the Upanisads, teachings of Buddha will have to be used.... In Buddha, we had the great, universal heart and infinite patience, making religion more practical and bringing it to everyone's door. In Shankaracharya, we saw tremendous intellectual power, throwing the scorching light of reason upon everything. We want today the bright sun of intellectuality, joined with the heart of Buddha, the wonderful infinite heart of love and mercy. This union will give us the highest philosophy. Science and religion will meet and shake hands. Poetry and philosophy will become friends. This will be the religion of the future...."

0.4 According to the above statement of Swami Vivekananda, Traditional Vedanta had "intellectuality", but was "lacking in love". The impractical feature of Vedanta was noticed by Indian scholars in the early years of the nineteenth century, after they had come into close contact with European scholars, who were exposed to revolutionary ideas of "democracy" and "liberty-equality-fraternity". Rammohun Roy was the first Indian scholar having a "modern approach"— he wrote in 1823—

> "How can youths be fitted to be better members of society, by Vedanta doctrines, which teach them

to believe that all visible things have no real existence, that as father, brother, etc. have no actual entity, they consequently deserve no real affection, and therefore, the sooner we escape from them, and leave the world, the better...."

0.5 In view of the above, the main point of departure to make Vedanta practical, was to change "escapism" into "activism", i.e. enthusiastic participation by people in worldly activities that are necessary for the prosperity, happiness and ethical progress of the society. In terms of the yogas, this obviously meant giving priority to Karmayoga, and furthermore, to emphasize the practical applications therefof. Swami Vivekananda adopted a comprehensive approach to "activism" which meant tackling (in due course of time), difficult social problems like untouchability as well as economic problems like poverty. He coined the term "Daridra-Narayana" (to tell the people — serve the poor, seeing God in them). He wanted, not only an "identification" of problems, but also their "solution". He was fully aware that such an all-round updating of Tranditional Vedanta was a long-term process, which called for effective steps to be taken, not only to start the process, but also to keep it moving till problems are solved. In 1897, he established Ramakrishna Mission, and thereby made "jagad-hitam" (good of the world) an integral part of Practical Vedanta. This meant adding a social dimension (based on activism), to the goal of human effort, which was so far individual-centered (based on escapism)

0.6 The concept of jagad-hitam, to be effective and meaningful, must include both spiritual and secular aspects, and in due course of time, the welfare of non human beings too. Continued efforts on a long term basis were therefore envisaged. Furthermore, since Ramakrishna Mission was established as a non-political organization, the need to extend Practical Vedanta to the political field, in the years to come, was implied.

0.7 Special remarks need to be made regarding the welfare of non-human beings. Swami Vivekananda pointed out that the widespread Indian practice of vegetarian food was a step in that direction. It was not exactly known when this practice had started, but it was definite that this aspect of Practical Vedanta was set in motion long before Shankaracharya. In the first lecture on Practical Vedanta, Swami Vivekananda expressed the hope that future progress of vegetarianism (whenever it is achieved) would form an integral part of the updating process. In his own words—

> "The ideal is not to eat flesh, not to injure any being, for all animals are my brothers. If you can think of them as your brothers, you have made a little headway towards the brotherhood of all souls, which Vedanta teaches."

0.8 Swami Vivekananda left this world in 1902. Thereafter, the work that he had started, continued to be done, not only by Ramakrishna Mission, but also by other Vedantins. We are of opinion that significant contributions to jagad-hitam were made in the twentieth century by Tilak-Aurobindo-Tagore-Gandhi-Nehru-Radhakrishnan. At this point, just a glimpse of these contributions need be given.

0.9 Two of the most important contributions of Tilak were—

(a) He started applying the Gita to the cause of the country's freedom. Thus he extended Practical Vedanta to the political field.

(b) He wrote "Gita-Rahasya or Karma-Yoga-Shastra", which put Karmayoga firmly in the front — and this provided support to the extended role of the Gita.

0.10 Aurobindo supported Tilak in the freedom struggle till 1910, when he went to Pondicherry. There he wrote "Essays on the Gita". Among the many outstanding features of this book, the one which is particularly relevant for our purpose, was his scholarly opinion against the jagat-mithya doctrine of Traditional Vedanta.

0.11 Tilak's and Aurobindo's writings made it clear that updating of Traditional Vedanta can be done largely on the basis of the Gita, and that the role of Buddhist texts was rather limited (although Vivekananda had thought otherwise in 1896). Swami Ranganathananda put it explicitly in 1995: "The yoga of the Gita is the essence of the philosophy of Practical Vedanta."

0.12 Tagore's "Gitanjali", after the award of the Nobel Prize, helped spread Vedantic messages all over the world. The message of one-ness of all beings was beautifully conveyed through hymn No. 63—

"When one knows Thee,
Then alien there is none,
Then no door is shut.
Oh, grant me my prayer
that I may never lose
the bliss of the touch of the one
in the play of the many."

Through hymn No. 10, he tried to awaken sympathy towards the poorest members of the society—

"Pride can never approach
to where Thou keepest company
with the companionless
among the poorest, the lowliest, and the lost."

0.13 "Tagore's deepest regret, when he approached the date of his death in 1941," writes Uma Das Gupta, "was that his work of village reconstruction could not remove social injustice. He put his absolute faith in

Gandhi's leadership to help the destitute millions."

0.14 Gandhi became the world-recognized champion of the Vedantic message of Ahimsa, to which he gave a path-breaking, socio-political role. He risked his life, while attempting to remove the centuries-old curse of untouchability. He also promoted vegetarianism.

0.15 Nehru made the untouchability-related reform of Gandhi, an integral part of the Indian constitution. Radhakrishnan dedicated his Gita-commentary to Gandhi, and provided the strongest scholarly support to the formulation of Practical Vedanta.

0.16 In the beginning of the 21st century, Western scholars and activists (drawing inspiration from Vedanta and other philosophies) have taken the lead in further updating of Vedanta, by attaching high priority to the welfare of non-human beings. This has been done by means of "Veganism", which is "non-dairy vegetarianism". With the publication of the book "The World Peace Diet", written by Will Tuttle in 2005, this bold initiative has acquired the effectiveness of a campaign. At our request, Chapter 9 of this book, entitled: "Living Vedanta: Will Tuttle and the World Peace Diet", has been written by Will Tuttle.

0.17 The above-mentioned contributions, made on a global basis, have been included in this study. This wider coverage is reflected in the title "Practical Vedanta Movement". The world "movement" was used by Yeats in 1912, when he admired "Gitanjali", and its author (Tagore) as a bright star in the "movement of thought" in India, in the realm of religion and philosophy. There are three common features of the various activities included here—

(a) The underlying approach of the activity is consistent with the Vedantic philosophy of oneness of all living beings.

(b) The aim is to contribute to the good of the world (jagad-hitam), both spiritual and secular, including world peace, and the welfare of non-human beings.

(c) The activity is carried on peacefully i.e. guided by Ahimsa.

0.18 The above-mentioned criteria imply that service-activities of several more Vedantins (including Vinoba Bhave and Pandurang Shastri Athavale) should be included in our study. Due to space-limitation, we can not do justice to them in the present volume, therefore we plan to study them in detail in a subsequent publication.

Contents

CHAPTER I

Shankaracharya's Vedanta – Selected Points

A Brief Life-sketch

1.1 Written accounts of Shankaracharya's life, that are available to us, were composed by his followers, more than five hundred years after he had left this world. None of these accounts can be called a biography. All the writers presented him as performing supernatural feats throughout his life. In fact, the words "Shankara-Vijaya" (meaning Victory of Shankara), occur in the title of all these accounts. We have to choose between summarizing these mythological writings or leaving out most of the material that is available to us. We have chosen the first alternative, hoping that our readers will see through the legends, to obtain some idea of what Shankaracharya did about 1200 years ago (actual dates being uncertain).

1.2 Most likely, Shankaracharya (Shankara, for short) was born in the year 788, in what is now known as Kerala state in south India, Kaladi is the name of the village where he was born (and we, like many others, have been there, as pilgrims). His father's name was

Shivaguru, and mother's name, Aryamba — both were Nambudri Brahmins. Having remained childless for several years, they invoked the help of their family deity, Shiva. One night, Shiva appeared to Aryamba in a dream, saying "you will have a son — would you prefer a long-lived unintelligent son or a short-lived genius?" Aryamba chose the genius. According to the legend, Shankara was Shiva's incarnation (Avatara).

1.3 When Shankara was only seven, his father died. So his mother brought him up and arranged for his education. According to the legend, Shankara showed remarkable talent, and mastered all the four Vedas by the age of eight.

1.4 Shankara developed a keen desire to become a samnyasin (monk) at an early age. But getting his mother's permission was very difficult. She was already a widow and she was worried that, if Shankara becomes a samnyasin, who will perform her last rites (Samskara). Shankara told her that, even if he becomes a samnyasin, he would break the normal rules (which prohibit a samnyasin from doing so), and come home to perform her last rites.

1.5 Still his mother wanted to delay any such move by Shankara. According to the legend, Shankara created a "vision", or rather an "illusion", to persuade his mother. One day, when they went to the river to take a bath, Shankara took a few steps towards the middle of the river and cried out, "Mother, a crocodile has attacked me and I am going to die. The only way to attain peace at this last moment is to obtain your permission and become a samnyasin." His mother had no choice, so she said, "I want you to be at peace". Apparently, this was just an illusion because the crocodile mysteriously vanished.

1.6 Shankara then left home in search of a Guru. Luckily

he soon found a famous Guru, named Govinda, on the banks of the river Narmada. In all his writings, Shankara paid homage, not only to his Guru, but also to his Guru's Guru, Gaudapada.

1.7 When Shankara completed his course of studies, his Guru advised him to go to Varanasi, the biggest center of learning. His knowledge of the Shastras (scriptures) was very impressive, so he attracted many pupils. According to the legend, the first famous disciple was given the name "Padmapada" — This expression literally meant "one whose feet (pada) were supported by lotus (padma) to enable him to walk over the river without drowning". Such a miracle occurred one day when Shankara wanted that his disciple should come to him urgently. But Padmapada was, at that time, on the opposite bank of the river Ganga. Nevertheless, the disciple started walking over the river and successfully reached where his Guru (Shankara) was, because lotuses miraculously supported his feet and saved him from drowning.

1.8 It was during his stay at Varanasi that Shankara wrote his famous commentaries on (i) ten Upanisads, (ii) Brahmasutras and (iii) Bhagavad-Gita. There is an interesting legend about his commentary on Brahmasutras. Vyasa, the reputed author of Brahmasutras, assumed the guise of a scholar, who called on Shankara and expressed his desire for shastrartha (i.e. philosophical discussion to decide whose interpretation is the right one). Shankara readily agreed. But both the scholars put forth countless arguments which seemed to go on and on. Then Padmapada recognized that the visiting scholar was Vyasa himself. Padmapada intervened and begged that the incarnations of Shiva (i.e. Shankara), and of Vishnu (i.e. Vyasa) should end the discussion. Modern writers infer from this legend that, since Shankara's interpretation of Brahmasutras was different from that of the other scholars, he had to face stiff opposition. The legend ends with a declaration by Vyasa that Shankara's interpretation was more profound.

1.9 Shankara visited many philosophical training centers in Varanasi. He noticed that too much emphasis was being placed on Sanskrit Grammar. There is a legend about his visit to one of the centres where a student was struggling to understand the fine points of grammar. Shankara's spontaneous comment was expressed in the form of a song containing twelve verses with the refrain: "Worship Govinda, the world's preserver. When you will experience a crisis in your life, you will realize that grammatical formulas can not help you".

1.10 Shankara frequently went and prayed at the Vishvanath temple in Varanasi. There is an interesting legend about one of these visits. One day, when Shankara was walking towards the temple, an untouchable, accompanied by four dogs, was also walking on the same path. Shankara's disciple asked the untouchable to move aside. Surprisingly, the untouchable replied, "Should I move my Atman or the body?" Shankara immediately recognised that the untouchable was Shiva in disguise, and the four dogs were the four Vedas. Shankara prostrated respectfully before Shiva, and composed five famous shlokas (verses), known as Manisha Panchakam, which contain the declaration, "I worship as my Guru, any one who has realized the self, be he a Brahmin or an untouchable".

1.11 Shankara loved poor men whom he employed as his care-takers. One such man was Trotaka, who washed clothes, fetched water and cooked food. Shankara saw in him a remarkable potential for learning although Trotaka took no interest in formal discourses.

Informally, Shankara taught him how to compose philosophical songs. One day, when Shankara thought of giving a talk, Trotaka was washing clothes, and so he did not show up. Shankara said, "I will wait". Shankara knew that Trotaka was composing a philosophical song. And this is exactly what happened — Trotaka came, singing a song that expounded Adhyatma-jnana (How to realize the self) in a deep and profound way, and was being sung in one of the toughest metres. Following in the foot-steps of Padmapada, Trotaka gradually became the second famous disciple of Shankara.

1.12 The third famous disciple of Shankara was, in his boyhood, "disabled". When the child was very small, his mother took him to the river to bathe. There the boy fell into deep water, and lost his ability to speak. His parents took him to Shankara, who told them, "His disability is temporary — he has a remarkable potential for learning". Shankara taught him, and the boy gradually developed the ability to explain Adhyatma-jnana in a simplified and easy-to-understand way. Shankara named him "Hastaamalaka" which literally means "one who feels that the task assigned to him is as easy as holding an "amala" (goose berry) in one's "hasta" (hand)"."

1.13 The fourth famous disciple of Shankara was a big scholar (Mandana Mishra) who, after being defeated in Shastrartha (philosophical debate), became Shankara's disciple named "Sureshvaracharya". This miraculous transformation has been narrated in the form of a long and interesting legend, which we summarize in the following nine paragraphs.

1.14 Shankara left Varanasi on a countrywide tour, to tell scholars about the greatness of Vedanta philosophy. His first stop was Prayaga (now called Allahabad), the holy city where Ganga-Yamuna-Saraswati rivers meet (and further flow to Varanasi as Ganga river). It was a coincidence that Kumarila Bhatta, the famous scholar of Mimamsa philosophy, was also at Prayaga at that time. Shankara thought of holding a debate with Kumarila Bhatta, but an unforeseen and strange problem presented itself. This itself is a long story, but we will summarize it below.

1.15 Kumarila Bhatta was a well-known Vedic scholar. He was unhappy to see that many persons were being converted from Vedic religion to Buddhism. He wanted to turn the tide by pointing out the comparative shortcomings of Buddhism. So he went to a famous Buddhist scholar and said, "Please teach me Buddhism". However, his intention was not to convert himself to Buddhism, but rather to obtain full knowledge of Buddhism so that he can effectively argue against it. Obviously, this was a sinful act which haunted him, so much so that he decided to burn himself. So he said to Shankara, "I am glad that you want to have a debate between Mimamsa and Vedanta. But I am ending life, so I suggest you hold the debate with my brother-in-law, Mandana Mishra, whom I consider to be my successor".

1.16 The debate between Shankara and Mandana Mishra was perhaps the most memorable event of Shankara's scholarly life. A unique feature of this debate was that, by mutual consent, Mandana Mishra's learned wife, Bharati, was requested to umpire. Bharati said, "I consider it a great honor that both of you asked me to umpire, but I am a busy person, so I will not be able to find time to listen to the full debate. Therefore, I propose to put a garland over the shoulder of each of you — whichever garland first shows signs of fading, it will signify the defeat of that person. I assure you that this procedure is fair and unbiased."

1.17 Both Shankara and Mandana Mishra gladly accepted Bharati's procedure, and started the debate. Since both of them were perfect masters in their respective field, the debate went on for seventeen days. At that point of time, Bharati noticed that Mandana Mishra's garland showed signs of fading. It is a sure sign of Bharati's impartiality that she gave a verdict against her own husband.

1.18 Then Bharati said to Shankara, "I congratulate you, but please understand that you have achieved only 50% victory — now you need to hold the debate with me." Shankara said, "I feel hesitant to hold a debate with a woman." Bharati replied, "According to our scriptures, women have the same rights as men." Shankara said, "I am happy that you have opened my eyes. I gladly accept your suggestion."

1.19 Thus began the second debate. According to the legend, this debate too, continued for seventeen days. Then Bharati said, "Shankara, our debate on dharma and moksa could go on and on. So I suggest that we change the topic of the debate — the next topic could be another Purushartha, say Kama (pleasure, psychological satisfaction)." Shankara replied, "But please allow me one month to prepare myself for a debate on Kama." Bharati said, "That's fine — please go and prepare yourself. We will meet after one month."

1.20 The legend about Shankara's preparing himself for a debate on kama is obviously a myth. But, without it, our story will remain incomplete. So let us continue.

1.21. In order to prepare himself, Shankara used a yogic technique of 'parakayapravesha', that is, to enter into the body of another person for a limited time. It was a coincidence that King Amaru had just died — as soon as Shankara entered into his dead body, the King came back to life. No one suspected that, for four weeks, Shankara was the king. This technique enabled Shankara to learn from the queens, complete details about kama. After one month, he re-entered into his (supposed) corpse, and came back to Bharati for the debate.

1.22 According to the legend, Bharati accepted defeat. Shankara utilized the deep knowledge of Mandana Mishra and Bharati, by assigning to them the task of running a vidyapitha (college), which Shankara established at Sringeri in South India. He also made arrangements that, after the death of Bharati, a temple in her memory would be erected there. This temple still stands, as a concrete expression of Shankara's respect for the learned Bharati.

1.23 After having summarized Shankara's famous encounter with Mandana Mishra, we now turn to his other "victories". Buddhism was losing popular support in India, because of its own degeneration. Shankara accelerated this process by defeating Buddhist scholars in debates. More significant encounters of Shankara were with Kapalika and Bhairava sects, in which human sacrifice was a common practice. While passing through Maharashtra, he nearly fell a victim to a fanatic of the notorious Kapalika sect. While Shankara was absorbed in deep meditation at a lonely spot, a Kapalika saw him and was about to kill him with an axe, when Padmapada fortunately arrived and killed the fanatic before his axe could fall on Shankara. However, Shankara's encounter with the Bhairavas of Ujjain achieved success peacefully. Shankara won over the local chieftains by argument, and they used their authority to put an end to their practice of human sacrifice.

1.24 We already mentioned that Shankara wrote commentaries on Upanishads, Brahmasutras, and

Bhagavad-Gita, which marked a unique, long-lasting contribution to the philosophical literature of the world. Shankara also established centres, assigning to them the important task of teaching Vedanta to people, all over India. Specifically, he established four Pitham (temples cum monasteries cum colleges) in the four regions of India—

(i) Jyotirmatha Pitham at Badrinath in the north, headed by Trotakacharya.

(ii) Govardhan Pitham at Puri in the east, headed by Padmapadacharya.

(iii) Sringeri Sharada Pitham at Sringeri in the south headed by Sureshvaracharya.

(iv) Dwarka Pitham at Dwarka in the west, headed by Hastaamalakacharya.

His contribution is comparable to that of Valmiki and Vyasa. By establishing centres in the four regions of India, he strengthened people's faith in the cultural unity of India.

1.25 Although Shankara was travelling all over India, he had made arrangements to receive regular reports about the health of his mother. As soon as he heard about her serious illness, he went to Kaladi. Although the Vedantic text, Nirvanashatkam, had declared that a Vedantin (having realized the self) considers himself as eternal and unborn, and has no mother and no father, nevertheless, Shankara fulfilled his putra-dharma (son's duty), disregarding the criticism of other Samnyasins (monks). He respectfully touched the feet of his mother, and when her end was near, he prayed to Shiva and Vishnu for her peace. His mother appreciated this very much, and gave her blessings to the son before leaving this world. Finally, Shankara himself performed the last rites of his mother, within the family compound. That site is now a popular center of pilgrimage. Whatever the samnyasins might say, common people of India admire Shankara for fulfilling his putra-dharma. All such (unorthodox) acts of Shankara strengthen our desire to study Practical Vedanta, because Shankara himself had realized that some of the messages contained in Vedantic texts were not "practical".

Shankaracharya's Vedanta — Selected Points

1.26 Innumerable volumes, in many languages, have been written about Shankaracharya's Vedanta. So we need not present his teachings in detail. Rather, since our focus in this book is on Practical Vedanta, we must concentrate on "selected points", based on which the concept of practicality has been developed during the last 120 years. In order to explain the "what and why" of selected points, we list below the main results of our study (reference chapter 10 of this book)—

(a) Practical Vedanta honours most of the philosophical points of Shankara (i.e. the basic mantras), except that the "jagat mithya" doctrine is omitted.

(b) Among the Purusharthas, Practical Vedanta modifies the definition of 'dharma' and 'moksa'.

(c) Practical Vedanta modifies the definition of 'Jnana'.

(d) Practical Vedanta modifies the definition of 'Sattvika karma'.

(e) Vivekananda specified 'jagat-hitam' (good of the world) as the most important element of Practical Vedanta — so the goal of human life is modified accordingly.

(f) Practical Vedanta puts Karmayoga at the top of all the yogas, and rules out karma-samnyasa.

(g) Vivekananda and Gandhi emphasized 'Seva'

(serving the poor, seeing God in them), therefore Practical Vedanta specifies 'Seva-yoga' as the most appropriate synonym of Karma-yoga for modern times.

(h) Practical Vedanta promotes the modern concept of 'Human Rights'.

(j) Practical Vedanta considers it extremely important to give moral support to the cause of 'world peace'.

(k) Since the scope of Practical Vedanta is wider than that of Shankara's Vedanta, two more scriptures (Shanti Parva, and Anu-Gita — both in the Mahabharata) are added, widening 'Prasthana-Traya' to 'Pancha-Shastra'.

1.27 To be "efficient", "selected points" should have a direct, one-to-one correspondence with the results. Secondly, they should fit into the approaches of chapters 1 and 10 (which deal with two different versions of Vedanta). Thirdly, since many Vedantins in India may not feel comfortable with English language, the purpose of writing this book will be better served if we write down the ten selected points in Sanskrit also, in chapters 1 and 10. In fact, we present below, first the Sanskrit version, and then the English one.

1.28 शंकराचार्यस्य वेदान्तः — दशांगिकं चयनम्

I के के मुख्य-मुख्य-मंत्राः ?

प्रश्नोत्तरं — चत्वारि महावाक्यानि तथा अन्ये मंत्राः

महावाक्यानि—

1. प्रज्ञानं ब्रह्म।
2. अयमात्मा ब्रह्म।
3. तत्त्वमसि।
4. अहं ब्रह्मास्मि।

अन्ये मंत्राः —

5. सर्वं खल्विदं ब्रह्म।

6. एकमेव अद्वितीयं ब्रह्म।

7. सोऽहं।

8. ब्रह्म सत्यं जगत् मिथ्या।

II पुरुषार्थानां परिभाषायां किंचित् परिवर्तनम्?

प्रश्नोत्तरं —

9. न हि।

III ज्ञानस्य का परिभाषा?

प्रश्नोत्तरं —

10. ज्ञानं अर्थात् अध्यात्मज्ञानम्।

IV सात्त्विककर्मणः का परिभाषा?

प्रश्नोत्तरं —

11. सात्त्विकं कर्म अर्थात् स्वधर्मः अर्थात् वर्णधर्मः।

V जीवनलक्षयस्य का परिभाषा?

प्रश्नोत्तरं —

12. जीवनलक्ष्यं मोक्षः।

VI भिन्नभिन्नयोगात् का उपलब्धिः?

प्रश्नोत्तरं —

13. मोक्षप्राप्तिः ज्ञानयोगेन।

14. ज्ञानप्राप्तिः अर्थात् कर्मसंन्यासः।

15. असम्भवः ज्ञानकर्मसमुच्चयः।

16. कर्मयोगेन चित्तशुद्धिः (न हि मोक्षः)।

VII दीनानां हिताय का विधिः?

प्रश्नोत्तरं —

17. दानं देयं दीनेभ्यः।

VIII मानवाधिकारं प्रति का दृष्टिः ?

प्रश्नोत्तरं —

18. शंकराचार्ययुगे अधिकाराश्रिता दृष्टिः न हि प्रचलिता।

IX विश्वशान्तिं प्रति का दृष्टिः ?

प्रश्नोत्तरं —

19. शंकराचार्ययुगे विश्वशान्तिप्रश्नः न हि विचारणीयः।

X के के आधाररूपाः ग्रन्थाः ?

प्रश्नोत्तरं —

20. प्रस्थानात्रयः वेदान्तदर्शनाधारः।

1.29 Shankaracharya's Vedanta — Ten Selected Points

I What are the main mantras?

Answer. Four Mahavakyas plus other mantras.

Mahavakyas.

1. Brahman is of the nature of consciousness
2. This Atman is Brahman
3. That thou art
4. I am Brahman

Other Mantras

5. All that is, is Brahman only
6. Brahman is the only Reality
7. I am That
8. Brahman is real, jagat is unreal

II Is there a need for any change in the definition of Purusharthas?

Answer.

9. No.

III What is the definition of jnana?

Answer.

10. Jnana means Realization of the identity of Atman and Brahman.

IV What is the definition of sattvika karma?

Answer.

11. Sattvika karma means Svadharma i.e. Varnadharma.

V What is the goal of human life?

Answer.

12. The goal of human life is Moksa.

VI What is the role of different yogas?

Answer.

13. Moksa is attained by Jnanayoga.
14. When jnana has been attained, then there is no need to engage in karma — that is, a state of karma-samnyasa is reached.
15. A combination of jnana and karma is impossible
16. By Karmayoga, one achieves self-purification (no Moksa).

VII How to help the poor?

Answer.

17. Give danam to the poor.

VIII What about human rights?

Answer.

18. At the time of Shankaracharya, human rights were not considered important.

IX What about world peace?

Answer.

19. At the time of Shankaracharya, world peace was not an important issue.

X What are the basic texts?

Answer.

20. Prasthanatraya i.e. Upanisads, Brahmasutras, and Bhagavad Gita.

Notes

1. We have made use of four sources—
   (a) Madhava-Vidyaranya, Sankara Digvijaya: The Traditional Life of Sri Sankaracharya. Translated by Swami Tapasyananda. Sri Ramakrishna Math, Madras, 2005.
   (b) Swami Agamananda, The Quintessence of Vedanta of Sri Sankaracharya, Sri Ramakrishna Advaita Ashrama, Kaladi, Fifth edition, 2002.
   (c) Y. Keshava Menon, The Mind of Adi Shankaracharya. Jaico Publishing House. Mumbai, Thirteenth Jaico Impression, 2012.
   (d) Internet

CHAPTER 2

Vivekananda's Vision to make Vedanta Practical

A Brief Life-sketch

Naren Prior to Meeting Sri Ramakrishna

2.1 Swami Vivekananda's pre-monkhood name was Narendra Nath Datta or Naren for short. The Dattas belonged to an aristocratic section of the Kṣatriya caste of Bengal, and they displayed several of the traditional characteristics of the Kṣatriyas, including a faith in leading an ostentatious life, in general, but also producing an occasional "Samnyāsin". For example Naren's grandfather, a rich and cultured man, had abandoned wife and children, a high position, fortune, and society at the age of twenty-five, to retire into "the forest" and became a "Samnyāsin", and from that day had never been seen by the family. Naren's father Visvanath Datta, a solicitor in the Calcutta High Court, was known for his varied interests and activities, and being conscious of his own superior position in the society, he exhibited a broad outlook on social and cultural matters, including a feeling of indifference to caste. Naren's mother, Bhuvaneśwarī Devī, was a highly educated woman of regal majesty, whose heroic spirit had been nurtured on the great Hindu epics. During private conversation with his disciples in America, Vivekananda later acknowledged the deep influence of his mother and said, "It is my mother who has been the constant inspiration of my life and work."[1]

2.2 Born in 1863, Naren exhibited in his boyhood, talents in several fields, and the rich family circumstances enabled him to cultivate as many of them as he could possibly do in the early years of his life. The type of personality which Naren developed by 1880 (that is, before he met Sri Ramakrishna for the first time) has been described by Romain Rolland in the following words:

> The possessor of physical courage and the build of an athlete, he [Naren] was a past master in all physical exercises. He could box, swim, row and had a passion for horses. He was the favourite of youth and the arbiter of fashion. He danced the great religious dances with consummate art, and had a delightful voice, which later was to charm the ear of Ramakrishna. He studied vocal and instrumental music for four or five years under famous Hindu and Mussulman professors. He wrote tunes and published a documented Essay on the science and philosophy of Indian music. Indeed he was everywhere regarded a musical authority... At college he was distinguished for his brilliant intellect, embracing with equal zest the sciences, astronomy, mathematics, philosophy, and Indian and Western languages. He read the English and Sanskrit poets. He devoured the historical works of Green and Gibbon. He was fired by the French Revolution and Napoleon. From his childhood up he practised, like so many Indian

children, the habit of meditation. At night he used to pore over the Imitation of Jesus Christ and the Vedanta. He loved philosophic discussions.[2]

2.3 A number of philosophic as well as practical questions arose in Naren's mind and he sought answers to such questions by consulting senior college students like Brajendra Nath Seal as well as leaders of the Brahmo Samaj, including Devendranath Tagore. The advice that Naren received through such consultations naturally varied, and each piece of advice seemed to provide partial help to Naren in his "search for truth". For example, Brajendra Nath Seal put forward the merits of rationalism, and he even spoke in terms of the "God of Reason". Romain Rolland describes how Brajendra's viewpoint could satisfy only Naren's "intellect" but not his "heart":

> Brajendra's rationalism was of a peculiar kind in that it claimed to be an amalgamation of the pure monism of the Vedanta, the Hegelian dialectic of the Absolute Idea, and the Gospel of the French Revolution: Liberty, Equality and Fraternity. He believed that the principle of individualism was "the evil", and Universal Reason "the good"... Brajendra's rationalism appealed to some sides of Naren's domineering nature, but the latter's tumultuous personality was not to be confined within such limits. Although his intellect certainly wished to accept (or impose) the sovereignty of universal reason and to make the foundation of morality an imperious negation of individualism, his life would not agree... Naren's heart and senses looked for the living revelation, the realization of the Absolute, God-made man—some holy Guru, who could say to him, "I have seen Him, I have touched Him, I have been He."[3]

2.4 In comparison to Brajendra Nath Seal's philosophy

of rationalism, the Brahmo Samaj spirit of "categorical reform" seemed to provide a way out of the orthodoxy and social divisiveness of the idol-worshipping Hindu. Naren joined the movement of young Brahmos in Bengal for the education and unity of the Indian masses without distinction of caste, race or religion. Some of them attacked orthodox Hinduism even more bitterly than did the Christian missionaries. Romain Rolland describes why the Brahmo spirit also failed to satisfy Naren's "heart":

> Naren's free and living intelligence quickly realised the unintelligent narrowness of the Brahmos, who were not free from cross-grained fanaticism, and Naren's spirit no less than his national pride was wounded by them. He could not subscribe to the abdication of Indian wisdom before the badly assimilated knowledge of the West. Although Naren continued to attend the meetings of the Brahmo Samaj, in his heart he was not at rest.[4]

2.5 As a last attempt to seek answers to the questions that made him live "in great turmoil of soul", Naren went to Devendranath Tagore and asked him: "Sir, Have you seen God?" Although Tagore recognized the depth of feeling and sincerity that prompted Naren to raise such fundamental issues, he gave no direct reply to his question and only said, "My boy, you have the eyes of a yogi. You should practise meditation."[5] Naren returned unsatisfied, and his inability to achieve the reconciliation of his mental struggles started showing up in the form of dreams, as he himself recalled in later days:

> From my youth up, every night just as I fell asleep, two dreams took shape. In one I saw myself among the great ones of the earth, the possessor of riches, honours, power, and glory; and I felt that the capacity to attain all these was in me. But the next

> instant I saw myself renouncing all worldly things, dressed in a simple loin-cloth, living on alms, sleeping at the foot of a tree; and I thought that I was capable also of living thus, like the Rishis of old. Of these two pictures, the second took the upper hand and I felt that only thus could a man attain supreme bliss... And I fell asleep in the foretaste of that bliss... And each night it was renewed...[6]

2.6 Such was the condition of Naren in November 1880 when a friend of his, Surendranath Mitra, a rich gentleman converted to Christianity, asked Naren to sing a religious hymn, in the presence of Sri Ramakrishna who had by that time been widely recognized as a great spiritual leader.

Sri Ramakrishna Prior to Meeting Naren

2.7 Sri Ramakrishna, whose pre-sainthood name was Gadadhar, was born in 1836 in a poor Brahmin family of a Bengal village. His father, Khudiram Chattopadhyaya, had been deprived of all that he possessed, because he had refused to bear witness to the advantage of the great landowner who was his neighbour. Khudiram died when Gadadhar was seven years old, and the latter had to depend on whatever his elder brother Ramkumar could earn as a teacher. Ramkumar tried to keep Gadadhar into school but without much success. Rather, the inner urge of Gadadhar's life was expressed in artistic emotions, so much so that a beautiful sight of snow-white cranes flying at the edge of a dark cloud made him lose his consciousness. Shortly thereafter, at the age of eight, Gadadhar was again seized with ecstasy when, playing the part of Śiva in the village festivities, he was carried away by devotional music and the sight of artistic images.

2.8 Poor family circumstances forced Ramkumar in 1855 to accept the paid office of a priest in a new temple, founded by Rānī Rasmani, a rich woman belonging to a low caste. This temple was dedicated to the Great Goddess, the Divine Mother, Kālī, and was located at Dakshineshwar, on the banks of the Ganga river near Calcutta. When Ramkumar died in 1856, his younger brother Gadadhar, the future Sri Ramakrishna, began his astounding career of spiritual disciplines and attainments, as a temple priest and devotee of Mother Kālī.

2.9. Of the total period of thirty years that Sri Ramakrishna spent at Dakshineshwar, the first half was devoted by him in personally verifying the efficacy of the diverse mode of *sādhanā* or spiritual discipline prescribed by the various religions. He was first initiated into the Tāntric mode of *sādhanā*. He practised it for two years, and passed successfully through all the stages till he was in a position to obtain from Mother Kālī answers to all his questions on many occasions. He then followed the mode of *sādhanā* laid down by the Vaiṣṇava cult, and is said to have obtained a vision of Śrī Kṛṣṇa. He was next formally initiated into ascetic life by Totāpurī, a great saint who had realized in his life the highest truths of Vedānta, and practised the Vedāntic *sādhanā*. Sri Ramakrishna was then initiated into the Sufi doctrine of Islam and followed all the rites prescribed by that religion. He ate and dressed like a Muslim, offered regular prayers to Allah, ceased to visit Hindu temples, and in three days, obtained the vision of God. Later, he practised similar *sādhanā* according to Christian rites, and on the third day obtained the vision of Jesus Christ. The significance of all these religious experiences has been summarized by Majumdar:

> Sri Ramakrishna made his own life a laboratory for

> the synthesis of different systems of religion—a wonderful synthesis of higher forms of spiritual discipline with rituals and ceremonies—of *sākāra* (God with form) with *nirākāra* (God without form); of Vedānta with devotion; of rationalism with emotion and intuition; of asceticism with social and domestic life.[7]

2.10 Another great distinguishing characteristic of Sri Ramakrishna's spiritual attainments was the spontaneity and depth of feeling with which he wanted to serve the poor. In 1868, when he travelled to holy cities like Varanasi and Allahabad with Mathur Babu, the master of his temple, the sight of human suffering aroused so much sympathy in his heart that he compelled his rich companion to do his best to alleviate at least a part of such suffering. Romain Rolland has described how Sri Ramakrishna's insistence on "sharing the fate" of the poor creatures brought about a change in Mathur Babu as well:

> When Sri Ramakrishna arrived at Deoghar with his rich companion, (Mathur Babu), he saw its almost naked inhabitants, the Santhals, emaciated and dying of hunger: for a terrible famine was ravaging the land. He told Mathur-Babu that he must feed these unfortunates. Mathur Babu objected that he was not rich enough to support the misery of the whole world. Ramakrishna thereupon sat down among the poor creatures and wept, declaring that he would not move from thence, but would share their fate. Croesus [Mathur Babu] was obliged to submit and to do the will of his poor priest.
>
> During the summer of 1870 Mathur Babu made the mistake of taking Ramakrishna in the course of another journey to one of his estates at the time of the payment of dues. The harvests had failed

> for two years running and the tenants were reduced to extreme misery. Ramakrishna told Mathur Babu to remand their dues, to distribute help to them and to give them a sumptuous feast. Mathur Babu protested but Ramakrishna was inexorable.
>
> "You are only the steward of the Mother," Ramakrishna said to the rich proprietor. "They are the Mother's tenants. You must spend the Mother's money. When they are suffering, how can you refuse to help them? You must do so."
>
> Mathur Babu had to give in.[8]

2.11 Swami Shivananda recalls how Sri Ramakrishna set a unique example of the most humble service that he himself rendered to a pariah:

> Sri Ramakrishna, a Brahmin, went to a pariah's house and asked permission to clean it. The pariah, overcome by the proposal, a criminal one in the eyes of an orthodox Hindu, which might have exposed his visitor and himself to the worst reprisals, refused to allow it. So Ramakrishna went to his house at night when all were asleep and wiped the floor with his long hair. He prayed: "O Mother, make me the servant of the pariah!"[9]

Naren and Sri Ramakrishna Together

2.12 Although Naren's singing of a religious hymn at Surendranath Mitra's house in November 1880 drew Sri Ramakrishna's attention, the latter had the capacity to peep into the "depth of Naren's unsatisfied soul", and he asked Naren to come and see him at Dakshineswar. At their next meeting, Naren's song moved the master deeply and he started the process of obtaining Naren's participation in his mission, to which Naren initially resisted. In later years, Naren recalled this occasion and described it thus:

> He (Sri Ramakrishna) said, 'Ah! you have come so late. Why have you been so unkind as to make me wait so long? My ears are tired of hearing the futile words of other men. Oh! how I have longed to pour out my spirit into the breast of somebody fitted to receive my inner experiences!...' He continued thus, sobbing the while. Then standing before me with folded hands he said, "Lord, I know that you are the ancient sage Nara, the incarnation of Nārāyaṇa, reborn on the earth, to take away the misery of humanity". I was amazed. "What have I come to see?" I am the son of Visvanath Datta. How dare he speak thus to me?"... But I remained outwardly unmoved and let him talk.[10]

2.13 A few minutes later, when the Master and Naren joined the group of friends assembled in the larger room, Naren heard the Master say (and these words were an answer to his own nocturnal strivings), "God can be realized. One can see Him and speak to Him as I speak to and see you. But who takes the trouble to do so? People will shed tears for a wife, children, or possessions. But who weeps for the love of God? Yet if a man weeps sincerely for Him, He will manifest Himself to him."[11]

2.14 Naren gradually felt that Sri Ramakrishna was "worthy of respect," but the former also wanted to be on his guard to escape the latter's "eccentric behaviour". The type of conflict between his "intellect" and "heart" that Naren had earlier experienced in his relations with Brajendranath Seal, now seemed to reappear, but in a reverse form, as Romain Rolland describes:

> Naren was struck by the incomprehensible power of Ramakrishna. It attracted him, as a magnet attracts iron, but he himself was made of stern metal. His reason would not submit to domination. If in his recent relations with the rationalist

> Brajendra Seal it had been his heart that strove against his intellect, now his intellect mistrusted his heart. He was resolved to maintain his independence, and to accept nothing from the Master except what could be rigorously controlled by his own reason. The uncritical faith of the others roused his contempt.[12]

2.15 Although several important developments took place to bring Naren and the Master closer and closer, a special mention needs to be made of what happened after Naren's father suddenly died in early 1884, leaving the family heavily indebted and facing starvation. In spite of the B.A. degree, Naren could not get any job and was hard put to it to maintain his widowed mother and younger brothers. At last, unable to bear the distress of the family, and in sheer desperation, he fell at the feet of Sri Ramakrishna and requested him to approach Mother Kālī on his behalf. Then, in Majumdar's words:

> Ramakrishna asked Naren to go himself and ask the favour of the deity. Naren went to the temple, but as soon as he stood before Kālī, he found in her the Mother Goddess in a living visible form. He forgot the worldly affairs and, prostrating himself before her, prayed that he might be endowed with true knowledge and a spirit of devotion and renunciation. When on his return he was questioned by Ramakrishna, he remembered that he had forgotten to pray to Mother to remove his misery. He was sent back, and again a third time, but with no better result... He was assured by Ramakrishna that his family would not be wanting in bare necessities of life, and so it turned out, as Naren could secure some jobs.[13]

2.16 Sri Ramakrishna gradually prepared Naren to be the

head of the group of sincere devotees who would carry out the Master's mission after he himself passed away. He never concealed his feelings about Naren's future destiny. When Naren implored the Master to show him the way to *nirvikalpa samādhi*— the attainment of final bliss after sundering all earthly ties—he was administered a sharp rebuke. "Fie on you!" exclaimed Sri Ramakrishna, "I never thought you so mean as to be anxious for your own salvation only whereas you have powers to do much good to mankind." At his insistent request the Master one day gave him a glimpse of it and said, "Just as a treasure is locked up in a box, so the realization of the supreme bliss will be locked up and the key shall remain with me. You have work to do."[14]

2.17 Sri Ramakrishna also taught Naren that the proper way of doing good to mankind was to view it as worship to God, and that it was sheer arrogance if any feeling of superiority were to be associated with compassion. As the Master put it, "Compassion! Who are you to be compassionate? God alone can have compassion for the mortal. But service to man should be done as worship to God—Jīva is none else than Śiva." Naren understood what the master had in mind, and he told his friends, "Today I have heard a new Truth of great significance. In time I shall broadcast this for humanity."[15]

2.18 A mysterious incident symbolizing the transmittal of special powers from Sri Ramakrishna to Naren, as confirmed by Vivekanand himself, has been described by Majumdar as follows:

> Knowing that his end was imminent, the Master, in order to endow Naren with the spiritual wealth which he himself had acquired after years of superhuman efforts and unprecedented austerities, called him to his side only three or four

days before his *mahāsamādhi.* Having seated him in front and looking intently into the eyes of his dear disciple, he fell into a deep trance. Naren felt the powerful impact of a tremendous force passing into his own body and soon lost all body consciousness. When, after a while, Naren came to himself, the Master was found shedding tears. When interrogated, Sri Ramakrishna softly replied, 'Oh Naren, today I have given you my all and have become a *fakir* (beggar). By the force of the power transmitted by me, great things will be done by you; only after that, will you go to whence you came.[16]

2.19 Naren also learnt from the Master the supreme lesson that it is more "glorious to help even one man" than to be freed from the cycle of birth and death. In the pre-Ramakrishna Hindu tradition as commonly understood (or rather misunderstood), personal salvation or Mukti was viewed as the highest attainment, and taking birth in the *saṇsāra* (for whatever reason) was considered a symbol of imperfection. Sri Ramakrishna, by his own example, helped revive the social service-oriented Hindu view, which was close to the Bodhisattva ideal of putting the salvation of all above one's own salvation. In the closing days of his worldly life, Sri Ramakrishna permitted visitors to seek his guidance on spiritual matters, even though doctors wanted him to take complete rest. As Romain Rolland puts it: He never turned anybody away. He said, "Let me be condemned to be born over and over again, even in the form of a dog, if so I can be of help to a single soul!"

And again, "I will give up twenty thousand such bodies to help one man. It is glorious to help even one man!"

He even reproached himself for his ecstasies, because they took time that might otherwise have been given to others: "O Mother, stop me from enjoying them! Let me stay in my normal state, so that I can be of more use in the world."

During his last days when his disciples protected him in spite of himself from the importunity of devotees, he said, "How I suffer because no one needs my help today!"[17]

2.20 Sri Ramakrishna also explained to Naren and to other disciples, the secret of reconciling worldly life with spiritual development, which in the Bhagvad-Gītā, has been identified as the technique of non-attachment or renunciation of the egoistic feeling of doer-ship. One of the parables which Sri Ramakrishna used to clarify his teaching on this subject was the following:

> As a wet-nurse in a rich family brings up the child of her master, loving the baby as if it were her own, but knows well that she has no claim upon it; so think ye also that you are but trustees and guardians of your children whose real father is the Lord God in Heaven.[18]

Vivekananda Carrying on Sri Ramakrishna's Work

2.21 The work done by Vivekananda during the sixteen-year period (1886-1902), after the passing away of the Master, to put into effect Sri Ramakrishna's Mission, can be broadly divided into four significant stages, namely,

(i) Initial attempts in India from 1886 onward, culminating in the Kanyakumari resolve of 1892.

(ii) First visit to the West, including speeches at the Parliament of Religions, and subsequent work (1893-1896).

(iii) Founding of the Ramakrishna Mission (1897)

(iv) Strengthening of the organization and worldwide network of activities and relationships (1898-1902), till his departure from this world in 1902.

2.22 For purposes of the present study, the most significant point is that Vivekananda revolutionized the traditional image of Samnyāsins by making social service an integral part of their life. Although a formal shape to his new ideas was given by Vivekananda in 1897, all his activities from 1886 onward helped prepare the ground for introducing so radical a change. A first-hand observation of the miseries of the poor in the various parts of the country culminated in what is commonly called "The Kanyakumari Resolve of 1892", and about which Vivekananda himself wrote in a letter from America:

> At Cape Comorin, sitting in Mother Kumari's temple, sitting on the last bit of Indian rock, I hit upon a plan. We are so many samnyāsins wandering about and teaching the people metaphysics—it is all madness. Did not our Gurudeva use to say, 'An empty stomach is no good for religion'? That these poor people are leading a life of brutes is simply due to ignorance. Suppose some disinterested samnyāsins, bent on doing good to others, go from village to village, disseminating education and seeking in various ways to better the condition of all down to the caṇḍāla, through oral teaching and by means of maps, cameras, globes and such other accessories— can't that bring forth good in time?... We, as a nation, have lost our individuality, and that is the cause of all mischief in India. We have to give back to the nation its lost individuality and raise the masses...[19]

Identification of the Social Problems of India

2.23 Vivekananda's assessment of the social problems of India was realistic, rather than academic, because he wandered all over the country for years, with a staff and a begging bowl in his hand. This was done prior to his journey to the West. Initially, after the passing away of his Master, he had thought of going on a pilgrimage to the holy places like Varanasi, Ayodhya, Vrindavan, and Ashramas of Yogīs in the Himalayas. However, after a couple of years spent on such visits, he turned his gaze to the common people for whom the struggle for survival itself was the basic reality. Romain Rolland has emphasized the significance of these travels which provided him with a first-hand knowledge of the poverty, ignorance, disease and misery of the masses:

> He wandered, free from plan, caste, home, constantly alone with God. And there was no single hour of his life when he was not brought into contact with the sorrows, the desires, the abuses, the misery, and the feverishness of living men, rich and poor, in town and field; he became one with their lives; the great Book of Life revealed to him what all the books in the libraries could not have done (for after all they are only collections), which even Ramakrishna's ardent love had only been able to see dimly as in a dream—the tragic face of the present day, the God struggling in humanity, the cry of the peoples of India.[20]

2.24 What bothered Vivekananda even more than the poverty itself, was the gulf between the rich and the poor, between the strong and the weak, and further, the ugly sight of the strong dealing a death-blow to those who are comparatively weak, without any standard of morality. Is this a country or hell, he asked, a country where millions of people live on the flower of the Mohuā plant, and a million or two of *sādhus*, and a hundred million or so of Brahmins suck the blood of these poor people, without even the least effort for their amelioration? This is our native land, he bemoaned, where huts and palaces existed side-by-side.

> Worn-out huts by the very side of palaces, piles of refuse in the near proximity of temples, the Samnyāsin clad with only a little loin-cloth, walking by the gorgeously dressed, the pitiful gaze of lustre-less eyes of the hunger-stricken at the well-fed and the amply provided![21]

2.25 With such a wide gulf between the rich and poor, asked Vivekananda, how can we have unity and fellow-feeling which are the secrets of national greatness? Born, as it were, a disunited mob, we cannot combine. All these dissensions pained Vivekananda and he remarked:

> If one of our countrymen stands up and tries to become great, we all try to hold him down, but if a foreigner comes and tries to kick us, it is all right. We have become used to such slavery, have we not?...
>
> We are intensely selfish. Not three of us can come together without hating each other, without being jealous of each other. Why should the Hindu nation with all its wonderful intelligence and other things have gone to pieces? I would answer you, Jealousy... Because of this we also lack organization and coordination of wills.[22]

2.26 Oppression of the masses, according to Vivekananda, was a big factor leading to the downfall of the country. Another equally significant factor was tyranny over women. The way they were kept under conditions of servile dependence on men made them so weak as to be "good only to weep at the slightest approach of a mishap or danger."[23] Evil customs were particularly injurious to women—child marriage, big gap in the ages of husbands and wives, ill-treatment of widows, and so on. What pained Vivekananda was that evil customs were being adhered to in the name of religion: "A girl of eight is married to a man of thirty and the parents are jubilant over it. And if any one protests against it, the plea is put forward, our religion is being overturned".[24]

2.27 Vivekananda lamented that, in contrast to the death-defying message of the Hindu scriptures—fearlessness and strength—the modern Indian society lived in a perpetual sense of fear. Lack of self-confidence and moral strength, according to him, could be partly traced back to physical weakness, which was identified by Vivekananda as "the cause of at least one-third of our miseries":

> In spite of the greatness of the Upaniṣads, in spite of the boasted ancestry of sages, compared to many other races, I must tell you that we are weak, very weak. First of all is our physical weakness. That physical weakness is the cause of at least one-third of our miseries. We are lazy, we cannot work... What we want is vigour in the blood, strength in the nerves, iron muscles and nerves of steel, not softening namby-pamby ideas.[25]

Tracing the Problems Back to Religious Perversion and Lack of Education

2.28 Of the many angles from which the social problems of India could be analysed—economic, political, sociological, historical, cultural, religious and spiritual—Vivekananda placed the greatest emphasis on the religious and spiritual. He based this on his interpretation of what has been the "nerve-centre" of India's life from time immemorial.

> We made our choice ages ago, and we must abide by it...

> Each nation, like each individual, has one theme in this life, which is its centre, the principal note round which every other note comes to form the harmony. In India, religious life forms the centre, the keynote of the whole music of national life... Social reform in India has to be preached by showing how much more spiritual a life the new system will bring; and politics has to be preached by showing how much it will improve the one thing that the nation wants—its spirituality.[26]

2.29 One of the commonest ways of expressing the state of degradation, using philosophical terminology, is by summarising it as "Tamas" which is one of the three *guṇas* of Prakriti, the other two *guṇas* being "Rajas" and "Sattva". Tamas denotes ignorance, inertia; Rajas denotes incomplete knowledge, intense activity; Sattva denotes right knowledge, peace. While introducing the "Problems of Modern India" to the readers of the Udbodhana, the Bengali journal of the Ramakrishna Order dated 14 January 1899, Vivekananda used the expressions "drowned in utter Tamas", "under the cloak of austerity", "taking the plea of Sattva":

> Do you not see—taking this plea of Sattva, the country has been slowly and slowly drowned in the ocean of Tamas or dark ignorance? Where the most dull want to hide their stupidity by covering it with a false desire for the highest knowledge which is beyond all activities, either physical or mental; where one, born and bred in lifelong laziness, wants to throw the veil of renunciation over his own unfitness for work; where the most diabolical try to make their cruelty appear, under the cloak of austerity, as a part of religion; where no one has an eye upon his own incapacity, but everyone is ready to lay the whole blame on others; where

> knowledge consists only in getting some books by heart, genius consists in taking the name of ancestors: do we require any other proof to show that that country is being day by day drowned in utter Tamas?[27].

2.30 The linkage between religion and social conditions has to be understood as explaining both the positive and the negative aspects, in the sense that, while social progress in the past rested on religious maturity, a deterioration in the social situation at present could be traced back to religious perversion. Vivekananda linked India's doom to ritual-centred priestcraft, orthodoxy, fanaticism, superstitions, and religious intolerance. Having forgotten the true spirit of religion, said Vivekananda, the priestly class made fools of common people by pushing them blindly from one ritual to another, from one evil custom to another. Caste distinctions became more and more rigid, and religious orthodoxy took pride in laying down hard and fast rules as to who can marry whom and who can dine with whom. People discussed for years such meaningless questions as whether to take food with the right hand or the left. If such a country does not go to ruin what else will? asked Vivekananda.[28] Religious perversion also appeared in the ugly forms of exclusiveness and touch-me-not-ism. Vivekananda asked the perpetrators of such a tyranny as well as the sufferers to "come out of your narrow holes":

> Hide your faces in shame. A race of dotards, you lose your caste if you come out! Sitting down these hundreds of years with an ever-increasing load of crystallised superstition on your heads, for hundreds of years spending all your energy upon discussing the touchableness or untouchableness of this food or that, with all humanity crushed out of you by the continuous social tyranny of ages—

> what are you? and what are you doing now?... Kick out the priests who are always against progress, because they would never mend, their hearts would never become big. Come out of your narrow holes, and look forward![29]

2.31 While the priestly class demanded blind adherence to evil practices in the name of tradition, a section of the city-dwellers took pride in aping the West and in denouncing India's past. No serious attempt was made to understand the good points in the spiritual tradition of the society. Kulandaival has summarized Vivekananda's views on the pitiable condition of such a blind imitator of the West:

> He laughs at the ancient sages. All Hindu thoughts to him are arrant trash, philosophy, mere childish prattle, and religion, the superstition of fools. He wants to imitate the West in his daily life and in his thought and actions. Anything coming from the West is good to him. This kind of imitation never makes for progress. It is a sign of awful degradation of man. When a man begins to hate himself and is ashamed of his ancestors, the end has come.[30]

2.32 But how did we create these two degrading extremes— the superstitious priest and the city-dweller imitating the West? Vivekananda identified the root cause as the lack of proper education. By education, he meant, not the amount of information that is put in the brain and runs rot there, undigested, all through life. What he wanted was life-building, man-making, character-making assimilation of ideas. This was not possible, said he, because, we have no hold on the education of the nation, neither secular nor spiritual:

> The education that you are getting now is entirely negative. A negative education or any training that is based on negation, is worse than death. The child

> is taken to school, and the first thing he learns is that his father is a fool, the second thing that his grandfather is a lunatic, the third thing that all his teachers are hypocrites, the fourth that all the sacred books are lies! By the time he is sixteen, he is a mass of negation, lifeless and boneless. And the result is that fifty years of such education has not produced one original man in the three Presidencies.[31]

2.33 While Vivekananda lamented the lack of "man-making" education in general, he felt even more strongly that the women of India were neglected by denying to them education, status, and opportunities of development. The evil of sex-discrimination, according to Vivekananda, represented a negation of the Vedāntic doctrine of the divinity of all human beings, men and women alike. Viewing women as the emblem of Divine Mother, he cried in agony: "The emblem of Divine Mother has been reduced to a slave to bear children. Why is it that our country is the weakest and the most backward of all countries? Because Shakti is held in dishonour here. There is no chance for the welfare of India unless the condition of women is improved. It is not possible for a bird to fly on one wing only."[32] In fact, Vivekananda's British disciple, Sister Nivedita, who was an educationist in England, was assigned the important task of opening a girls' school in Calcutta, where "real" education could be given.

2.34 Non-adherence to moral and social values, by large sections of the Indian society, was partly due to a wrong interpretation of the Hindu scriptures, and in particular of the Karma doctrine. Vivekananda had a chance to point this out when in February 1897, an enthusiastic preacher belonging to the society for the protection of cows came to Calcutta for an interview with him. Bengal was at that time in the grip of a famine, and hundreds of thousands of people were falling into the jaws of death. So Vivekananda suggested to the preacher that, since their society had plenty of resources, they could provide food to the starving people. The preacher's reply and Swami Vīvekananda's comments thereon have been recorded by Sharatchandra Chakravarty:

> **Preacher:** No, we do not help human beings because this famine broke out as a result of their karma, their sins. It is a case of "like karma, like fruit".
>
> Hearing the words of the preacher, sparks of fire, as it were, scintillated in Swamiji's large eyes; his face became flushed. But he suppressed his feelings and said: Those associations which do not feel sympathy for men and, even seeing their own brothers dying from starvation, do not give them a handful of rice to save their lives, while giving away piles of food to save birds and beasts, I have not the least sympathy for, and I do not believe the society derives any good from them. If you make a plea of karma by saying that men die through their karma, then it becomes a settled fact that it is useless to try or struggle for anything in this world; and your work for the protection of animals is no exception. With regard to your cause also, it can be said that the mother-cows through their own karma fall into the hands of the butchers and die, and we need not do anything in the matter.
>
> The preacher was a little abashed and said: "Yes, what you say is true but the Shastras say that the cow is our mother."
>
> Swamiji smilingly said, "Yes, that the cow is our mother, I understand; who else could give birth to such accomplished children?"

The preacher did not speak further on this subject, perhaps he could not understand the point of Swamiji's poignant ridicule.

After the departure of the preacher, Swami Vivekananda told his disciples: "Do you see how much abused the karma theory of our Hinduism has been?"[33]

Plan of Action Based on Practical Vedanta

2.35 By January 1897 when Vivekananda returned from the West to India, he had made up his mind to initiate a plan of action based on an harmonization of spirituality and social service. The underlying views of Vivekanda can , in the terminology of the Gītā, be also called "the Karma-yoga-based socio-spiritual approach to India's problems". In a speech in Madras he announced:

> My plan is to follow the ideas of the great ancient Masters. They were the great originators of society... Circumstances have become a little different, and in consequence the lines of action have to be changed...
>
> The first work that demands our attention is that the most wonderful truths confined in our Upaniṣads must be brought out from the monasteries and scattered broadcast all over the land...
>
> One word more. This national ship, my countrymen, has been ferrying millions and millions of souls across the waters of life. But today, perhaps through our own fault, this boat has become a little damaged, has sprung a leak. If there are holes in this national ship, this society of ours, we are its children. Let us go and stop the holes. Say not one harsh word against this society. I love

> it for its past greatness... I do not dare to put myself in the position of God and dictate to our society, "This way thou shouldst move and not that. Ours is only to work, as the Gītā says, without looking for results."[34]

2.36 By making special mention of the Upaniṣads and the Gītā, Vivekananda made it clear that his plan represented an harmonization of Vedānta and Karma-yoga, or "Practical Vedānta" as he called it. He also called it "real worship", as he explained in his address at Rāmeśwaram temple: "It is in love that religion exists and not in ceremony, in the pure and sincere love in the heart. External worship is only a symbol of internal worship; but internal worship and purity are the real things... This is the gist of all worship—to be pure and to do good to others."[35]

2.37 One of the ways in which Vivekananda brought out the distinction between the "monastery-based Vedānta" and "Practical Vedānta" was how he identified the root cause of misery. Whereas in the former (i.e. monastery-based Vedānta) the root cause of misery is only "ignorance", Vivekananda (explaining Practical Vedānta) specified "ignorance" as well as "wickedness" as being equally responsible for human bondage and suffering:

> You must be pure and help anyone who comes to you, as much as lies in your power. And this is good Karma. By the power of this, the heart becomes pure (*Citta-śuddhī*) and then Śiva who is residing in everyone will become manifest. If there is dirt and dust on a mirror, we cannot see our image. So ignorance and wickedness are the dirt and dust that are on the mirror of our hearts.[36]

2.38 Vivekananda's intention in putting as much emphasis on wickedness as on ignorance was to say that a true knowledge of Vedānta must be reflected in compassionate behaviour. He knew that many of the orthodox scholars who knew Vedāntic scriptures by heart were as much guilty of unkind treatment towards the low-caste, poor countrymen as other high-caste Hindus who were not scholars. "Practical Vedānta", according to Vivekananda, meant theoretical knowledge as well as practice:

> Raise once more that mighty banner of Vedānta for on no other ground can you have that wonderful love until you see that the same Lord is present everywhere. The nation is sinking, the curse of unnumbered millions is on our heads—the unnumbered millions to whom we have talked of Vedānta and whom we have hated with all our strength, to whom we have talked theoretically that we are all the same and all are one with the same Lord, without even an ounce of practice ... Throw away everything, even your own salvation, and go and help others. Ay, you are always talking bold words, but here is Practical Vedānta before you. The first part of this is that you should go to the sinking millions of India, and take them by hand, remembering the words of Lord Krishna.
>
> Even in this life they have conquered relative existence whose minds are firm-fixed on the sameness of everything, for God is pure and the same to all, therefore such are said to be living in God. (*Gītā*, V. 19)[37]

2.39 On other occasions, Vivekananda gave the same message (Help the poor to the extent of giving up your own salvation) under the title of "unselfishness". There is an obvious parallel to the Bodhisattva ideal of Mahāyāna Buddhism which refers to "one who treads the Path not for his own salvation alone but for the salvation of all." [38] As Vivekananda explained his concept of "sharing with others":

> Does one feel happy to taste of a good thing all by oneself? One should share it with others. Granted that you attain personal liberation by means of the realisation of the Advaita, but what matters it to the world? You must liberate the whole universe before you leave this body. Then only you will be established in the eternal Truth. Has that bliss any match, my boy? You will be established in that bliss of the Infinite which is limitless like the skies. You will be struck dumb to find your presence everywhere in the world of soul and matter. You will feel the whole sentient and insentient world as your own self. Then you can't help treating all with the same kindness as you show towards yourself. This is indeed Practical Vedānta.[39]

2.40 Vivekananda characterized "unselfishness" as the test of religion. According to him, the philosopher, the worker, and the devotee, all meet at one point, that one point being "self-abnegation". Conveying the same idea from another angle, he characterised "selfishness" as the chief sin:

> Selfishness is the chief sin, thinking of ourselves first. He who thinks, "I will eat first, I will have more money than others, and I will possess everything", is the selfish man. Similarly, he who thinks, "I will get to heaven before others, I will get Mukti before others", is the selfish man. The unselfish man says, "I will be the last, I do not care to go to heaven, I will even go to hell if by doing so I can help my brothers." This unselfishness is the test of religion. He who has more of this unselfishness is more spiritual, whether he is learned or ignorant, he is nearer to Śiva than anybody else.[40]

2.41 As another example of the terminological variation

used by Vivekananda to convey the same message, he coined the famous phrase "Daridra-Nārāyaṇa" which meant that the service of the poor was the service of God. To Śiva-worshippers he said, "Jīva is Śiva," and explained it further:

> He who sees Śiva in the poor, in the weak and in the diseased, really worships Śiva; and if he sees Śiva only in the image, his worship is but preliminary. He who has served and helped one poor man, seeing Śiva in him, without thinking of his caste, or creed, or race, or anything, with him Śiva is more pleased than with the man who sees Him only in temples.[41]

2.42 By thinking of the poor man as God, said Vivekananda, the risk of arrogance on the part of the helper is minimized. By having faith in God, one gives up the fruits of work unto the Lord, and worshipping Him thus, one does not expect any reward from mankind for the work one does:

> So drive out of your mind the idea that your are doing something for the world; the world does not require any help from you. It is sheer non-sense on the part of any man to think that he is born to help the world; it is simply pride, it is selfishness insinuating itself in the form of virtue.[42]

2.43 Expecting no reward for the work done, as taught by the Gītā, is a relatively easier way of giving up attachment to the fruits of work. Not that the work will not bear fruit; in fact, the law of karma says that any action done cannot be destroyed until it has borne its fruit. A karma-yogin does take into account what effect his actions will have on others, but he does not hanker after deriving selfish gains therefrom.

2.44 A favourite idea of Vivekananda was that we do good deeds in the world, apparently to help the world, but really to help ourselves:

> The main effect of work done for others is to purify ourselves; this forgetfulness of self is the one great lesson we have to learn in life... Every act of charity, every thought of sympathy, every action of help, every good deed, is taking so much of self-importance away from our little selves and making us think of ourselves as the lowest and the least; and therefore it is all good. Here we find that jñāna, bhakti, and karma— all come to one point. The highest ideal is eternal and entire self-abnegation, where there is no "I", but all is "Thou", and whether he is conscious or unconscious of it, karma yoga leads man to that end.[43]

2.45 Within the range of deeds that can be done to help others, Vivekananda included a wide variety, providing material benefits as well as giving knowledge, both secular and spiritual. He recognised the changing needs of the society with the passage of time. Speaking in terms of the Hindu terminology of the four *yugas* or time-periods, he interpreted Vyāsa's words as: "What is needed in this Kaliyuga is giving, helping others, the highest of gifts is the giving of spiritual knowledge, the next is the giving of secular knowledge, next to that is the saving of life, and the last is giving food and drink."[44] However, leaving aside Vyāsa's order of priorities, Vivekananda said, on another occasion, "First bread and then religion": "What we want is not so much spirituality as a little of the bringing down of the Advaita into the material world. First bread and then religion. We stuff them too much with religion, when the poor fellows have been starving. No dogmas will satisfy the cravings of hunger."[45]

2.46 To pay attention to both the secular and the spiritual needs of the society is a special feature of Practical Vedānta. Similarly, it seeks to harmonize science and religion. In a lecture delivered in England, Vivekananda declared:

> Science and religion will meet and shake hands... When the science teacher asserts that all things are the manifestation of one force, does it not remind you of the God of whom you hear in the Upaniṣads: As the one fire entering into the universe expresses itself in various forms, even so that one Soul is expressing itself in every soul and yet is infinitely more besides? Do you not see whither science is tending?[16]

2.47 Although in the interest of those who are in a position to serve others, Vivekananda advised them to do their utmost, but with humility, still from the viewpoint of the receivers of such service, and also in general, he stressed the importance of self-help and self-confidence. Commenting on the Gītā verse VI.5, he called "self-help" as the "greatest lesson":

> It is a tremendous error to feel helpless. Do not seek help from anyone. We are our own help. If we cannot help ourselves, there is none to help us. The Gītā says, "Thou thyself art thy only friend, thou thyself thy only enemy. There is no other enemy but this self of mine, no other friend but myself." This is the last and greatest lesson, and Oh, what a time it takes to learn it! We seem to get hold of it, and the next moment the old wave comes. The backbone breaks. We weaken and again gasp for that superstition and help. Just think of that huge mass of misery, and all caused by this false idea of going to seek for help.[47]

2.48 "Self-confidence" was given so much importance by

Vivekananda that, in Practical Vedānta, it plays the same role as "faith in God". For achieving success in his plan of action (referred to in para 2.35), Vivekananda's main requirement was "men who believe in themselves". In fact, the essence of Practical Vedānta was viewed by him to be a "man-making religion":

> What we want is muscles of iron and nerves of steel. We have wept long enough. No more weeping, but stand on your feet and be men. It is a man-making religion that we want. It is man-making theories that we want. It is man-making education all round that we want.
>
> Men, men, these are wanted: everything else will be ready, but strong, vigorous, believing young men, sincere to the backbone, are wanted. A hundred such and the world becomes revolutionized. The will is stronger than anything else. Everything must go down before the will, for that comes from God and God Himself; a pure and strong will is omnipotent.[48]

Institutional Commitment to Social Service—A Novelty Achieved After Fraternal Resistance

2.49 Hindu tradition speaks of *bhaktas* and saints loving all creatures and helping the needy. But these were generally individual efforts without much organizational support. Also, many of these *bhaktas* felt as if they were being pulled in two directions, one represented by worship of God's image, reading of scriptures, meditation, and preaching to devotees, and the other represented by rendering service to the sick, the poor and the neglected. With the worsening economic and social conditions in India, the importance of rendering service was recognised by reform movements like Brahmo Samaj, but some of its leaders gave the impression that the inspiration for rendering service came mainly from Western influences including Christian missionaries. Therefore such movements could not arouse mass support all over the country on a long-term basis.

2.50 Ramakrishna Mission founded by Vivekananda in 1897 distinguished itself as a religious organisation in Modern India which adopted social service as one of its main goals and which drew the inspiration for this mainly from the Indian tradition. In fact, six sources of inspiration have been mentioned, namely, their Master Sri Ramakrishna, other *bhaktas*, wandering monks, the Upaniṣads, the Bhagavad-Gītā, and the Buddha. Although Vivekananda gave a concrete shape to the social service programme of the Ramakrishna Mission, he said he was only carrying out the teaching of his Master Sri Ramakrishna. The strong emphasis on Karma-Yoga in the entire approach of the Ramakrishna Mission is a clear indicator of the impact of the Bhagavad-Gītā. While Vivekananda based the doctrine of Karma-yoga mainly on the Gītā, he often referred to the Buddha as an 'Ideal Karma-yogin'.

2.51 Sri Ramakrishna was characterised by Vivekananda as one who saw God in every being, whose heart wept for the poor, for the weak, for the downtrodden. But Sri Ramakrishna did not thrust such ideas on his disciples. When the problem of awakening spirituality in the hearts of the common people was raised with the Master, he had said, "Religion is not for empty bellies."[49] Sri Ramakrishna had also declared: "The day when Naren comes in contact with suffering and misery, the pride of his character will melt into a mood of infinite compassion."[50]

2.52 In 1886, when Sri Ramakrishna had fallen seriously ill, his intimate disciples (twelve in number) organized themselves under the leadership of Naren to serve the Master with utmost care, love and veneration. This whole-hearted love of God and devotion to the Master and his ideas led to the formation of the brotherhood, which soon after the Master's departure from this world developed into a Maṭh (Monastery of the Ramakrishna Order). However, its members were often on move with no coordinated and systematic plan of work and it took Naren several years of wandering throughout India and of sharing the misery and privations of the oppressed classes before he was able to assert in 1892 that, to care for the poor and to raise them is the first duty of religion. Subsequently Vivekananda's coining of the phrase "Daridra-Nārāyaṇa" elevated the service of the poor to be equal in importance and value to the service of God, or in Vivekanand's words: "The only God that exists, the only God in whom I believe... my God the miserable, my God the poor of all races."[51] Furthermore, Vivekananda constantly reminded his brother disciples (who wanted to carry out the teachings of the Master) that the only way to help the poor was through the spirit of *niṣkāma* Karma of the Gītā:

> Why should we expect anything in return for what we do? Be grateful to the man you help, think of him as God. Is it not a great privilege to be allowed to worship God by helping our fellowmen? If we were really unattached, we should escape all this pain of vain expectation, and could cheerfully do good work in the world.[52]

2.53 Following the successful visit to the West, and after witnessing the keen interest that the people in South India expressed in his plan of action, Vivekananda arrived in Calcutta in February 1987. At that time the central idea in his mind was to put into practice what he had so long preached, by making the monks devote themselves to an active life of service for the masses and thus to make the monastic organisation a potent instrument for social and spiritual regeneration. His vision of utilizing the energies of the monks for spreading education among the illiterate, helping them fight against poverty and disease, removing social evils and inequities, and raising them to a higher level of morality, meant an innovation in the monastic practices as commonly understood in those days. It was not surprising, therefore, that there were voices of dissent among his brother-disciples. Nikhilananda explains what lay behind this fraternal resistance to Vivekananda's plan of action:

> The dissenting monks were individualists, eager for their personal salvation. They wanted to practise austerities and penances, enjoy peaceful meditation, and lead a quiet life of detachment from the world. To them God was first, and the world came next. At least that was the way they had understood Sri Ramakrishna's teachings. These young monks thought that for one who had taken the monastic vows, the world was māyā; therefore all activities, including the charitable and philanthropic, ultimately entangled one in worldly life.[53]

2.54 Vivekananda knew that the narrow vision of the young monks, focusing on an exclusive search for *mukti*, could only be widened by giving clearer instructions and sincere assurances. Therefore, he repeatedly pointed out to his brother-disciples that to worry about personal liberation was unworthy of those who called themselves disciples of Sri Ramakrishna. Karma-yoga activities carried out with a sense of dedication to the Almighty were as efficacious a means of salvation as meditation and austerities. With so much of misery and ignorance prevailing in the society, the duty of Sri Ramakrishna's disciples, as Vivekananda explained to his colleagues, was to serve the needy as the visible manifestations of God. He also told them that he wanted to create a new brand of monks, who would take not only the traditional vow of personal salvation, but also a new vow of service to humanity.

2.55 After a good deal of clarification, Vivekananda's views prevailed, and he proceeded to give institutional shape to his plan of action. He explained his ideas at a representative meeting of the monks and lay devotees held at Calcutta on 1 May 1987. He was convinced, he said, that lack of organization was a serious defect in the Hindu society. He also cited the example of the Buddhist organization which spread that religion in large areas of the world. He therefore asked for the cooperation of all in order to organize the educational, philanthropic and religious activities which had hitherto been carried out in an unsystematic way. The meeting unanimously approved of Vivekananda's proposal, and in a subsequent meeting on 5 May 1897, formally established the Ramakrishna Mission with the following aims and methods of action.

The aim of the Mission is to preach those truths which Shri Ramakrishna has, for the good of humanity, preached and demonstrated by practical application in his own life, and to help others to put these truths into practice in their lives for their temporal, mental and spiritual advancement.

The duty of the Mission is to conduct in the right spirit the activities of the movement inaugurated by Shri Ramakrishna for the establishment of fellowship among the followers of different religions, knowing them all to be so many forms only of one undying Eternal Religion.

Its methods of action are:

(a) To train men so as to make them competent to teach such knowledge or sciences as are conducive to the material and spiritual welfare of the masses;

(b) To provide and encourage arts and industries; and

(c) To introduce and spread among the people in general Vedāntic and other religious ideas in the way in which they were elucidated in the life of Shri Ramakrishna.

Indian work Department and Foreign Department.

The activities of the Mission should be directed to the establishment of *maṭhas* and *āśramas* in different parts of India for the training of Samnyāsins and such of the householders as may be willing to devote their lives to educate others, and to the finding of the means by which they would be enabled to educate the people, by going about from one province to another.

Its work in the Foreign Department should be to send trained members of Order to countries outside India to bring about a closer relation and better understanding between India and foreign countries.

The aims and ideals of the Mission being purely spiritual and humanitarian, it shall have no connection with politics.

Anyone who believes in the mission of Shri Ramakrishna, or who sympathises or is willing to cooperate with the above-mentioned aims and objects of the Association, is eligible for membership.[51]

2.56 Side by side with the setting up of the Ramakrishna Mission, Vivekananda also wanted to systematize the working of the Maṭha. Although the Maṭha (monastery) had nominally come into existence in 1886, it had to be shifted from one location to another and its functioning was guided largely by unwritten rules based on an implicit understanding of Vivekananda's wishes. In December 1898, when the Maṭha shifted to Belur on a permanent basis, Vivekananda strengthened its organisation by putting down in writing an elaborate set of rules. The Maṭha being a purely monastic institution, the rules provided for disciplined life and spiritual practices, and emphasized the needs of strength of character, self-reliance, and faith in the Master. For new monks also the training to be imparted in the Maṭha clearly reflected the wider vision of Vivekananda, as the following two rules show:

> This Maṭha is established to work out one's own liberation, and to train oneself to do good to the world in every way, along the lines laid down by Bhagavan Shri Ramakrishna. For the women too there will be started a similar Maṭha.
>
> The root of all misery in India is the wide gulf between the lower and upper classes. Unless this difference is made up, there is no hope of any well-being for the people. Therefore we must send preachers to all places to give the masses education and religious teaching.[55]

2.57 Although all the monks appeared to be satisfied with the way Vivekananda explained to them his new concept of religion, namely, the worship of God through the service of the needy, a lingering doubt was still bothering some of them whether the real formulator of this concept was Vivekananda or Sri Ramakrishna. They had heard Sri Ramakrishna speak time and again against preaching, excessive study of the scriptures, and charitable activities, and exhort aspirants to intensity their love of God through prayer and meditation in solitude. Therefore they regarded Vivekananda's activities as out of harmony with the

Master's teachings. One of them said bluntly to Vivekananda, "You did not preach our Master in America; you only preached yourself". Vivekananda retorted with equal bluntness, "Let people understand me first; then they will understand Sri Ramakrishna".[56]

2.58 But things came to a climax one day at Balram's house in Calcutta, when Jogananda, a brother-disciple whom Sri Ramakrishna had pointed out as belonging to his 'inner circle' of devotees, said that the Master had emphasized bhakti alone for spiritual seekers and that philanthropic activities, organizations, homes of service for the public good, and patriotic work were Vivekananda's own peculiar ideas, the result of his Western education and travel in Europe and America.

2.59 Vivekananda at first replied to it in good humour. But he suddenly flared up. "You think you have understood Sri Ramakrishna better than myself!.. Your Bhakti is sentimental nonsense which makes one impotent. Hands off! Who cares for your Ramakrishna? Who cares for your Bhakti and Mukti? Who cares what the scriptures say? I will go into a thousand hells cheerfully, if I can rouse my countrymen, immersed in Tamas, to stand on their on their own feet, and be men inspired with the spirit of Karma-yoga. I am not a follower of Ramakrishna or anyone, I am a follower of him only who carries out my plans! I am not a follower of Ramakrishna or any one, but him only who serves and helps others, without caring for his own Bhakti and Mukti."[57]

2.60 Nikhilananda describes what happened next:

The Swami's voice was choked with emotion, his body shook, and his eyes flashed fire. Quickly he went to the next room. A few moments later, some of his brother-disciples entered the room and found him absorbed in meditation, tears flowing from his half closed eyes. After nearly an hour the Swami got up, washed his face, and joined his spiritual brothers in the drawing-room. His features still showed traces of the violent storm through which he had just passed; but he had recovered his calmness. He said to them softly: "When a man attains bhakti, his heart and nerves become so soft and delicate that he cannot bear even the touch of a flower: ... I cannot think or talk of Sri Ramakrishna long without being overwhelmed. So I am always trying to bind myself with iron chains of jñāna, for still my work for my motherland is unfinished and my message to the world not fully delivered. So as soon as I find that those feelings of bhakti are trying to come up and sweep me off my feet, I give a hard knock to them and make myself firm and adamant by bringing up austere jñāna. Oh, I have work to do! I am a slave of Ramakrishna, who left his work to be done by me and will not give me rest till I have finished it.[58]

2.61 So profound and convincing was the impression created by this incident that no protest was afterwards made against Vivekananda's plans and methods of work. The Karma-yoga-based socio-spiritual approach to India's problems formulated by Vivekananda was thus fully adopted by Ramakrishna Mission.

2.62 Although the right technique of rendering *sevā* is given by Karma-yoga, an ultimate answer to the question: "Why should we render *sevā* to the poor?" is provided by jñāna-yoga or bhakti-yoga. A common argument put forward by *bhaktas* in India is, that although a knowledge of the identity of Ātman in all beings does provide an intellectual base for *sevā*, this by itself is not enough because *sevā* also calls for a feeling of compassion. The *bhaktas* therefore feel that the rendering of *sevā* (service) with compassion is achieved more easily in the path of devotion, as compared to the path of knowledge. The Indian tradition seems to provide general support to this. Moreover, although monks of the Ramakrishna Mission combined Advaita Vedānta with *sevā*, they too have an element of Bhakti. In fact, Vivekananda believed in a harmonious development of Karma, Bhakti and Jñāna, and in his final message to the disciples, he clearly gave priority to *sevā* over other aspects of these paths when he said: "Let the reading of the Vedānta and the practising of meditation and the like be left to be done in the next life! Let this body go in the service of others."[59]

2.63 As we mentioned in para 2.55, the Ramakrishna Mission, under Vivekananda's guidance, kept itself aloof from politics. Whatever might have been the reasons underlying this policy, it averted a likely threat of dissolution of the Mission by the British Government in 1916. Rolland gives a graphic account of what happened after Vivekananda's death and how the revolutionary political agitators (who tried to use the Gītā as a proof of their alleged link with the Ramakrishna Mission) placed the Mission on a collision course with the British Government:

> 1905, the year of the division of the Province of Bengal, marked the beginning of the Swadeshi movement and political unrest. The (Ramakrishna) Mission refused to take part in them. In 1908 it was obliged to make a rule not to receive strangers at night in its establishment, because it feared some were abusing its hospitality in order to prepare their political offensive. It transpired from the answers of political prisoners that more than one, disguised under the robe of a samnyāsin, had cloaked their designs under the name of its work and religion. Copies of the Gītā and Vivekananda's writings were found on several

of them...

In 1916, the Governor of Bengal announced that revolutionaries were joining the Ramakrishna Mission in order to achieve their ends. Fortunately, friends in high places intervened and the danger of dissolution of the Mission was averted.[60]

Exemplary Dedication and Widening Coverage of Service Activities

2.64 Practical Vedānta was the foundation on which the whole structure of the new organisation was sought to be built by Vivekananda from May 1897 onward. Reference has already been made above to the opposition of some of the brother-disciples to this new mode of salvation propounded by Vivekananda. He, however, not only stuck to his guns, but even went to the other extreme of denouncing every other form of salvation. His retort to his critics, that he would follow this path even if it went against the teachings of Ramakrishna indicates the depth of his feeling in the matter. The same spirit of dedication was expressed by him in letters written to his friends. For example, in a letter to Mary Hale dated July, 1897 he expressed a feeling of satisfaction:

Only one idea was burning in my brain—to start the machine for elevating the Indian masses, and that I have succeeded in doing to a certain extent. It would have made your heart glad to see how my boys are working in the midst of famine and disease and misery—nursing by the mat-bed of the cholera-stricken pariah and feeding the starving caṇḍāla, and the Lord sends help to me, to them, to all.[61]

2.65 However, difficult tests of the organization's capability to fulfil its mission against heavy odds were still to come. In April, 1898, when Vivekananda was in

Darjeeling to recoup his health, news reached him of the outbreak of plague in Calcutta. On May 3 1898, Vivekananda reached Calcutta, although his health was not good. He thought he might be of help to his people. They were terror-stricken by the plague and dismayed by the plague regulations. It was as if a storm were about to burst over Calcutta. People were fleeing in panic. Troops were called to quell riots. Vivekananda grasped the gravity of the situation at once. On the day of his arrival at the Maṭha he drafted a plague manifesto in Bengali and in Hindi. He wanted to start relief operations immediately to help the afflicted. When a brother-monk asked him, "Swamiji, where will the funds come from?", he replied with a sudden fierceness of decision: "Why, we shall sell the newly-bought Maṭha grounds, if necessary! We are samnyāsins; we must be ready to sleep under the trees and live on daily Bhikṣā (alms) as we did before. What! Should we care for Maṭha and possessions when by disposing of them we could relieve thousands suffering before our eyes!"[62] Fortunately, this extreme step was not necessary, for Vivekananda soon received promises of ample funds for this immediate work.

2.66 When plague again broke out in 1899, the Ramakrishna Mission undertook relief work under the leadership of Sadananda, assisted by Sister Nivedita and others. About Sister Nivedita's part in the work, we have it on the authority of the historian, Sir Jadunath Sarkar, an eyewitness, "that when the sweepers had fled away, he chanced upon a white woman one day clearing the streets with broom and basket in hand. This was none other than Nivedita, whose courage and sense of civic duty spurred the local youths to take up the cleansing of the lanes and streets, following her example, and make their quarters free from the threat of the pestilence".[63]

2.67 Sadananda himself similarly set an unprecedented example. If the stench of garbage accumulated in a narrow lane repelled even the practised sweepers, he would non-chalantly snatch the basket and spade from one of them and set about removing the decomposed heap till the sweepers too would step forward to help him. At the end, he would congratulate them and embrace them warmly, regardless of their social distance and dirty bodies. Or if there was an uncared-for patient, he would hug him and nurse him to recovery.

2.68 The above incidents bring out in bold relief the ideal of service enunciated by Vivekananda and the exemplary spirit of his close associates, which showed the steadily growing strength of the new organization.

2.69 Almost 120 years have elapsed since the Ramakrishna Mission faced the initial challenges of rendering service to the needy under the most difficult circumstances. The fact that this institution not only maintained the spirit of dedication but also widened the coverage of service activities is a tribute to Vivekananda and his followers: Although a detailed account of such developments is beyond the scope of the present study, it is of interest to note that the social work activities of the Ramakrishna Mission now cover as many as six broad areas, namely:

(i) Educational work
(ii) Health
(iii) Cultural activities
(iv) Rural uplift
(v) Tribal welfare
(vi) Youth movement

Indira Patel, after describing the work being done by the Ramakrishna Mission in each field, singles out 'the inculcation of the right attitude' as a special feature of the Mission's training:

> One point which should be made clear is that the Mission's centers enlist youths or disciples and train them as social workers, the only difference between the academic training and the training imparted in the Maṭha lies in the initial emphasis on discipline, both mental and physical, with a view to inculcating the right attitude over and above generating a sensitivity, so essential in all social work.[64]

2.70 Mention should be made of Swami Ranganathananda's famous book entitled "Practical Vedanta and the Science of Values", published by Advaita Ashrama, Publications Department, Calcutta, in 1995. This book was based on four lectures that Swamiji delivered in 1992—these lectures were in the nature of "follow-up" to four lectures that Swami Vivekananda had given in London in 1896 (where the Practical Vedanta Movement can be considered to have been launched, because the opening statement contained the words "This series of lectures is intended to be a basis").

Monks as Pillars of Ramakrishna Mission

2.71 Renunciation and service are, according to Vivekananda, the twofold national ideals of modern India. "To practice and preach these ideals"—this is how the work of Ramakrishna Mission can be described. Organizationally, the principal workers of the Mission are monks or samnyāsins. In a speech to newly initiated monks in Calcutta towards the end of April 1897 (that is, just a couple of days before the establishment of Ramakrishna Mission), Vivekananda spoke of the glory of renunciation.

"The real aim of samnyāsa is "*ātmano mokṣārthaṁ jagad-hitāya ca*", that is, for one's highest freedom and for the good of the world.[65] Without having Samnyāsa, none can really be a knower of Brahman—this is what the Vedas and the Vedānta proclaim. Don't listen to the words of those who say: We shall both live the worldly life and also be knowers of Brahman. That is the flattering self-consolation of crypto-pleasure-seekers. He who has the slightest desire for wordly pleasures, even a shred of some such craving, will feel frightened at the thought of the path you are going to tread; so, to give himself some consolation he goes about preaching that impossible creed of harmonizing Bhoga (enjoyment) and Tyāga (renunciation)... No freedom without renunciation. Highest love for God can never be achieved without renunciation. Renunciation is the word. *Nānyaḥ panthāḥ vidyate ayanāya,* that is, there is no way other than this. Even the Gītā says: *kāmyānāṁ karmaṇāṁ nyāsaṁ saṁnyāsaṁ karvayo viduḥ,* that is, the sages know samnyāsa to be the giving up of all work that has desire for its end."[66]

2.72 In a speech in California in January 1900, on the subject of "My life and Mission", Vivekananda explained that the Indian concept of Samnyāsa is as old as the Vedas. Gradually a regulation was established that every man and woman towards the end of their lives, must get out of social life altogether and think of nothing except God and their own salvation. This was to get ready for the great event—death. So old people used to become samnyāsins in those early days. Vivekananda pointed out how a big change in the functioning of samnyāsa was brought about by Buddha. He (Buddha) being a young samnyāsin did not sit and think of death, he went about preaching and helping people. So that, according to Vivekananda, was a great reform.

2.73 In the later part of the same California speech, Vivekananda admitted that monastic systems in modern India have merits as well as defects. What he wanted was a balance between the monastics and the householders. Specially for purpose of preaching, he said, the monks are more suitable because of the long tradition:

> The whole national soul in India is upon monasticism. You go to India and preach any religion as a householder: the Hindu people will turn back and go out. However, if you have given up the world, they say: 'He is good, he has given up the world. He is a sincere man, he wants to do what he preaches.' What I mean to say is that monasticism represents a tremendous power... The monk in India is greater than the prince. There is no reigning sovereign in India who dares to sit down when the yellow "robe" is there. He gives up his seat and stands. Now, that is bad, so much power, even in the hands of good men—although these monastics have been the bulwark of the people. They are the centers of knowledge and reform. But better methods need to be worked out... What we can do is just to transform the monastic system, give it another form. This tremendous power in the hands of the Samnyāsins of India has got to be transformed, and it will raise the masses up.[67]

2.74 Monasticism transformed to serve the Indian masses—this is how Vivekananda conceived of the Ramakrishna Mission. It is only because the monastic institution exists in the country, said Vivekananda, that great men like Shri Ramakrishna are born here. He raised a question: Why is it that in spite of its faults, this noble institution stands yet supreme over all the other institutions of life? And he also provided an answer: It is because the true Samnyāsins forgo even their own liberation and live simply for doing good to the world. Emphasizing this to the newly initiated Samnyāsins at

Calcutta, Vivekananda concluded his address:

> For the good of the many, for the happiness of the many is the Samnyāsin born. His life is all vain, indeed, who, embracing samnyāsa, forgets this ideal. The Samnyāsin, verily, is born into this world to lay down his life for others, to stop the bitter cries of men, to wipe the tears of the widow, to bring peace to the soul of the bereaved mother, to equip the ignorant masses for the struggle for existence, to accomplish the secular and spiritual well-being of all through the diffusion of spiritual teachings and to arouse the sleeping lion of Brahman in all by throwing in the light of knowledge.. So achieve the consummation of human life before you pass off. Arise, awake, and stop not till the goal is reached.[68]

Summary of Vivekananda's Contribution to Practical Vedanta

2.75 (a) He coined the term "Practical Vedanta", and was "The Founder of the Practical Vedanta Movement."

(b) He introduced 'jagad-hitam' as the distinguishing feature of Practical Vedanta. Implicitly, he rejected the 'jagat-mithya' doctrine of Shankaracharya.

(c) His vision of 'jagad-hitam' was comprehensive, and covered both spiritual and secular aspects. Among secular issues, he mentioned untouchability, poverty, education, and women's status in society.

(d) He coined the term "Daridra-Narayana" and appealed to the people to "serve the poor, seeing God in them". Because of his initiative, "Seva-yoga" became the most popular synonym of Karma-yoga.

(e) He started the open-ended process of making Vedanta Universal.

(f) He established Ramakrishna Mission and made sure that the work he had started was installed on a permanent footing.

(g) His writings and speeches (which have been published) are a valuable addition to the world's inspirational literature.

Notes

1. Romain Rolland, The Life of Ramakrishna. Advaita Ashrama, Calcutta, Eighth edition, 1970, p. 222.
2. Ibid. pp., 223-4
3. Ibid., pp., 226.
4. Ibid., p. 228.
5. Swami Nikhilananda, Vivekananda: A Biography. Advaita Ashrama Mayavati, third edition, 1975, p. 16
6. Romain Rolland, The Life of Ramakrishna, op. cit., pp. 228-9.
7. R.C. Majumdar, Swami Vivekananda: An Historical Review. General Printers, Calcutta, 1915, p. 13.
8. Romain Rolland, The Life of Ramakrishna, op. cit, pp. 84-5.
9. Ibid., p. 85.
10. Ibid., p. 220.
11. Ibid., p. 231.
12. Ibid., p. 234.
13. R.C. Majumdar, Swami Vivekananda: An Historical Review, op. cit., pp. 18-9.
14. Ibid., pp. 19-20.
15. Indira Patel, Vivekananda's Approach to Social Work. Sri Ramakrishna Math, Madras, 1987, p.1.
16. R.C. Majumdar, Swami Vivekananda: An Historical Review, op. cit., pp. 20-1.
17. Romain Rolland, The Life of Ramakrishna, op. cit., pp. 258-9.

18. R. C. Majumdar, Swami Vivekananda: An Historical Review, op. cit., p. 12.
19. D.S. Sarma, The Renaissance of Hinduism, Banaras Hindu University, 1944, p. 265.
20. Romain Rolland, The Life of Vivekananda and the Universal Gospel, Advaita Ashrama, Calcutta, 1970, p. 21.
21. Swami Vivekananda, Complete Works (eight volumes). Advaita Ashrama, Calcutta, fourteenth edition, 1972, vol., V, p. 441.
22. R.C. Majumdar, Swami Vivekananda: An Historical Review, op. cit., p. 121.
23. Ibid., p. 132.
24. Ibid., p. 132.
25. Ibid., p. 115.
26. Swami Vivekananda, Complete Works, op. cit., vol. III, pp. 220-2.
27. Ibid., vol. IV, p. 405.
28. Seminar on Swami Vivekananda's Teching. Sri Ramakrishna Vidyalaya, Coimbatore, 1964, p. 109.
29. Swami Vivekananda, Complete Works, op. cit., vol. V, p. 10.
30. Seminar on Swami Vivekananda's Teaching, op. cit., p. 98.
31. Swami Vivekananda, Complete Works, op. cit., vol. III, p. 301.
32. R.C. Majumdar, Swami Vivekananda: An Historical Review, op. cit., p. 132.
33. Swami Vivekananda, Complete Works, op. cit., VI, pp. 450-2.
34. Ibid., vol. III, pp. 213-27.
35. Ibid., vol. VII, p. 163 and vol. III, p. 141.
36. Ibid., vol. III, pp. 142-3.
37. Ibid., vol. III, pp. 430-3.
38. Sri Krishna Prem, The Yoga of the Bhagavad Gita. Penguin Books, Baltimore, 1958, p. 217.
39. Swami Vivekananda, Complete Works, op. cit., vol. VII, p. 163.
40. Ibid., vol. III, p. 143.
41. Ibid., vol. III, p. 142.
42. Swami Vivekananda, Karmayoga, Advaita Ashrama, Calcutta,

seventeenth impression, 1984, p. 91.

43. Ibid., p. 83.
44. Swami Vivekananda, complete works op. cit., vol. III, p. 133.
45. Ibid., vol. III, p. 432.
46. Ibid., vol. II, p. 140.
47. Ibid., vol. I, p. 478.
48. Ibid., vol. III, pp. 223-4.
49. Romain Rolland, The Life of Vivekananda and the Universal Gospel, op. cit., p. 286.
50. Ibid., p. 10.
51. Ibid., p. 285.
52. Swami Vivekananda, Karmayoga, op. cit., p. 72.
53. Swami Nikhilananda, Vivekananda: A Biography. op. cit., p. 236.
54. R.C. Majumdar, Swami Vivekananda: An Historical Review, op. cit., pp. 69-70.
55. Ibid., p. 71.
56. Swami Nikhilananda, Vivekananda: A Biography, op. cit., p. 244.
57. Ibid., p. 246.
58. Ibid., pp. 246-7.
59. Romain Rolland, The Life of Vivekananda and the Universal Gospel, op. cit., p. 166.
60. Ibid., pp. 324-5.
61. R.C. Majumdar, Swami Vivekananda: An Historical Review, op. cit., p. 111.
62. Life of Swami Vivekanana by his Eastern and Western Disciples. Advaita Ashrama, Calcutta, fifth edition, 1981, vol. II, p. 328.
63. R.C. Majumdar, Swami Vivekananda: An Historical Review, op. cit., p. 72.
64. Indira Patel, Vivekananda's Approach to Social Work, op., cit. p. 92.
65. Swami Vivekananda, Complete Works, op. cit., vol. VI, p. 504. This famous Sanskrit phrase was coined by Vivekananda to

summarize the Karmayoga-based socio-spiritual approach to India's problems.

66. Ibid., vol. VI, pp. 504-5.

67. Ibid., vol. VIII, p. 89.

68. Ibid., vol. VI, pp. 511-2.

CHAPTER 3

Tilak's Use of the Gita for the Freedom Struggle

A Brief Life-sketch

3.1 In an attempt to trace the likely causes of Tilak's revolutionary ideas in politics, a good deal of attention is often devoted to the fact that he was a Chitpāvan Brahmin of Maharashtra. Leaving aside the mythological links of this community with Parashurama, who preceded Rāma as an avatar of Viṣṇu, the historical records speak of the glory that the Chitpāvans attained in the eighteenth century, as Peshwas. Although Shivaji was the founder of the Marāthā power in the second half of the seventeenth century, a big expansion of the territory under the control and influence of the Marāthās occurred in the days of the Peshwas in the eighteenth century. Unlike Shivaji, the Peshwas were Brahmins. These Brahmins left their ancestral home in Konkan, and joined the army of Shivaji's grandson, and in course of time, assumed a commanding position. The most famous of the Peshwas was Bajirao Bhat, who defeated the Nizam of Hyderabad and conquered large areas of territory from the Moghul Emperor. Wolpert characterizes the Chitpāvan community as "unique among India's priestly class", because they assumed temporal as well as spiritual power over the people.[1] The reign of the Peshwas came to an end in 1818 when the British administration was established in this part of the country.

3.2 Bal Gangadhar Tilak (or Bal for short) was born at Ratnagiri in 1856. His grandfather Ramchandrapant not only taught him how to read and write but also told him about the events of the "Indian Mutiny or the first war of independence" which occurred in 1857 and in which the Maratha chiefs played a significant role.

3.3 Bal's father, Gangadhar, was a school teacher who used his great knowledge of Sanskrit, mathematics and grammar to write textbooks for students. Bal's mother, Parwatibai, was a very religious woman. Tahmankar has narrated how Bal mourned his mother's death when he was only ten:

> "Bal's mother was never strong and, perhaps owing to the habit of frequent fasting, and the other penances which she practised, her health gave way and she died in 1866, soon after her husband was transferred from Ratnagiri to Poona. Bal who was then barely ten years old, has left behind a Sanskrit poem in which he mourns his mother's loss.[2]

3.4 Only six years after his mother's death, Bal lost his father and became an orphan at the age of sixteen. Recollections of this tragedy became prominent in Bal's mind when, forty years later, he was in Mandalay jail and his two sons practically became orphans when their mother (i.e. Tilak's wife) died at Poona. In his message to his nephew from Mandalay jail, Tilak said in 1912: "Let them (Tilak's sons) remember that I was left an orphan when I was much younger than either of them. Misfortunes should brace us for greater self-dependence... See that their time is not lost in useless grief".[3]

3.5 After completing his Bachelor's and the Law degrees, Tilak started his career as a teacher in the New English School in Poona in 1880. This was a private school opened by a famous Marathi writer Chiplunkar, in partnership with Tilak, Agarkar and Namjoshi. All four colleagues wanted to proclaim a principle—that Indian education should be carried out by Indians and for Indians. Limaye characterizes the New English School as unique in the country at the time: "No school through the length and breadth of India perhaps can boast of a group of founders of such great personality. The rejuvenation of the land of their birth was their goal and they looked upon education, properly conceived and properly conducted, as the surest way leading to it."[4]

3.6 Although Tilak gained reputation as a teacher, he, along with his colleagues, also ventured into journalism. They launched two newspapers in 1881, the *Kesari* written in Marathi, and the *Mahratta* in English. Tahmankar outlines the distinguishing features of the two newspapers:

> The tone and temper of the *Kesari* were democratic, its aim was popular education and public agitation. The *Mahratta* was to serve as the authoritative organ of educated public opinion in Maharashtra. It discussed comprehensively every question of high politics, and offered its readers a selection of the views of foreign and Indian journals and publicists on the questions of the day.[5]

3.7 The success of the two papers was immediate. By the end of 1882 *Kesari* had the largest circulation of any vernacular paper in the country, and the *Mahratta* was well on the way to becoming the leading organ of native public thought in western India. The two newspapers owed their success, according to Tahmankar, to virile impassioned writing, animated at all times by lofty patriotism and the courage of conviction.

3.8 The next important activity with which Tilak was closely associated was the establishment of the Deccan Education Society in 1884, and the founding of the Fergusson College in 1885. Parvate describes how the spirit of sacrifice that Tilak and his colleagues displayed in working for a private educational institution, at nominal pay, was appreciated by leading scholars:

> Dr. Bhandarkar spoke highly of the self-sacrificing and self-effacing venture of the young and patriotic founders of the Deccan Education Society and referring particularly to Tilak he said: This first class graduate in law would easily have become a Rao Saheb and amassed a fortune, had he chosen to serve private and personal ends only, instead of embarking on the career of an educationist in a private institution.[6]

3.9 However, Tilak's association with the Deccan Education Society came to a close in 1890, and there was, at the root of it, a conflict between him and Gokhale. According to Wolpert, "superficially, the cause of conflict was monetary, though actually more basic questions of the power and principle were involved."[7] Ideological differences between Tilak and Gokhale persisted thereafter—Tilak championing the cause of revolution, and Gokhale, the cause of reform. Acute differences between Tilak and Agarkar also arose due to their different outlook on social reform. Agarkar gave up the editorship of *Kesari*, with the result that both the *Kesari* and the *Mahratta* now belonged to Tilak and occupied much of his time.

3.10 In 1891, the Age of Consent Bill, which sought to put legal restriction on child marriages, saw Tilak and the social reformers argue strongly and present the opposing points of view. The social reformers, including eminent scholars like Dr. Bhandarkar, were in favour of collaborating with the British authorities in removing evil customs from the Hindu society. However, Tilak wanted the Hindus to introduce reforms on their own, without letting a non-Hindu government interfere in their religious and social affairs.

3.11 In 1893, Tilak gave to the traditional Gaṇapati festival of the Hindus a revivalist look, so as to make it an effective means of creating cultural enthusiasm, religious consciousness and social solidarity. In the traditional way of worshipping the Elephant God, Gaṇeśa, the festivities were mostly confined to households. By making this a public function, Tilak attracted large gatherings of people, by providing artistic displays and music, and this facilitated the giving of lectures, not only on religious topics but also covering other issues, including anti-British propaganda. Barnouw sees in this a "second aim", namely, Hindu solidarity vis-a-vis the Muslims, but he assesses this to be "less significant" than anti-British consciousness.[8]

3.12 Having successfully launched the Gaṇpati festival, which was mainly directed to revive the religious enthusiasm of the Hindu community. Tilak turned his attention to organising the enthusiasm of the people in secular matters. In 1895 he organised a public meeting in Poona and resolved to raise a memorial fund to rebuild Shivaji's tomb at Raigarh, which was then in a very dilapidated condition. Encouraged by a good public response, the 1896-

celebrations of the Shivaji festival were on a grand scale, as Wolpert summarizes:

> The festival had all the trappings of a typical Hindu religious celebration with songs, dances, gymnastic events, readings from the scriptures, and distribution of sweets and betel leaves. In addition, however, ballads exalting Shivaji's heroic deeds, and lectures on the highlights of Marāthā history were delivered. Symbolizing the joint political and religious character of the celebration, huge painted portraits of Shivaji and his Brāhmin guru Ramdas were carried side by side in procession up to the mountain fortress where Shivaji had been coronated "Chhatrapati" (Lord of universe) in 1674.[9]

3.13 The year 1987 can be characterised as bringing to the forefront the impact of the Gītā on Tilak's political views. Although Tilak's family background had acquainted him with the Gītā at an early age, this only exposed him to the traditional interpretation, the inadequacy of which he realised only when he made his own studies. This is how he recalled his boyhood exposure to the Gītā:

> When I was quite a boy, I was often told by my elders that strictly religious and really philosophic life was incompatible with the humdrum life of everyday.... I was also told that Bhagavad-Gītā was universally acknowledged to be a book containing all the principles and philosophy of the Hindu religion. The question that I formulated for myself to be solved was: Does my religion want me to give up this world and renounce it before I attempt to, or in order to be able to, attain the perfection of manhood?[10]

3.14 Tilak's new interpretation of the Gītā, although still

in his mind and not yet formulated in the form of a book, got linked with the Shivaji festival of 1897, and ironically resulted in Tilak's arrest, trial and imprisonment. When Tilak addressed a big public meeting in Poona, he portrayed Shivaji not only as a great national hero but also as an adherent to the Karma-yoga teachings of the Gītā. He further said, among other things, that since Shivaji murdered Afzul Khan for the good of the society, and not for selfish gain, his action was blameless, according to the Bhagavad-Gītā. A few days after this speech, a British Officer, Rand, was murdered in Poona by Damodar Chapekar, to take revenge for atrocities committed on the public, as Chapekar put it. Although the police found no direct connection between Tilak's speech (in Marathi) and Chapekar's action, the non-Marathi-speaking jury found Tilak guilty of sedition and he was sentenced to eighteen months' imprisonment.

3.15 After the 1897-trial and imprisonment, Tilak became, on the one hand, a recognized enemy of the British, and on the other, 'Lokamānya' (Revered by the People) in Indian public opinion. His advocacy of 'Extremist' ideas was reinforced by similar views of Bipin Chandra Pal and Lala Lajpat Rai, and the three of them became known as "Lal-Bal-Pal". After the Bengal partition of 1905, Aurobindo also joined the Extremist group.

3.16 The anti-partition agitation in Bengal lasted six years till the partition was annulled in 1911. This agitation got widespread support from all sections of the society, including those who believed in the cult of the bomb. One such person was Khudiram Bose whose bomb-throwing at Muzaffar Pore (Bihar) in April 1908 later became known as the Alipore Conspiracy Case. Tilak was one of the leaders arrested in the aftermath of this incident, and although no link could be established between him and the bomb-thrower, Tilak was sentenced to six years' imprisonment and sent to Mandalay (Burma).

3.17 Two statements made by Tilak in 1908 have become inextricably linked with his name in Indian history. As Sarma puts it:

> Two of Tilak's utterances have justly become famous and are cherished by the nation. One is"Swarāj is my birthright and I will have it". And the other is his reply to the judge who convicted and transported him for six years in 1908:
>
> "In spite of the verdict of the jury, I maintain I am innocent. There are higher powers that rule the destinies of things, and it may be the will of Providence that the cause which I represent should prosper more by my suffering than by my remaining free".[11]

3.18 During the long imprisonment in Mandalay, Tilak had to undergo all sorts of hardships. When the news of his wife's death in Poona in 1912 reached Tilak in Mandalay, he wrote back:

> "I am used to take my misfortunes calmly, but I confess that the present shook me considerably."[12]

The only bright side of this tragic story was that Tilak wrote his commentary on the Gītā, called *Gītā-Rahasya,* while still in Mandalay.

3.19 The years 1916-18 saw Tilak as the "Uncrowned king of India", and even the Secretary of State, Mr. Montagu, wrote in his diary: "He (Tilak) is the politician who probably has the greatest influence of any person in India."[13]

While Tilak was away in England, during most of 1919, the Gandhian era in India's freedom struggle began, and it was a significant coincidence, that the first All-

India Non-cooperation movement under Gandhi's leadership started on 1st August 1920, just a few hours after Tilak breathed his last. As Sarma puts it: "Doubtless, it is Tilak's mantle that has fallen on Mahatma Gandhi, and not that of Gokhale, though the Mahatma regards Gokhale as his political guru."[14]

A Paradoxical Combination of Politics, Religion, Philosophy and Opposition to Ruler-Reformer-Collaboration

3.20 Tilak was perhaps the most controversial figure in the political history of modern India. Abundant praise as well as ridicule has been showered upon him. On the one hand, he has been described as 'the Father of the Indian Revolution', 'the Maker of Modern India', 'the First Great Mass Leader in the Freedom Movement', and so on. The popular title 'Lokamānya' itself means 'Revered by the People'. It was he who gave to the whole of India the famous slogan 'Swarāj is my birthright and I will have it'. On the other hand, his political opponents called him an 'Extremist' determined to destroy the Congress Organization if he cannot control it. The British government considered him to be the greatest enemy of the empire.

3.21 Similar disagreements exist about Tilak's role in the realms of religion, philosophy, and social reform. Panikkar gives him the primary credit for the rediscovery of the Bhagvad-Gītā as the political and social gospel of Hindu India:

> The revolutionary interpretation of the Bhagvad-Gītā was primarily the work of Bal Gangadhar Tilak, the father of Indian Nationalism.... It fulfilled the urgent need to endow the Hindu people as a whole with a new ethic and a message for social

> action and to discover a dynamic doctrine which, while providing Hindus with modern social ideals, could enable them to transform their society.... The philosophy of the Hindus, so long considered to be contemplative and world-denying, was interpreted by Tilak as a dynamic doctrine for action for the welfare of the world.... the *Gītā-Rahasya* gave to modern India a scripture which, at once orthodox and universally accepted, was also, so to say, a handbook of revolution.[15]

3.22 However, Tilak's activist interpretation of the Gītā has not found favour with orthodox Advaitins who follow Śaṁkara. For example, Mahadevan contends that if Karma were obligatory as Tilak holds, then many passages in the Gītā would be unintelligible. From an Advaitin's point of view, the very purpose of Śrī Kṛṣṇa's teaching was to lead Arjuna to a knowledge of the indestructible self, which is eternal and has neither birth nor death. The problems of temporal existence are insignificant from this lofty angle. In the divine command to "surrender all thy works to me", Mahadevan sees the need for renunciation on the part of one who seeks release.

3.23 Similarly opponents of Tilak's approach criticized him for being a reactionary in social and religious matters. For example, Paranjpye found fault with Tilak's concentration on politics and accused him of neglect of other aspects of national uplift work:

> In my opinion, Tilak's want of appreciation of the need of work among ourselves shows the bankruptcy of his statesmanship and the futility of the claim made for him as the greatest national leader. He opposed the Age of Consent Bill, he attacked well-known social reformers like Justice Ranade and Dr. Bhandarkar, he did not allow the social conference the use of the Congress *mandap*,

> and he did not cooperate with the Plague Inoculation Team. He organized anti-Muslim festivals devoted to Ganesh and Shivaji. No attempt was made by him to look at the aspirations of the backward castes in a sympathetic spirit and he poured ridicule and abuse on those who inveighed against the caste system.[16]

3.24 What lay behind such conflicting assessments of Tilak's role? The choice of priority was certainly a key factor. Right from the start Tilak had contended that the lack of political freedom was the root of all the evils in the country. He therefore decided to pursue the difficult path of politics to the exclusion of everything else. He explained this further, in reply to Paranjpye's criticism:

> Without the power to shape our own destiny, our national regeneration in a larger sense cannot, in my opinion, be effected and I have throughout my career tried to preach and emphasize this view. When I opposed the Age of Consent Bill, I did so mainly on this ground. I did not then think, nor do I think now, that a legislature which is not wholly responsible to the public is competent to deal with social questions. Another point involved in that controversy was Dr. Bhandarkar's interpretation of certain Sanskrit texts. It is well known that Government obtained the opinions of their own Paṇḍits on the matter, and when they were found to be in my favour, Government eventually decided to be wrong with Dr. Bhandarkar than right with me.[17]

3.25 Tilak asked Paranjpye to recall how the Moderates (who called Tilak an Extremist), mostly led by Government servants and pensioners in those days, never thought of going beyond a mild and diffused criticism of some measures of official administration with a view to getting them dropped or improved. They did not then have the courage to put forward the ideal of self-government before the people, and to educate public opinion in accordance therewith. On the contrary, they tried to obstruct the political work of the "Extremists" by misrepresenting them and also by backbiting them whenever possible. Tilak particularly mentioned how the word "Swarāj" was mistranslated by the Moderates who formed an unholy alliance with the Anglo-Indians to overwhelm the Extremists, until the Grand Old Man of India, Dada Bhai Naoroji declared from the Congress platform that Swaraj should be our goal. Even then the Moderates, according to Tilak, were not prepared to declare this ideal for practical work, nor to accept any scheme for the realisation thereof.

3.26 Tilak also explained how his group "the Nationlists" wanted to build on old foundations. Reform based on utter disrespect for the old did not appeal to them as constructive work. They did not want to Anglicize their institutions and so denationalize them in the name of social and political reform. He reminded Paranjpye that the latter's colleagues (Moderates) favoured alien methods even in offering prayers to God. As against this, the Nationalists desired to emphasize and preserve the national sentiment by giving due credit to all that was good in the old system but without detriment to progress and reform needed for the national uplift. In Tilak's view, the festivals of Gaṇapati and Shivaji were means to keep and maintain a proper pride in the doings of the ancestors. The large gatherings in the festivals provided an opportunity to the Nationalists to talk indirectly on the current problems also.

3.27 Leaving aside the other points contained in Tilak's

reply to Pranajpye, a recent American writer, William Holland, has observed that religion played an important role in India's freedom struggle because the nationalist movement was characterised by a strain of Hindu revivalism. Like all empires the British suppressed political meetings but they generally observed a hands-off policy with regard to religion. This provided a loophole which nationalists like Tilak exploited to the full for political purposes.

3.28 Tahmankar has cited several instances that reveal Tilak's sympathetic behaviour towards the weaker sections of the society. One of these relates to the Gaṇapati festival of 1894. While walking along with thousands of persons in the religious procession. Tilak saw a boy of seven or eight crying loudly from a window of a house while his mother was trying to pacify him. Tilak stopped to ask why the boy was crying. The mother told Tilak that her son wanted his Gaṇapati to be taken to the river for the immersion ceremony along with other Gaṇapatis, but she dared not let him do this as her family belonged to the untouchable class. Tilak was moved to tears; he could not bear to see an innocent child suffer. He went into the house, took the Gaṇapati idol and placed it by the side of his own and the boy joined the procession holding on to Tilak's hand.

3.29 Another instance cited by Tahmankar relates to a special conference for untouchables in Bombay where Tilak declared before an audience of more than seven thousand people:

> If God were to tolerate untouchability, I would not recognize Him as God at all.... Although I have appeared amongst you in person for the first time, believe me you have been in my mind all the time. I do not deny that it was the Brahmin rule that introduced the practice of untouchability. This is

> a cancer in the body of Hindu society and we must eradicate it at all costs.[18]

3.30 Still another instance is the description that Tilak gave of his political ideal as "the Swaraj of oilmen and sellers of betel-nut leaves", by which he meant the toiling masses, irrespective of caste and creed.[19] What people like Pranjpye found paradoxical was that, on the one hand, Tilak had declared that he was for removing all caste distinctions regarding interdining and untouchability, still on the other, he refused to sign a manifesto condemning untouchability. Tahmankar therefore describes "Tilak's career.... as a whirlpool of controversy, sometimes about social reforms, sometimes about political ideals and ways and means of achieving them and sometimes about purely personal matters".[20] Wolpert's explanation of Tilak's attitude, which was found paradoxical by Paranjpye, runs as follows:

> While Tilak may sincerely have believed in the beneficence of the many causes he so ably popularised, at times he appears to have been motivated less by his own faith in the inherent worth of a particular cause, than by the belief that championing it would prove most expedient in winning him the support of the majority of his fellow countrymen. Conversely, while he personally may not have believed that every social reform he condemned was in itself harmful or unnecessary, he appears to have been supremely aware of the fact that a potent method of achieving swift popularity was by criticizing unpopular innovations.[21]

3.31 Arvind Sharma, after comparing the approaches of Tilak and Rammohun Roy on the issue of British governmental interference in Hindu social life, has found "a basic identity" overpowered by "differences in detail". Sharma observes that the position of these two leaders "have, to a certain extent, been misrepresented" with the result that:

> In much of modern historiography about British India, Raja Rammohun Roy has the image of an ardent social reformer and Bal Gangadhar Tilak at least that of a social conservative, if not that of a social reactionary.[22]

3.32 Rammhun Roy's role as a social reformer is well known. He tried his best to create Hindu public opinion in favour of the social reform (suttee-abolition). He did not want the British government to assume the role of a law-maker on this issue, fearing that such an interference might assume undesirable forms in future. Rammohum Roy conveyed this "privately" to the Governor-General. However, the Hindu society was too slow to change its ways, and the British government did not want any delay in stopping the evil custom. Sharma summarizes "Rammohum Roy's attitude on the point of British government's interference in Hindu social life as one of ex-ante objection but ex-post approbation".[23]

3.33 Sharma has concentrated his attention on the role of Tilak in the controversy surrounding the Age of Consent Bill. According to Sharma, the suttee-abolition legislation of 1829 and the Age of Consent Bill of 1891, both represent landmarks in the social history of India. The purpose behind the Age of Consent Bill (which represented close collaboration between the British authorities and the Indian social reformers) was to put legal restriction on child-marriages. Tilak proposed before a public meeting in October 1890 that Hindus voluntarily agree to marry their daughters at the age of sixteen (which was higher than the age of twelve suggested in the Bill), and their sons at the age of twenty. However,

Tilak objected to the Bill publicly on the same ground on which Rammohun Roy had objected privately to suttee-legislation. Tilak explained this in many statements, two of which are:

> We would not like that Government should have anything to do with regulating our social customs or ways of living, even supposing that the act of Government will be a very beneficial and suitable measure....
>
> This we have to admit if we look at the Age of Consent Bill. The Muhammadans forced the Hindus to grow beards after cutting off Hindus' locks of hair by taking a sword in one hand and a Koran in the other. So also our subjugation to others gives evidence that our brave English people have the power to send us to "our Father in Heaven" after making us drink red water (wine) instead of the sacred water of the Ganges.[24]

3.34 Tilak's biographer, Ram Gopal, has stated that Tilak performed the marriage of his daughters after they had attained the age of sixteen. In doing so, he was not guided by the Age of Consent Act but by his own suggestion of voluntary agreement among Hindus to raise the minimum age of marriage in Hindu society.

3.35 Tilak's biographer, Parvate, has given interesting details about a school devoted to female education, which initially received full support from social reformers, but when exposed by Tilak's newspapers *Kesari* and *Mahratta* as a proselytizing activity under the garb of education, fell into disrepute in the eyes of the social reformers also. Paravate's version (with some deletions) is reproduced below:

Ramabai Dongre established a school for Indian girls, particularly widows. It was a residential school and the inmates of the school were constantly thrown in the company of the Christian missionary teachers of the Sharada Sadan which she established in Poona. Tilak did not like it very much, but Ranade, Bhandarkar and Agarkar were very enthusiastic about it. They became members of its advisory committee. Tilak also enrolled his name among the sympathizers of the school after satisfying himself that the Indian girls were not compelled to attend Christian prayers and the education imparted to them was only secular. He soon discovered that this condition was not being observed and the institution was functioning as a proselytizing body. He brought this to the notice of Ranade and Bhandarkar. They protested against it. Ramabai explained that only four girls were learning the Christian scripture. The matter was referred to the headquarters of the missionary society in America. The society backed Ramabai and invested her with full powers to conduct the Sharda Sadan as she thought best. The *Subodha Patrika* and *Sudharak* wrote tauntingly about Tilak, questioned his motives and called him an opponent of women's education. Tilak paid them in the same coin through the columns of the *Kesari* and the *Mahratta.* Ultimately even the social reformers found that it was impossible to support Ramabai's activities and shield her against public resentment.[25]

First Political Imprisonment, Ironically Linked with the Gita

3.36 Tilak's imprisonment in 1897 was the first instance when an eminent Indian political leader was put behind bars by the British administration, and ironically, this was linked, among other things, with Tilak's new interpretation of Karma-yoga. It can be viewed as a coincidence that the following two events occurred in Poona during 1897, and although there was no direct connection between these two, they were put together by the British authorities to justify Tilak's imprisonment:

(i) Occurrence of the deadly epidemic "plague" in Poona in the spring of 1897, appointment of Walter Rand as Chairman of Plague Committee, resentment among the residents of Poona against the offensive behaviour of Rand and the British soldiers working with him, Rand's murder by Damodar Chapekar on 22 June 1897, Damodar's arrest and trial and subsequent hanging.

(ii) Celebration of Shivaji festival in Poona on June 12, 1897 under the presidentship of Tilak, speech by Tilak in Marathi that Shivaji's killing of the Moghul General Afzul Khan in 1659 was not a sin according to his (i.e. Tilak's) interpretation of Karma-yoga, publication of Tilak's speech, together with other material, in the Marathi newspaper *Kesari* of which Tilak himself was the editor.

3.37 In order to help understand the plague-related events as well as the significance of Tilak's speech on Shivaji festival, some details of the Rand story need to be given, as also the ethical issues connected with the killing of Afzul Khan. First, the Rand story together with Tilak's role therein. Most of Tilak's biographers agree, that the chairman of plague committee, Rand, although a man of great energy and courage, unfortunately lacked the finer qualities of a good administrator and did not respect the feelings of the people for whose welfare he was working. He employed British soldiers to go round the city and inspect the houses where plague cases had occurred or were suspected. The soldiers used rough and ready methods, and ignorant of the Marathi language, showed contempt of the customs, sentiments and religious susceptibilities of the people. While removing people from the affected houses into segregation camps, they herded together indiscriminately in the same camp, all sorts of people—for instance, expectant and nursing mothers were crowded together with men. Before long, the people of Poona began to dread the reign of terror of Rand and his search parties more than the epidemic itself. Added to all these, Rand and his committee were guilty of the supreme sin of failure, for without a vaccine to prevent it, plague continued taking its toll.

3.38 Tilak saw Rand with a citizen's deputation to explain to him the growing resentment of the public and made suggestions for minimizing people's hardships. He also organized the establishment of a separate private hospital for the Hindus with the support of people of different persuasions and creeds.

3.39 In the meantime, a determined group of reckless young men was planning to avenge in its own way the humiliation and distress of the people of Poona. They chose 22 June 1897, the diamond jubilee of Queen Victoria's succession to the throne, which was being celebrated in a big way all over the country. That night, when Rand and his assistant were returning from the party, Damodar Chapekar shot them dead.

3.40 The authorities immediately put the city under a curfew and imposed a punitive police force on the citizens of Poona. A prize announced for providing information about the murderer attracted one of the acquaintances of Damodar, and on the basis of the information received by the police, Damodar was arrested, and put on trial, sentenced to death and hanged.

3.41 Secondly, the Afzul Khan-Shivaji encounter of 1659.

The Moghul General Afzul Khan was sent at the head of a mighty Bijapur army to wipe out, once and for all, the guerilla force of Shivaji. Afzul's army advanced to Wai, hoping to engage Shivaji on the open plain, but by the time they arrived there, the Marathas were gone, retreating to Pratapgarh, a fort on a hill. Afzul knew that it would be unwise to launch a frontal assault against the lofty ramparts of Pratapgarh. Recognizing his general's dilemma, a Brahmin in the Bijapur camp named Pantoji Gopinath suggested that he be sent to Shivaji to try to convince him of the wisdom of surrender before his forces were starved out of that retreat. Afzul agreed, and Pantoji was admitted to the fortress to confer with Shivaji, who then appealed to Pantoji's Hindu faith, and thereby won him over to the Maratha cause. Returning to the Bijapur camp, Pantoji told Afzul that Shivaji wanted to meet the Bijapur general, man to man, to discuss ways of settling the dispute. Afzul agreed to have his army at the base of the hill, and to advance alone to a level spot more than half way up to the fort, where he and Shivaji came together. What happened next is not firmly established but in the encounter Afzul was dead. The leaderless Bijapur army suffered a defeat and Maratha power was firmly established.

3.42 Ethical issues raised by historians in the Afzul-Shivaji encounter are: Who struck first? Did both of them come armed to destroy the enemy or was Shivaji the only one so armed? Was Afzul's murder an act of bravery or treachery or a little bit of both? Tilak's answer to these questions is contained in his speech at Shivaji festival, on 12 June 1897, relevant extracts from which are given in para 3.44 below.

3.43 Why was it necessary for the British authorities to link Rand's murder with Tilak's speech? Because the police authorities of Bombay failed to find any basis whatsoever to establish a direct connection between Tilak and Rand's murder. The only possible justification for arresting Tilak then appeared to rest on the argument suggested first by British-owned newspapers that his speech at the Shivaji festival, though apparently referring to an historical incident, was an attempt to excite feelings of disaffection towards British rule. The Governor of Bombay, Lord Sandhurst, did not initially accept the validity of such an argument. Not only did he refuse to order Tilak's arrest, he even sanctioned Tilak's election to the Legislative Council. But the clamour in the *Times of India* and other British-owned newspapers for Tilak's arrest became louder and louder. According to one report, the British community of Bombay threatened to ostracize the Governor socially if he persisted in his "policy of weakness". Similar threats had forced the liberal Viceroy, Lord Rippon, a few years earlier, to drop the idea of giving more powers to Indian magistrates. In the present case, too, Lord Sandhurst had to accept the validity of the argument suggested for Tilak's arrest and prosecution.

3.44 But what exactly had Tilak said about Shivaji's killing of Afzul Khan which could be interpreted as an incitement to a murderous attack against the British? The relevant portion of Tilak's speech of 12 June 1897 is reproduced below:

> Let us even assume that Shivaji first planned and then executed the murder of Afzul Khan. Was this act of the Maharaja good or bad?... Did Shivaji commit a sin in killing Afzul Khan or how? The answer to this question can be found in the Mahābhārata itself. Shrimat Kṛṣṇa's advice in the Gītā is to kill even our teachers and our kinsmen. No blame attaches to any person, if he is doing deeds without being actuated by a desire to reap

the fruits of his deeds. Shri Shivaji Maharaj did nothing with a view to fill the small void of his own stomach (i.e. from interested motives). With benevolent intentions, he murdered Afzul Khan for the good of others. If thieves enter our house and we have not sufficient strength in our wrists to drive them out, we should, without hesitation, shut them up and burn them alive. God has not conferred upon the Mlecchas (the foreigners) the grant inscribed on a copper-plate (having long-term validity) of the kingdom of Hindustan. Shivaji Maharaj strove to drive them away from the land of his birth; he did not thereby commit the sin of coveting what belonged to others. Do not circumscribe your vision like a frog in a well. Get out of the Penal Code, enter into the extremely high atmosphere of the Shrimat Bhagavat Gītā, and then consider the action of great men.[26]

3.45 Judge Strachey agreed that there was "no reason why a person (Tilak) should not discuss, in a proper moderate way, whether the assassination (of Afzul by Shivaji) was justified. But although there are subjects of legitimate comments and discussion, you will readily recognize that these are delicate subjects for a man of importance, a leader of the people; that is to say, he ought to be careful as to the spirit in which they are discussed in the audience. It is one thing to discuss it amongst philosophers, it is another thing to discuss it amongst an ignorant mob."[27]

3.46 Tilak's biographers have analyzed in detail whether there was any justification at that time to connect Damodar's act of "political terrorism" with Tilak's views on "ethical relativism" as understood by him from the Gītā and applied by him to Shivaji-Afzul encounter. Obviously, the political factor was more weighty than the legal. That is why, Tilak's speech in Marathi was not translated by a language expert for the benefit of the non-Marathi speaking jurors. Tilak protested, but to no avail. Wolpert summarizes how the trial ended with Tilak's imprisonment and subsequent political implications:

> Tilak's protest was as much political as it was linguistic. The trial had aroused widespread journalistic and popular interest, attracting vast crowds to Bombay's High Court, especially in its final days.... Tilak was sentenced to eighteen months of rigorous imprisonment. A poll of despair settled over his political opponents in Congress as well as on his followers. At the Amraoti Congress that year, the President Surendra Nath Banerjee said, "For Mr. Tilak my heart is full of sympathy, my feelings go forth to him in his prison-house. A nation is in tears."[28]

3.47 By his Sanskrit scholarship and defence of orthodoxy, as Wolpert puts it, Tilak had won the respect and approbation of the elders of his community. By his trial and imprisonment he won the reverence and love of the young and the unlettered to whom suffering and sacrifice were the supreme signs of greatness. From now on, Tilak was called "Lokamānya" meaning 'revered by the people'.

3.48 Tahmankar is of opinion that Tilak's trial of 1897 and his consequent imprisonment was a turning point in the history of India's fight for independence and democracy. Highlighting this in his "Prelude" to Tilak's biography, he characterizes this trial as the first clash in a decisive struggle between History and Destiny. Tahmankar continues:

> Fate had placed in Tilak's hands the threads of India's fate, and the weaving of them was, over the next fifty years, to change the course of history.

> In him fate had made a good choice, for in his fingers the threads did not slip or waver as the complex pattern of India's independence was being worked out by the people.[29]

3.49 In those days the Indian Penal Code made no special provision for political prisoners. Tilak was, therefore, not entitled to any concessions, even by way of providing him with a vegetarian meal (free from onions and garlic). In less than two months, his weight came down from 135lbs to 110lbs, and when the news of his worsening health leaked out, people began to fear the worst. The news shocked European Sanskrit scholars and there was some talk in the universities of Oxford and Cambridge in favour of taking effective steps to get him released. Professor Max-Müller, the world's great authority on Vedas, was in correspondence with Tilak when the latter published his first essay in the field of Vedic research. Professor Max-Müller, with the help of two sympathetic members of British Parliament, organized a petition to the Queen, signed by a number of influential men, asking for clemency for a learned scholar, Tilak. This, together with other considerations which the British government might have had, led to Tilak's release from prison, about six months before the completion of his term. Also, in due course of time, (nearly twenty-two years), political prisoners got recognition as a special category under the Indian Penal Code. The process of achieving this was set in motion because of Tilak's suffering as an ordinary prisoner during 1897-98.

Second Imprisonment and the Writing of Gita-Rahasya

3.50 In the eventful life that Tilak led, two aspects stand

out prominently, namely, his new interpretation of the Karma-yoga doctrine, and his fight with the British authorities leading to his imprisonment. It was noted in Para 3.36 that Tilak's brief explanation of Karma-yoga in 1897 practically became a cause of his trial and first political imprisonment. This cause-effect relationship between those two was, in a way, reversed in 1908 when his second imprisonment (which lasted six years) became a cause of his monumental elucidation of Karma-yoga. Wolpert draws attention to the fact that the doctrine of "ethical relativism", first propounded by Tilak prior to his imprisonment in 1897, was "reiterated and elaborated upon" in the Mandalay prison (where Tilak stayed during 1908-1914), the final outcome of which was *Gītā-Rahasya* (published in 1915).[30]

3.51 The chain of events leading to Tilak's trial of 1908 can be said to have begun when the Governor-General, Lord Curzon, announced the partition of Bengal as of 16 October 1905. On the grounds of administrative efficiency, a new province called Eastern Bengal and Assam was to be carved out of Bengal. The British government knew that the idea of partitioning Bengal was bound to be extremely unpopular, but they went ahead nevertheless. The "Bengal Revolution" which followed, marked a new highpoint of united popular agitation in that province. The national slogan "Bande Mātaram" (Salutation to Mother India) which originally occurred in Bankim Chandra's novel *Ānandamaṭha* was suddenly on the lips of every agitator. Rabindranath Tagore also participated in making the following declaration.

> Whereas the Government has thought fit to effectuate the partition of Bengal, in spite of universal protests of the Bengali nation we hereby

> pledge and proclaim that we as a people shall do everything in our power to counteract the evil effects of the dismemberment of our province and to maintain integrity of our race. So God help us.[31]

3.52 The repercussions of the Bengal agitation rolled wave-like across the whole of British India. Mass protest meetings were held, and government was warned of the plan to boycott British goods if partition was actually carried out. "It was", declared Tilak, "a critical time. We must act and not only hold meetings".[32] Within a few months, three major planks emerged in the platform of militant nationalism: boycott, Swadeshi, and national education. Tilak called upon all the countrymen "to give the Bengalis all necessary help", and explained the significance of the three elements which constituted the new plan of action. He suggested that the idea of boycott be considered a sacred practice. To make it successful, he said, we must try to learn how much produce is imported from England, how to manufacture those goods in India, (Swadeshi), and if they cannot be manufactured here, whether we can import them from non-English places. He also supported the idea of establishing "a University of our own, independent of Government aid and subject to no other control but that exercised by the best cultivated independent intelligence in the country."[33] The principal idea underlying national education, was according to Tilak, to give such education to the children of the land as will make them good patriots, who will serve the national cause of freedom.

3.53 Although the Congress broke up in two, namely, the moderate and the Extremist wings in 1907 (called the "Surat Split" because it occurred at Surat), it had no adverse effect on Tilak's activities in support of boycott, Swadeshi, and national education. On May

2, 1908 he made, for the first time, in a speech at Akola, the famous statement:

> Swaraj is my birthright and I will have it".[34] Furthermore Sarma gives Tilak credit for being the first political leader to visualize the likely form of "non-cooperation with the foreign ruler", which would be a step beyond the Congress policy of boycott. Tilak spoke of such an idea, in Calcutta on January 2, 1907:

> What the new party wants you to do is to realize the fact that your future rests entirely in your own hands. If you want to be free, you can be free; if you do not mean to be free, you will fall and be for ever fallen. So many of you need not take arms, but if you have not the power of active resistance, have you not the power of self-denial and self-abstinence in such a way as not to assist this foreign government to rule over you? This is boycott and this is what is meant when we say, boycott is a political weapon. We shall not give them assistance to collect revenue and keep peace. We shall not assist them in fighting beyond the frontiers or outside India with Indian blood and money. We shall not assist them in carrying on the administration of justice. We shall have our own courts and when time comes we shall not pay taxes. Can you do that by your united efforts? If you can, you are free from tomorrow.[35]

3.54 Just as Rand's murder by Damodar Chapekar in 1897 resulted in Tilak's imprisonment, a similar tragedy occurred in 1908. In the midst of the agitation that was going on because of the Bengal partition, a young Bengali man, Khudiram Bose, threw a bomb, on 30 April 1908, into a carriage at Muzafferpore (now in Bihar, but at that time within the province of Bengal). He wanted to kill Kingsford, who, as Chief Presidency

Magistrate, had ordered some young men to be severely flogged for a comparatively minor offence. Khudiram Bose threw a bomb at a carriage which resembled that of Kingsford, but really belonged to one Kennedy, with the result that the wife and daughter of the latter were killed. Khudiram Bose and many others were arrested. Since the trial was conducted at Alipore, it became known as the Alipore Conspiracy Case. Khudiram Bose was hanged. Tilak was arrested in Bombay on 24 June 1908, and charged with sedition for ideas expressed in two of his editorials in *Kesari*, dated May 12 and June 9, 1908.

3.55 A jury of seven Europeans and two Parsis tried Tilak's case. Tilak could find no barrister to argue his case the way he wished. He wanted to establish that the Anglo-Indian press was guilty of defaming India and Indian people, which was as much a libel, and the Government did not take any steps against them. When he asked Muhammad Ali Jinnah, barrister of Bombay, to serve as his counsel and to focus attention on the failings of the Anglo-Indian press, Jinnah, "refused to adopt any line, as a counsel, except what I considered best for his defence"[36] So Tilak decided to plead on his own behalf. Wolpert sees in this defence the echo of the 'Svadharma' doctrine of the Gītā:

> Lokamānya's statement deserves an honoured place in the history of his nation's struggle for independence.... In traditional Hindu terminology it may be viewed as an exposition of the dharma of the newspaper editor, who like every other person in Hindu society had his special duty or religion to perform because of his occupational status. Just as the king's dharma was to rule wisely, and the warrior's to fight valiantly, so the newspaper editor's was to speak his mind on topical issues

without fear of reprisal. Tilak's statement moreover, was an explanation as well of the dharma of the juror, and of the political agitator.[37]

3.56 The seven European jurors found Tilak guilty, while the two Parsis did not. Assured that there was no possibility of making the verdict unanimous by sending the jury back, Justice Davar asked Tilak if he had anything to say before sentence was passed. What Tilak stated in reply, on July 22, 1908 has since become a famous declaration of the belief in the ancient Hindu doctrine of Tapas or willingness to suffer for a just cause:

> What I wish to say is that in spite of the verdict of the jury I maintain that I am innocent. There are higher powers that rule the destiny of things and it may be the will of Providence that the cause which I represent may prosper more by my suffering than by my remaining free.[38]

3.57 What followed can be briefly summarised. Tilak was sentenced to deportation for six years. As the news of Tilak's conviction spread, mills in Bombay struck in sympathy for him. The cloth, grain, freight, and stock markets as well as the cotton exchange, all closed down. This was the first mass political strike in recent Indian history. The agitation against the partition of Bengal continued unabated, and finally the British Government had to annul the partition in 1911.

3.58 Although Tilak's imprisonment in Mandalay jail in Burma was a period of much suffering and pain to him (his wife died at Poona while he was far away), it did provide, at the same time, "compulsory time off" from the busy life that Tilak had led in India. He made the best use of it for writing *Gītā-Rahasya*, and this was facilitated by the permission to receive non-political books that was granted to him by the British authorities after some delay. Tilak himself highlighted this in a press interview that he gave in Poona after his release in 1914.

> Even before I was imprisoned, a conviction was growing on me that the meaning of the Gītā, adumbrated by all the many commentaries and expositions, was not the correct one. I had long wanted to give concrete shape to my ideas on the meaning of the Gītā, together with a comparative study of the eastern and the western philosophies. I could do that only at Mandalay....
>
> I do not know what would have happened to me if I had not been allowed to have books, because the room and the compound had become my entire world for the duration of my imprisonment; outside the compound, there was, so to speak a big void.... In the case of books, there were three orders issued; when I complained to the government, I was allowed to have the books I wanted for writing Gītā-Rahasya.
>
> I have now written this book in Marathi; it took me four to six months to write but much time was spent in thinking out its plan and then again in revising it. The manuscript is with the government—they did not give it to me at the time of my release.[39]

3.59 Tilak's ideas as contained in *Gītā-Rahasya* are consistent with a lifetime of thought and action. He also believed that, unlike Śaṁkara, Rāmānuja, and Madhva, he had no pre-conceived theory to substantiate: "I approached the book with a mind prepossessed by no previous ideas about any philosophy, and had no theory of my own for which I sought any support in the Gītā". It soon became clear to him that "the Gītā was preached to desponding

Arjuna to make him ready for the fight—for the action".[40] Luckily for him, he found that the thirteenth century Maharashtrian philosopher, Jñānadeva, had also attacked the renunciatory interpretation of Śaṁkara. In a renowned commentary on the Gītā, the *Jñāneśvarī*, and in his *Amṛtānubhava,* Jñānadeva had rejected Śaṁkara's concept of an illusory and meaningless world and described the material universe and man as "natural expressions of Reality". Even the *Jīvanmukta,* or liberated soul, of Śaṁkara and Vedāntists, fails in Jñānadeva's opinion, to achieve the bliss of a devotee living in the material world. In *Gītā-Rahasya,* Tilak cites Jñānadeva's description of the devotee, as an elaboration of the Gītā-concept of a perfect man engaged in actions for the welfare of the society. Tilak also refers to the Maharashtrian poet Tukārāma who was deeply influenced by Jñānadeva. The fact that Jñānadeva had written his Gītā commentary in Marathi, to reach the masses, had a special appeal to Tilak. This is not to imply that *Gītā-Rahasya* (written in Marathi) agreed with *Jñāneśvarī* in all respects. Far from it, because Tilak's emphasis was on unselfish action for social welfare rather than on devotee action and compassionate behaviour for individual salvation.

New Ideas on Social Action and Lokasamgraha

3.60 Since the draft of *Gītā-Rahasya* had to pass through the censorship of the British authorities, Tilak had to avoid references to what his new ideas could imply in terms of political action. He therefore confined himself to discussions of a philosophic and religious nature, and talked of the needs of the society in a general way. But in earlier writings in *Kesari* and *Mahratta,* and in his political speeches, there were ample indications that he considered political independence as the paramount need of the Indian society at that time. The arguments in *Gītā-Rahasya,* making no direct mention of foreign rulers, were aimed at refuting the socio-religious approaches of two broad groups of Indians, namely,

(a) The traditional interpreters of the Gītā who had accorded a lower status to Karma-yoga as compared to Jñāna and Bhakti, and

(b) The Indians who had received modern education and who felt that the Hindu society could be pulled out of the mess mainly by means of social reform and by borrowing the philosophy of social action from the Christians and other liberal thinkers of the west.

3.61 Out of a large number of issues which Tilak raised to achieve his objective, four main topics can be identified for purpose of summarizing his message:

(i) Dharma-Kṣetra or the field where the battle for dharma or righteousness is fought.

(ii) Avatāra or God's incarnation to re-establish dharma from time to time.

(iii) Niṣkāma Karma or action without attachment to fruits of a selfish nature.

(iv) Lokasaṁgraha or the goal of the good of the society.

Dharma-Ksetra

3.62 This is the first word in the Gītā and its traditional meaning was 'the sacred field', which the place 'Kurukṣetra' was supposed to be. There is a story in the Mahābhārata according to which Indra gave a blessing to Kuru that all those who die on that field in war or while performing religious austerities would obtain heaven. As a result of this blessing, this place came to be called sacred. Another common interpretation was that Kurukṣetra became sacred because the Mahābhārata was fought there to establish dharma and justice, and also because Lord Kṛṣṇa imparted the sacred teaching of the Gītā at that place. The word 'Kṣetra' in the Gītā occurs also in the thirteenth chapter, in the sense of 'human body' and Śaṁkara associated several meanings with 'Kṣetra', for example, that which is protected against injury, or that which perishes or wastes away, or that in which the results of actions get fulfilled as in a field. The word 'dharma' in the Gītā has two distinct aspects, namely, individual or particular, and social or universal. When Arjuna admits in the second chapter that he is confused about his dharma, he is referring to the individual aspect. However, when Śrī Kṛṣṇa explains the concept of Avatāra or incarnation, in the fourth chapter, and links it with the need to protect dharma, the emphasis obviously is on the social or universal aspect.

3.63 When Śrī Kṛṣṇa refers to the conditions which call for divine intervention, he mentions 'the decline of dharma' as well as 'the rise of adharma'. Subsequently, in the sixteenth chapter, one of the main characteristics of those who follow the path of *adharma* is stated to be 'doing harm and bringing about the ruin of the world'. This is consistent with the etymological derivation of the word dharma, signifying that which holds the society together. Tilak emphasizes dharma as a moral law which maintains the society, and warns against the evil consequences of adharma:

> When this dharma ceases to be observed, the binding ropes of society may be said to have become loose, and when these binding ropes are loosened, society will be in the same position as the planetary system consisting of the sun and planets would be

in the sky without the binding force of gravitation or as a ship would be on the ocean without a rudder.[41]

3.64 What Tilak did was to ask every member of the society to generalize the predicament of Arjuna and raise the issues of dharma in relation to present-day problems. The significance of Tilak's call to view the whole society as *dharmakṣetra* has been highlighted by Thomas: "Tilak was the first Indian national leader to bring out the meaning of the righteous war (*dharmayuddha*) in the *dharmakṣetra*, for modern India. He boldly stated that not only one's immediate field of activity but the whole of India is the *dharmakṣetra* of modern Indians".[42]

Panikkar not only refers to Tilak's wider interpretation of *dharmakṣetra*, but also finds a parallel between Arjuna's spirit of unmanliness at Kurukṣetra and the inactivity which gripped the Indian society when Tilak wrote *Gītā-Rahasya:*

To Tilak India was the *dharmakṣetra*—the field of righteousness—and the inactivity which seemed to have gripped India was but a reflection of the unmanliness that Arjuna felt on the field of battle. The Gītā helped Arjuna to get rid of his dejection. The same purpose it can now fulfil on this new field of righteousness. To Tilak it was clear that it was only through the message of the Gītā that India could save herself.[43]

Avatara

3.65 The doctrine of Avatāra or God's incarnation arises from Śrī Kṛṣṇa's famous declaration in the fourth chapter of the Gītā: "Whenever dharma decays and unrighteousness prospers, I appear in successive ages for the purpose of destroying evil-doers and re-establishing the supremacy of the moral law". In pre-

Tilak days the tendency was to interpret this doctrine literally as a promise of God to take human shape to set matters right. Like many other teachings of Hinduism it was perverted into a doctrine for the passive acceptance of the present conditions, howsoever bad, on the plea that when it suits God He will be born into the world and change things by His direct intervention. It became therefore in the hands of sectarian teachers another argument for passivity, reinforcing fatalism connected with an equally damaging interpretation of the law of Karma.

3.66 Tilak linked the concept of Avatāra with the repeated call of Śri Kṛṣṇa to Arjuna "Matkarma Kuru" or "do my work". To those who believed in the Vedāntic declaration that "a knower of Brahman himself becomes Brahman", Tilak appealed for taking up in hand the same tasks as an Avatāra does, namely, to help the righteous and to prevent evil-doers from harming the society. Otherwise, said Tilak, such "Knowers of Brahman" are selfish:

> It is pure selfishness for a man to be engrossed in the happiness of meditation while there are millions of people to whom he is bound by an inseparable bond, the bond of the all-pervading self... It is natural that noble sentiments of sympathy towards all beings must arise in the minds of people who know that there is only one Ātman in all created beings and the trend of his mind must naturally be towards universal welfare.[44]

3.67 Panikkar believes that the Avatāra doctrine, together with the social interpretation thereof as initiated by Tilak, gradually led to the formulation of a doctrine of rejuvenation of society. Viewed from this angle, the Gītā foresees the inevitable decay of all institutions and the necessity at different times of revolutionary changes to restore the harmony of life. While the Gītā emphasizes that there are permanent social values, it does not give support to the doctrine that what exists is always the best and that change in itself is something to be resisted. It goes much beyond this. It emphasizes that social institutions are liable to decay and petrifaction when the original values are lost sight of and social chaos follows as a result of which the purposes behind social organization begin to be misunderstood or misinterpreted. At such times, qualitative change or revolution according to the Gītā is a divinely ordained process. Panikkar attaches great importance to this doctrine of change:

> This sublimation of the doctrine of change is one of the major contributions of the Gītā to modern India. To a static society held down by custom and tradition and suffocated by the accretions of ages, the teaching that change is divinely ordained when society had decayed came as a life-giving revelation. There it was provided in the most authoritative text that dharma requires to be restated in every age and society must be reorganized to suit new needs. No stronger weapon could have been put in the hands of those who desired to reshape Indian society and give it purpose and vitality.[45]

Niskama Karma

3.68 Tilak recognised, as did the other commentators, that the Gītā actually advocates at least three paths of conduct for the seeker of perfection: *niṣkāma* karma or unselfish work, jñāna or knowledge, and bhakti or devotion to a supreme being. The main question was thus of allocation of priority. The commentary of Śaṁkara, based on the philosophy of Advaita Vedānta, had declared jñāna and renunciation of action to be the ultimate truth of the Gītā. Rāmānuja's Viśiṣṭādvaita commentary had stressed bhakti or devotion as the central theme. Madhva's commentary following the Dvaita school of philosophy also arrived at a similar conclusion in support of bhakti. What Tilak attempted to show was that each of these commentators had twisted the meaning of some of the verses of the Gītā "to advocate a pet theory of his own". A forced interpretation of the Gītā was also important for the classical Vedāntist commentators because they wanted to show that the basic philosophy of the Gītā was the same as that of the Upaniṣads and the Brahma-sūtras—the three authoritative scriptures together being called *prasthāna-traya*. Tilak questioned the validity of such an approach, because, if the Gītā contained nothing different from the other two elements of the *prasthāna-traya,* what would be the point in mentioning the Gītā separately as an authoritative scripture in its own right?

3.69 The concept of *niṣkāma* karma is based on the universality of action, that no man alive is free from performing his dharma, directed towards his own release and the welfare of world. All human actions are motivated by the desire to attain happiness, whether material or spiritual. Tilak distinguishes between desires of two types:(a) desire for the fruit of our action, and (b) desire which motivates us to the right action. The device or skill, *kauśalaṁ* of giving up only selfish desire for the fruit, which causes unhappiness, and of performing one's duty (right action) according to one's status in life is known as yoga or Karma-yoga. The Gita, according to Tilak, asks us to give up only selfish desire or attachment to the fruit, but not all desires nor all actions:

> Actions in the gross material world, which are lifeless in themselves, are not by themselves the root cause of unhappiness. The true root of unhappiness is the hope for result, desire or

attachment with which man performs those actions. It naturally follows that in order to prevent this unhappiness, it is quite enough if a person by controlling his mind, gives up attachment, desire or hope of result entertained by him towards the objects of pleasure. It follows logically that it is not necessary to give up all objects of pleasure or actions or desires as prescribed by the Samnyāsa school.[46]

3.70 Tilak stated that the concept of *niṣkāma karma* or *svadharma* may be specifically related to the four castes when such an arrangement existed, as in the Gītā period, but that it applies nevertheless to all persons in all societies, with or without caste. Thus, by implication, caste rules are not the final sources of duty in modern India: "that duty which has fallen on one's shoulders or which, being possible, may have been taken up by one as a duty, of one's own choice, becomes a moral duty."[47] He cited the example of the Brahmin Madhavrao Peshava who was praised by Rāma Śāstrībuva for taking up the duties of a soldier instead of religious duties when Maratha affairs were in a crisis.

Lokasamgraha

3.71 While *niṣkāma karma* provides the technique of performing one's duty, Lokasaṁgraha provides the goal, the direction, and therefore also the content of actions that constitute the duty. Tilak was the first Gītā-commentator to have identified and highlighted this important concept which occurs in the third chapter of the Gītā. The compound word Lokasaṁgraha means social harmony and welfare as well as world preservation, because its two component words *loka* and *saṁgraha* have more than one meaning each. For example, *loka* denotes mankind or the world, and *saṁgraha* stands for protecting, keeping, regulating, etc. Lokasaṁgraha thus epitomizes, in the Gītā, the social and universal dimension of Śrī Kṛṣṇa's teaching. Panikkar has rightly described Lokasaṁgraha as the special contribution of the Gītā, even beyond what the Vedas and Upaniṣads had given in this field, and the credit for declaring this to the modern Hindus and to everyone else goes to *Gītā Rahasya*. In Panikkar's words:

> Lokasaṁgraha or the welfare of the world as the motive and object of all action is the special contribution of the Gītā to Hindu religious and social thought. It follows naturally from the doctrine of unattached action which is the central theme of Kṛṣṇa's teaching. If action is to be selfless and is to be without reference to the fruits thereof (in relation to the actor) then the question naturally arises, why should anyone persist in a course of action? The old theories of yajña or sacrifice provided a simple answer: action is to please the gods and to derive worldly benefits through them. Since that was not *niṣkāma* karma or action without reference to the results for the actor, the Gītā rejected it and supplied the answer that the object of all action should be Lokasaṁgraha or the welfare of the world.
>
> The social theory behind the Loksaṁgraha doctrine of the Gītā is most important. The conception of a world order which it is the duty of the individual to uphold by dedicating his activity towards that end, runs all through the teachings of the Gītā. The earlier Vedic religion had no such conception. Nor did the later thinkers who built up the comprehensive structure of Upaniṣadic thought devote any attention to social development. For the first time the Gītā gives a

social content to religion and emphasizes the welfare of the world as the purpose of all action. The doctrine of sacrifice is thus given a wholly different meaning in the Gītā, where action dedicated to God is called Brahmayajña.[48]

3.72 Tilak's elaboration of Lokasaṁgraha was intended to show to the social reform-oriented, educated Indians that their attempts at copying the west arose only because they had not understood their own scriptures properly. In the nineteenth century, the reformist thinkers were, to begin with, impressed by the social purpose and wide humanism of Chiristianity, and the earliest spiritual stirrings of educated India were towards a dilution of Hindu religion with Christian thought which was best exemplified by one of the phases of the Brahmo-samāj. Brown explains why, in Tilak's opinion, the Lokasaṁgraha approach was better suited to India than the social action philosophy borrowed from the west:

> Tilak rejects the Activism of the West adopted by his Brahmin rival, Gokhale, who believed in gradual social reform as a precedent to swaraj or Indian independence. The Lokamānya insisted on the ousting of the British and upon self-rule as prerequisite to all else. He characterised Western-type Activism as devoted merely to improving worldly existence, whereas the Karmayoga of the Gītā was devoted to self-realization through service to mankind. The Western Energism was thus rājasa or emotional while the Indian variety was sāttvika or intelligent.[49]

Viewing Householders as Pillars for Social Action

3.73 Although Tilak himself broadly accepted the

metaphysical concept of the Advaita philosophy of Śaṁkara, whom he called "a superman and a great sage," the Gītā-commentary of Tilak, being Karma-yoga-oriented, was so different from the jñāna-centred commentary of Śaṁkara. Furthermore, as part of his argument establishing the inadequacy of "jñāna without karma," Tilak also criticized Śaṁkara for removing the prohibition on Samnyāsa or renunciation as a stage of life. Tilak quoted *smṛti* texts to assert that, in the Kaliyuga, that is after the days of the Kauravas and the Pāṇḍavas, the path of renunciation was prohibited. In fact, five things were forbidden: cow slaughter, meat eating at the Śrāddha ceremonies, honouring the ancestors; Agnihotra or maintenance of the perpetual sacred fire; niyoga or begetting offspring from another's wife; and samnyāsa. Of these, Śaṁkara retained the first four prohibitions, but removed that on samnyāsa, which according to Tilak was partly responsible for a lukewarm attitude to the philosophy of activism as taught by the Gītā. In Tilak's approach, the main responsibility for Lokasaṁgraha activities has to be borne by householders, not samnyāsins.

3.74 Tilak's contention was that, not only in Kaliyuga but even prior to that, warnings were given about the disadvantages likely to be caused to the society by a widespread recourse to samnyāsa. This practice (of renunciation) was encouraged by Buddhists and the Jains. In the Bhagavad-Gītā, only an attitude of renunciation concerning the fruit of action is recommended, not renunciation of worldly duties as such. This Gītā way of harmonizing the two ancient doctrines—pravṛtti or karma, and nivṛtti or renunciation—was, in Tilak's opinion, more beneficial to the society than that attempted by Smṛti writers through the scheme of four Āśramas.

3.75 Smṛti writers like Manu devised the scheme of four Āśrama, out of which the second (Gṛhastha) would concentrate on Karma, and the fourth Āśrama (Samnyāsa) would concentrate on Jñāna. However, these writers had fully realised the fact that if there was an inordinate increase in the desire of the people to take up samnyāsa, the activity in the world would be adversely affected and society would ultimately be tamed. Therefore, Manu placed definite restrictions as to when Samnyāsa Āśrama could be entered into. In fact, he compared the Gṛhastha Āśrama to the sea and other three Āśramas to rivers. (Manu.6.90) Inasmuch as the state of the householder provides the other three states with food, Manu enjoined the performance of all worldly activities, including acts of valour and of universal welfare, during Gṛhastha Āśrama. He argued that in coming to birth, every man brings on his back three debts which he owes to Ṛṣis, his ancestors, and the Vedic deities. He must discharge these debts by fulfilling his obligations, namely, to the Ṛṣis by the study of Vedas; to the ancestors by the procreation of offspring; and to the deities by the performance of sacrificial ritual. If he takes to Samnyāsa without having discharged his obligations, he will go to pedition. Two visible signs as to when a man might be ready for Samnyāsa are indicated by Manu, namely, when a man's body becomes covered with wrinkles, and he has seen his own grand-children. (Manu.6.2).

3.76 There are indications that in many cases the preconditions for taking to Samnyāsa were not observed. Tilak refers to a story in the Ādiparva of the Mahābhārata that Jaratkaru did not discharge his debt to the ancestors, and started austere religious practices preparatory to Samnyāsa, before marrying; that as a result of his having thus destroyed his possible children, he saw his ancestors dangling in the air, and that, in performance of their injunctions he later married.[50] Tilak also mentions another story that occurs in the Bhāgavata. Nārada advised the sons of Dakṣa Prajāpati to take to the path of Samnyāsa before they had married. Dakṣa Prajāpati reprimanded Nārada for this unlawful and objectionable behaviour, and laid a curse on him.[51]

3.77 In later times, many instances of people taking to Samnyāsā as an easy way of escaping from worldly responsibilities must have occurred. Tulsidās in Rāmacaritamānas refers to people who, after the death of their wife, and realising that they are unable to maintain themselves as householders, shave off their head and become Samnyāsin (Uttarakāṇḍa, 99.3). It was in anticipation of such occurrences that the *Smṛti*-writers had made samnyāsa a *kali-varjya,* that is prohibited in Kaliyuga. Tilak's *Gītā-Rahasya* strongly supports such prohibition against Samnyāsa, which was, however, removed by Śaṁkara.

Summary of Tilak's Contribution to Practical Vedanta

3.78 (a) His use of the Gita for the freedom struggle was a contribution of historic importance.

(b) His monumental book "Gita-Rahasya or Karma-Yoga-Shastra" was a very valuable addition to Gita-literature.

(c) He strengthened the Practical Vedanta movement by pointing out that Shankaracharya's Gita-commentary suffered from serious methodological errors—

(i) Shankaracharya did not follow the standard method of interpretation based on "upakrama-upasamhara-phala."

(ii) Shankaracharya used the method of "arthavada" in an incorrect manner.

(iii) Shankaracharya started with a pre-determined conclusion and so had to twist the meaning of important shlokas.

Notes

1. Stanley A. Wolpert, Tilak and Gokhale: Revolution and Reform in the Making of Modern India. University of California Press, 1962, p. 2.
2. D.V. Tahmankar, Lokamanya Tilak, Father of Indian Unrest and Maker of Modern India. John Murray, London, 1956, p. 11.
3. Ibid., p. 205.
4. Ibid., p. 24.
5. Ibid., p. 27.
6. T.V. Parvate, Bal Gangadhar Tilak. Navajivan, Ahmedabad, 1958, p 23.
7. Stanley A. Wolpert, Tilak and Gokhale, op. cit., p. 29.
8. D.V. Tahmankar, Lokamanya Tilak, op. cit., p. 62.
9. Stanley A. Wolpert, Tilak and Gokhale, op. cit., p. 81.
10. Ainslie T. Embree (ed.) The Hindu Tradition, Random House, Newyork, 1872, p. 310.
11. D.S. Sarma, The Renaissance of Hinduism, op. cit., p. 145.
12. Stanley A. Wolpert, Tilak and Gokhale, op. cit., p. 15.
13. D.V. Tahmankar, Lokamanya Tilak, op. cit., p. 253.
14. D.S. Sarma, The Renaissance of Hinduism, op. cit., p. 143.
15. K.M. Panikkar, The Foundations of New India, Allen and Unwin, London, 1963, p. 36.
16. T.V. Parvate, Bal Gandakar Tilak, op. cit., p. 475.
17. Ibid., p. 477.
18. D.V. Tahmankar, Lokamanya Tilak, op. cit., pp. 49-50.
19. Ibid., p. 50.

20. Ibid., p. 50.
21. Stanley A Wolpert, Tilak and Gokhale, op. cit., p. 302.
22. Arvind Sharma (with A. Ray, A. Hejib and K. Young), Sati, Historical and Phenomenological Essays. Motilal Banarsidass, Delhi, 1988, pp. 43-8.
23. Ibid., p. 48.
24. Ibid., p. 46
25. T.V. Parvate, Bal Gangadhar Tilak, op. cit., pp. 42–3.
26. D.P. Karmarkar, Bal Gangadhar Tilak: A Study. Popular Book Depot, Bombay, 1956, pp. 107-8.
27. Ibid., p. 111.
28. Stanley A. Wolpert, Tilak and Gokhale, op. cit., p. 101.
29. D.V. Tahmankar, Lokamanya Tilak, op. cit., Prelude.
30. Stanley A. Wolpert, Tilak and Gokhale,op. cit., pp. 96 and 259.
31. D.P. Karmarkar, Bal Gangadhar Tilak: A study, op. cit., pp. 133-4.
32. Stanley A. Wolpert, Tilak and Gokhale, op. cit., p. 170.
33. Ibid., p. 169.
34. Ibid., p. 191.
35. D.S. Sarma, The Renaissance of Hinduism, op. cit., pp. 143-4.
36. Stanley A. Wolpert, Tilak and Gokhale, op. cit., p. 220.
37. Ibid., p. 221.
38. T.V. Parvate, Bal gangadhar Tilak, op. cit., p. 213.
39. D.V. Tahmankar, Likamanya Tilak, op. cit., p. 196.
40. B.G. Tilak, Writings and Speeches. Ganesan, Madras, 1922, pp. 259-61.
41. B.G. Tilak, Gita Rahasya. Tilak Brothers, Poona, sixth edition, 1986, pp. 90-1.
42. P.M. Thomas, Twentieth Century Indian Interpretations of Bhagavad Gita: Tilak, Gandhi and Aurobindo. Indian Society for Promoting Christian Knowledge, Delhi, 1987, p. 188.
43. K.M. Panikkar, The Foundations of New India, op. cit., p. 43.

44. B.G. Tilak, Gita Rahasya, op. cit., pp. 460-1.
45. K.M. Panikkar, The Foundations of New India, op. cit., p. 42.
46. B.G. Tilak, Gita Rahasya, op. cit., p. 151.
47. Ibid., p. 697.
48. K.M. Panikkar, The Foundations of New Delhi, op. cit., pp. 39-40.
49. D. Mackenzie Brown, "The Philosophy of Bal Gangadhar Tilak: Karma vs. Jnana in the Gita Rahasya", in The Journal of Asian Studies, vol. XVII, No. 2, (Feb. 1958), p. 202.
50. B.G. Tilak, Gita Rahasya, op. cit., p. 404.
51. Ibid., p. 469.

CHAPTER 4

Aurobindo's Rejection of the Jagat-Mithya Doctrine

A Brief Life-sketch

4.1 A good deal of significance is often attached to Aurobindo's date of birth (15 August) as well as to his ancestry. When the date fixed for India's Independence (15 August 1947) happened to be the same as Aurobindo's seventy-fifth birthday, he himself felt that "this coincidence" was not merely "a fortuitous accident":

> August 15th 1947, is the birthday of free India....
>
> August 15th is my own birthday and it is naturally gratifying to me that it should have assumed this vast significance. I take this coincidence, not as a fortuitous accident, but as the sanction and seal of the Divine Force that guides my steps on the work with which I began life, the beginning of its full fruition.[1]

4.2 Among Aurobindo's ancestors, the direct or indirect influences exerted on him by his own father, and by his mother's father, pulled Aurobindo in practically opposite directions. Majumdar has described in detail how the "strongly anglicized" father of Aurobindo gave "strict instructions" to provide for Aurobindo a thoroughly Western education to fit him for public service under the British Government:

> Aurobindo's father, K.D. Ghose, an England-returned medical officer, was so strongly anglicized that he sent Aurobindo to England at the age of eight....
>
> Aurobindo, as a child, spoke only English, and under the strict instructions of his father he was brought up in England in such a way that he knew nothing of India and her culture.[2]

4.3 In comparison to the strong and direct influence which Aurobindo's father tried to exert on his son in his childhood, (but without a long-lasting effect), the influence of Aurobindo's mother's father, Rajnarain Bose, can only be characterized as indirect and implicit, but ultimately proving more effective. Majumdar speaks of Rajnarain Bose "as the father of nationalism in Bengal", who "turned the tide" against Keshab's followers who might otherwise have "proved to be a highly denationalizing element in the body-politic, owing to their tendencies towards European ethics and theology":

> Rajnarain Bose held out before his countrymen a complete and comprehensive picture of nationalism, touching almost every aspect of life, in a prospectus which he issued in 1866 with a view to the establishment of a "Society for the promotion of national feeling among the educated natives of Bengal". The object of this Society was to resist the powerful tendency of imitating the west, by reviving old ideas, traditions and customs in every walk of life.... Rabindranath Tagore says in his autobiography that he and his elder brother

> joined a secret society founded by Rajnarain Bose and got from him their first inspiration to free India.[3]

4.4 What stirred the souls of "a large number of Hindus" was a public lecture delivered by Rajnarain Bose in 1872 (the year of Aurobindo's birth), in which the idea of basing Indian nationalism on the Hindu religion was vehemently formulated. The concluding lines of this lecture of Rajnarain Bose were: "I see in my mind the noble and puissant Hindu nation rousing herself after sleep, and rushing towards progress with divine prowess".[4]

4.5 Majumdar speaks of "the effect produced by this lecture of Rajnarain Bose" on many persons, including Bankim Chandra Chatterji who wrote: "Let there be a shower of flowers and sandal on the pen of Rajnarain Babu".[5] Although Rajnarain Bose's influence on Aurobindo might be indirect, the way it was reinforced by Bankim Chandra Chatterji and others, made it more penetrating, and its full effect became visible in Aurobindo's views after about thirty five years. As Majumdar summarizes:

> Rajnarain Bose played a significant role in the birth of nationalism in Bengal... but it was his daughter's son Aurobindo who became the high-priest of the new cult of nationalism.[6]

4.6 Karan Singh has given details of how Aurobindo "managed to get himself disqualified for ICS," and started, instead, to utilize his stay at Cambridge University for participating in the activities of the Indian Majlis:

> At Cambridge, Aurobindo passed the First Part of the Classics Tripos in the first division after two years, and also won college prizes for English and literary ability. He was working simultaneously for

the I.C.S. examination and passed all its terminal examinations. Finally he passed the open competition with distinction, but did not qualify for the service because he did not pass the riding test. As he puts it, he 'felt no call for the I.C.S. and was seeking some way to escape from that bondage. By certain manoeuvres he managed to get himself disqualified for riding, without himself rejecting the service which his family would not have allowed him to do.'

When he went to Cambridge he came into contact there with an organization known as the Indian Majlis founded in 1891. He took an active part in the activities of the Majlis of which he also became Secretary. Along with several other hot-blooded young men he participated in its debates, and it seems that he delivered several speeches against British imperialism that can only be described as revolutionary.[7]

4.7 Sarma views Aurobindo's stay at Cambridge as a tussle between "his erring father" on the one hand, and "Mother India" on the other. Since Aurobindo was soon to switch over his interests from Europe to India, and in particular, from Greek to Sanskrit, Sarma quotes a poem written by Aurobindo during 1890-92, which shows that he had already heard "the call of Saraswati" for quitting the "Athenian lanes" in favour of the "shores of the Ganges":

For in Sicilian olive-groves no more
Or seldom must my foot-prints now be seen,
Nor tread Athenian lanes, nor yet explore
Parnassus or thy voiceful shores, O Hippocrene.
Me from her lotus heaven Saraswati
Has called to regions of eternal snow
And Ganges pacing to the Southern sea,

Ganges upon whose shores the flowers of Eden blow.[8]

4.8 Aurobindo's stay in India from 1893 to 1950 constitutes three successive phases, namely,

(i) The Preparatory phase (1893-1905)
(ii) The Bengal-partition phase (1905-10)
(iii) The Pondicherry phase (1910-50)

Regarding the beginning of the preparatory phase, Aurobindo recalled later how he arrived in India only to hear of his father's death and find his mother too ill to recognize him. But another event happened to him the moment he touched Indian soil; the darkness which had encompassed him all of his years in England lifted, and he had his first spiritual experience. In Aurobindo's own words: "Since I set foot on the Indian soil on the Apollo Bunder in Bombay, I began to have spiritual experiences, but these were not divorced from this world but had an inner and infinite bearing on it, such as a feeling of the Infinite pervading material space and the Immanent inhabiting material objects and bodies."[9]

4.9 Aurobindo's first job in India was in the princely state of Baroda, in the secretariat to start with and later as Professor of English and French and also as Vice-Principal of Baroda College. It was during these twelve years that he laid the foundations for his future work by learning Sanskrit and several of the modern Indian languages and, above all, by assimilating the spirit of Indian civilization and Hindu religion. He wrote a series of strong articles attacking the moderate policies of the Indian National Congress. He and his younger brother Barindra also tried to organize secret revolutionary groups in Bengal. Aurobindo's occasional practice of Yoga in this phase was motivated partly as a spiritual endeavour and partly to gain an inner power for political use.

4.10 During the Bengal-partition phase, Aurobindo shared the leadership of the Nationlists, or the Extremists, as they were called, with Tilak, Lajpat Rai and Bipin Chandra Pal. Like Tilak, Aurobindo attained fame not only as a great political leader but also as a journalist whose writings won mass support for the nationalist cause, and it was the same act of bomb-throwing by Khudiram Bose at Muzaffarpore (Bihar) in April 1908 which resulted in Tilak's trial in Bombay and Aurobindo's trial in Calcutta.

4.11 During 1908-1909, Aurobindo was kept in the Alipur jail as an under-trial prisoner for about a year. Aurobindo later characterized this period of detention in the jail as the most momentous period in his life. In jail he read the Bhagavad-Gītā and it deeply affected him. He also had a profound religious experience which totally altered the course of his life. He saw in a vision the familiar form of Śrī Kṛṣṇa of the Gītā. As Aurobindo recalled in his famous Uttarpārā speech delivered immediately after his acquittal in 1909:

> Then He placed the Gītā in my hands. His strength entered into me and I was able to do the Sādhanā of the Gītā.... It was Vāsudeva who surrounded me. I walked under the branches of the tree in front of my cell.... It was Śrī Kṛṣṇa whom I saw standing there and holding over me His shade. In the court, it was not the Magistrate whom I saw.... it was not the Counsel for the prosecution that I saw, it was Śrī Kṛṣṇa who sat there.... He smiled and said, 'I am guiding, therefore fear not. Turn to your own work for which I have brought you to jail and when you come out, remember never to fear, never to hesitate. Remember that it is I who am doing this, not you nor any other....[10]

4.12 Referring to Aurobindo's acquittal itself, Karan Singh notices "an ironic twist of destiny" by virtue of which the District and Sessions Judge trying the case was one Mr. Beachcroft who was at Cambridge with Aurobindo and had stood second to him in Greek. Furthermore, Aurobindo's lawyer, C.R. Das, had the keen vision to foresee that Aurobindo was no ordinary political prisoner but a remarkable person of high destiny. Accordingly C.R. Das's speech for defence, which was spread over eight days, concluded with a prophetic appeal to the judge in the following words:

> My appeal to you is this, that long after the controversy will be hushed in silence, long after this turmoil and agitation will have ceased, long after he is dead and gone, he will be looked upon as the poet of patriotism, as the prophet of nationalism and the lover of humanity. Long after he is dead and gone, his words will be echoed and re-echoed, not only in India, but across distant seas and lands. Therefore I say that the man in his position is not only standing before the bar of this court, but before the bar of the High Court of History.[11]

4.13 Aurobindo emerged from the Alipur jail with the firm conviction that he was merely an instrument in the hands of the Divine, and that the Divine power was intimately and irrevocably working in the national movement, the success of which was therefore assured whether or not he as an individual remained on the scene. This new consciousness transformed his approach to the political problems of the day, and soon to the very problem of political activity itself. Although he took to journalism again to carry forward the nationalist cause, the eight month period from June 1909 to February 1910 can be viewed as a preparation for his final withdrawal from active politics.

4.14 The weekly paper, the *Karmayogin*, which Aurobindo started editing in June 1909, clearly showed the impact of the Gītā. Not only was the name of the paper taken from the Gītā, its motto also was the famous Gītā aphorism '*Yogaḥ karmasu Kauśalaṁ*,' meaning 'yoga is skill in action'. The cover illustration showing Śrī Kṛṣṇa driving Arjuna's chariot at Kuruskṣetra, proved highly effective as a religious symbol. Besides writing on political, social, economic and cultural topics of the day, Aurobindo published a series of essays on 'the Ideals of the Karmayogin'. Comparing 'the Karmayogin' with 'Bande Mātaram' (the paper with which Aurobindo was associated prior to his imprisonment), Karan Singh remarks: "While in the Bande Mātaram, the political had been predominant and the spiritual an undercurrent, in the Karmayogin the roles were reversed."[12]

4.15 Parvate is of opinion that Aurobindo had envisaged the desirability, if not the feasibility, of winning India's independence through an unarmed revolution. In one of his speeches, Aurobindo had said, "On their fidelity to Swadeshi, to boycott, to passive resistance, rested the hope of a peaceful and spiritual revolution. On that it depended whether India would give the example unprecedented in history of a revolution worked only by moral force and peaceful pressure".[13] However, Aurobindo realized that neither he nor any of the other leaders who were in India at the time seemed capable of leading such a 'spiritual revolution'. Almost prophetically he wrote in the Karma-yogin on 31 July 1909 that the country 'must wait for the man who is to come':

> The party is there, not less pervading and powerful than before but in want of a policy and a leader. The first it may find, the second, only God can give. The men who have led hitherto, have been

> strong men of high gifts and commanding genius, great enough to be protagonists of any other movement; but even they were not sufficient to satisfy one which is the chief current of a world-wide revolution. Therefore, the Nationalist Party, custodians of the future must wait for the man who is to come, calm in the midst of calamity, hopeful under defeat, sure of eventual emergency of triumph and always mindful of the responsibility which they owe not only to India, but to the world.[14]

4.16 Aurobindo's final decision to quit politics and to make his contribution to the cause of the humanity in the spiritual field came with apparent abruptness in February 1910. Writing 'On Himself' he gives a first-hand account of how he 'suddenly received a command from above':

> Here are the facts of that departure. I was in the Karmayogin office when I received the word, on information given by a high-placed police official, that the office would be searched the next day and myself arrested. (The office was in fact searched but no warrant was produced against me: I heard nothing more of it till the case was started against the paper later on, but by then I had already left Chandernagore for Pondicherry). While I was listening to animated comments from those around on the approaching event, I suddenly received a command from above, in a Voice well-known to me, in three words, "Go to Chandernagore". In ten minutes or so I was in the boat for Chandernagore.... Afterwards, under the same "sailing orders" I left Chandernagore and reached Pondicherry on April 4, 1910.[15]

4.17 The fact that 'the progress of humanity' remained Aurobindo's goal was confirmed by Aurobindo himself when he gave Romain Rolland the following reason for his withdrawal from 'mediocre politics':

> India possesses in its past, a little rusty and out of use, the key to the progress of humanity. It is to this side that I am now turning my energies, rather than towards mediocre politics. Hence the reason for my withdrawal. I believe in the necessity for tapasyā (a life of meditation and concentration) in silence for education and self-knowledge and for the unloosing of spiritual energies. Our ancestors used these means under different forms; for they are the best for becoming an efficient worker in the great hours of the world.[16]

4.18 During the Pondicherry phase of Aurobindo's life, the year 1914 is significant because Paul Richard, a French writer, came with his wife Mira Richard to Pondicherry to collaborate with Aurobindo in the starting of the philosophical journal, the *Ārya* (Review of the Great Synthesis). The aims of this journal were to give the reader:

(i) A systematic study of the highest problems of existence;

(ii) The formation of a vast synthesis of knowledge, harmonizing the diverse religious traditions of humanity, occidental as well as oriental. Its method will be that of realism, at once rational and transcendental, a realism consisting of the unification of intellectual and scientific disciplines with those of intuitive experience.

4.19 But soon after the journal *Ārya* was started, the First World War broke out and Richard and his wife returned to France. Aurobindo continued the journal, publishing therein the result of his meditations, thoughts and experiences. In the next six years he published many of his famous writings, including Essays on the Gītā, the Life Divine, The Ideal of Human

Unity and new interpretations of the Upaniṣads. About his written works Aurobindo later said, "I have made no endeavour in writing, I have simply left the higher power to work."[17]

4.20 In 1920, Mira Richard returned from France to join Aurobindo in the spiritual work she had envisioned as needed for the world. During the last ten years in Pondicherry, Aurobindo had progressed for himself, but he could not do much by way of helping others. With the help of Mira Richard (who became The Mother of the Āśrama), Aurobindo was able to give to the world the spiritual message representing the result of his *sādhanā*. With the Mother in charge of the Āśrama, Aurobindo found the proper atmosphere and time that he needed to fulfil his mission—to prepare the physical earth plane for the new supramental age, the kingdom of heaven on earth. He wrote thousands of letters to the followers and also completed the epic *Sāvitrī* (23,806 lines of inspired poetry).

4.21 Following his retirement into a secluded portion of the Āśrama, Aurobindo faced accusations of escaping the harsh world of reality and suffering, and of retreating into a pleasant, painless, non-abrasive seclusion. Aurobindo clarified and pointed out that such accusations arose out of an "illusion":

> But what strange ideas again! —that I was born with a supramental temperament and that I have known nothing of hard realities! Good God! My whole life has been a struggle with hard realities, from hardships, starvation in England and constant dangers and fierce difficulties continually cropping up here in Pondicherrry, external and internal. My life has been a battle from its early years and is still a battle: the fact that I wage it now from a room upstairs and by spiritual means as well as

others that are external makes no difference to its character. But, of course, as we have not been shouting about these things, it is natural, I suppose, for others to think that I am living in an august, glamorous lotus-eating dreamland where no hard facts of life or Nature present themselves. But what an illusion all the same![18]

4.22 In the world-wide message that Aurobindo sent on 15 August 1947, he spoke of his "dreams", which clearly showed how deeply devoted he always was to the ideals of "individual perfection, perfect society, human unity, and spiritual regeneration of the world".

> The first of these dreams was a revolutionary movement which would create a free and united India. India today is free, but she has not achieved unity....
>
> Another dream was for the resurgence and liberation of the people of Asia and her return to her great role in the progress of civilization....
>
> The third dream was a world-union forming the outer basis of a fairer, brighter and nobler life for all mankind.... The momentum is there.... A new spirit of oneness will take hold of the human race.
>
> Another dream, the spiritual gift of India to the world has already begun... amid the disasters of the time more and more eyes are turning towards her with hope and there is even an increasing resort not only to her teachings, but to her psychic and spiritual practice.
>
> The final dream was a step in evolution which would raise man to a higher and larger consciousness and begin the solution of the problems which have perplexed and vexed him since he first begin to think and to dream of individual perfection and perfect society. This is

> still a personal hope and idea, an ideal which has begun to take hold both in India and in the West on forward-looking minds. The difficulties in the way are more formidable than in any other field of endeavour, but difficulties were made to be overcome.[19]

4.23 Aurobindo "withdrew from the physical body" on 5 December 1950. However, the Mother of the Pondicherry Āśrama continued implementing Aurobindo's ideas, two of which need special mention, for purposes of the present study:

(i) Śrī Aurobindo International University Centre was started on 24 April 1951. It was later called 'Śrī Aurobindo International Centre of Education'.

(ii) Auroville, "the Cradle of a new World", was founded on 29 February 1968.

Viewing Politics as God's Work, with Stress on Religious Symbols

4.24 Although Aurobindo's direct involvement in the nationalist movement was only during five years (1905-10), he made a significant contribution to the freedom struggle by viewing it as "God's work" and by exhorting all his countrymen to plunge into the fight as "instruments of God." He told the people that the real leader of the movement was God, who was inspiring persons like Aswini Kumar Datta of Barisal (East Bengal) and Bal Gangadhar Tilak of Poona (the chief spokesman of the Extremist wing of the Congress in the country):

> It is God who rides on the wings of the hurricane, it is the might and force of the Lord that manifested itself and His almighty hands that seized and shook the roof so violently over our

> heads.... Repression is nothing but the hammer of God.... They do not know that great as he is, Aswini Kumar Datta is not the leader of this movement, that Tilak is not the leader—God is the leader.... It is because God has chosen to manifest Himself and has entered into the hearts of His people that we are rising again as a nation... It will move forward irresistibly until God's will in it is fulfilled...
>
> Nationalism is a religion that has come from God.... If you are going to be a nationalist, if you are going to assent to this religion of nationalism, you must do it in the religious spirit. You must remember that you are the instruments of God.[20]

4.25 The enthusiastic acceptance which Aurobindo's approach received in the country, and particularly in Bengal, grew out of the mood of patriotic awakening and religious revival, stirred up by the partition of Bengal. Lord Curzon's scheme of dividing the province of Bengal into two, although formally announced on 20 July 1905, was to take effect from 16 October 1905. The entire Bengali community felt a strong concern about a matter directly affecting their province such as they had never experienced before. Hundreds of public meetings were held and all sorts of ways of putting pressure on the government were talked of. Four methods of protest found strong support, namely boycott of British goods, greater use of Swadeshi or goods made within the country, starting institutions of national education not controlled by the government, and observing the partition day as a day of mourning. Patriotic feelings were aroused by these methods of protest. Side by side with these, the following four "religious symbols" became prominent, almost spontaneously or inspired partly by the occurrence of festivals and partly through religious literature:

(a) "Rākhī" not only as a traditional festival but also as a religious symbol highlighting the indelible unity of the Bengali race and the promise of mutual protection (of *Rakṣā*).

(b) "Pūjā", the most important Bengali festival symbolically remodelled so as to include a grand "yajña" ceremony and a mass prayer to the Goddess to give to Her devotees strength at this critical hour.

(c) "Bande Mātaram" adopted from Bankim Chandra Chatterji's novel "Ānandamaṭh" as the symbolic war-cry of the peaceful fighters for the Motherland.

(d) "Vivekananda" as a symbol of the new Hinduism, emphasizing "sevā" or service of fellow-brethren as an essential feature of religion, and also "fearlessness" as the message of the Upaniṣads and the Gītā.

4.26 Each of the above-mentioned symbols, and action programmes associated therewith, contributed, in its own ways, in giving religious orientation to patriotic feelings and in making the people mentally prepared to listen to Aurobindo's declaration that the movement is God's work. Furthermore, Rabindranath Tagore's active association with these programmes was also of great significance. For example, Tagore himself issued to the public a letter in Bengali, indicating how the Rākhī festival was to be given a new shape, for affirming that the bond of union between East Bengal and West Bengal was "implanted by Providence".

> On the 30th of Āświn, Bengal will be partitioned by legislation. To prove, however, that God did not ordain the serverance of the race, it is proposed that the day should be commemorated by an observance of Rākhī Bandhan, to indicate the

> indelible unity of the Bengali race....
>
> The mantra to be uttered on the occasion of tying the sacred Rākhī thread on the arms of one another is: 'Brothers live united'.... Let that day be commemorated to indicate the indissoluble brotherhood between East Bengal men and West Bengal men, between rich and low, between Christians, Mohammedans and Hindus, born of soil.... The Rākhī ceremony will indicate that no monarch's sword, howsoever powerful, can cut asunder the bond of union implanted by Providence amongst people forming one and the same race.[21]

4.27 The Pūjā ceremony, held at the Kalighat temple on 28 September 1905, was also given a new shape, including prayers to the Goddess for averting the doom of partition, and the taking of a solemn vow to discard all foreign clothes. The *Amrita Bazar Patrika* of Calcutta highlighted the following aspects of the Pūjā festival of that year:

> The gathering was estimated to be more than 50,000. It was not a gathering of boys, nor of illiterate people. It was a respectable and representative gathering of the Hindu inhabitants of Calcutta and the neighbouring places, including the landed Hindu aristocracy, barefooted and dressed in holy silken clothes...
>
> But it was not a mere matter of crowds. The feeling was intense. This vast assembly, consisting of all grades of society, was led to congregate before the Goddess on that auspicious day—the Mahālaya day—to offer up to the Goddess prayers for averting the doom of partition and to take a solemn vow to discard all foreign clothes....
>
> The Pūjā was followed by the Homa (yajña)

> ceremony which was a grand sight, a huge fire was burning to which ghee and other offerings, incense, and sandalwood were incessantly supplied, accompanied by the offering of mantras by thousands of voices. They invoked the aid of the Goddess, the centre of all power, to give them strength at this critical hour....
>
> The Brahmins in the temple uttered the following invocation in Sanskrit: Worship the motherland before all other deities, give up sectarianism, all religious differences, animosities, and selfishness; adopt one and all the pledge of serving the mother country and devote your lives to relieve her distress.
>
> Standing in front of the Mother in the temple, the following vow was taken in batches: I solemnly promise that to the best of my power I will never use foreign articles, that I will not purchase such articles from foreign shops which are to be had at Indian shops, that I will not employ foreigners for work which could be done by my countrymen.[22]

Majumdar, the author of the *History of the Freedom Movement in India* looks upon this solemn vow as the first declaration of war against the British—and this paved the way for Aurobindo to make his own contribution thereto as a karmayogin.

4.28 The adoption of "Bande Mataram", meaning "Hail Mother", as a greeting and slogan, for use by the agitators, played a long-lasting role in reminding all Indians that worshipping and serving the motherland was the highest form of religious devotion. This greeting forms part of a hymn to Mother Goddess in the Bengali novel *Ānandamaṭha* written by Bankim Chandra Chatterji. This hymn is really a song addressed to the motherland, Bengal and India, conceived not only as a geographical unit, but as the fountain source of everything that is dear to man, namely physical strength, spiritual devotion, knowledge, religion, feeling, perception.

"Who says that the Mother is weak and helpless? Harken to the war-cry from seven (later changed to thirty) crores of voices, backed up by weapons held in hands twice that number".

The novelist Bankim Chandra makes one of the characters in the novel utter a remark: "But this is not mother—it is a country", to which the singer of the hymn replies: "A patriot knows no other mother, no other object of devotion".[23]

4.29 The Congress adopted this hymn of Bankim Chandra Chatterji as the National Song. (After independence, Tagore's song "Jana-Gaṇa-Mana" was adopted as the National Anthem). The symbolic expression of patriotism by means of the greeting "Bande Mātaram" became such a strong force that British authorities took repressive measures to stop this practice. It was one such occurrence in Barisal (East Bengal) where the local leader Aswini Kumar Datta tried, for purposes of holding a conference, to arrive at a compromise with the British administration whose main demand was that "Bande Mātaram" should not be used in the streets by the processionists. However, the authorities started beating boys for saying "Bande Mātaram" even inside their homes and schools, with the result that, ultimately the conference organised by Aswini Kumar Datta, became, in the words of Congress leader Surendranath Banerji, "a story of acts of repression, one of the darkest in the annals of the Government of East Bengal."[24]

It was mainly with reference to this incident that Aurobindo described Aswini Kumar Datta as an instrument of God (see para 4.24 above). Barisal provided one of the strongest evidences of how effective and powerful the slogan "Bande Mātaram" was during the freedom struggle. The great contribution of Bankim Chandra, whose novel was the original source of "Bande Mātaram" was recognized by Aurobindo in the following words: "He (Bankim Chandra) bade us leave the canine method of agitation for the leonine".[25] Even school-boys behaved like lions when they insisted on saying "Bande Mātaram".

4.30 Although Vivekananda himself had avoided direct involvement in political activities, his teaching relating to "sevā", "fearlessness" and "strength" were found to be particularly inspiring by the students and other groups of young patriots who were anxious to do something worthwhile for the motherland. Majumdar finds a parallel between what these young persons picked up from the writings of Bankim Chandra and Vivekananda. Bankim Chandra's message of religious devotion to motherland, and the action-generating call of Vivekananda based on the philosophical teachings of the Upaniṣads and the Gītā—these became the sacred canon of the young patriots of Bengal. To a group of young men who had asked Vivekananda for advice, he had said, "Be strong, my young friends; that is my advice to you. You will be nearer to heaven through football than through the study of the Gītā.... You will understand the Gītā better with your biceps, your muscles, a little stronger."[26] On another occasion he had said, "Remember the soul-stirring death-defying Mantraṁ—Abhīḥ—fearlessness—and shake off age long vestiges of slave-mentality, superstition and inferiority complex".[27]

4.31 Majumdar has highlighted Vivekananda's influence on the young patriots:

> The Bhagavad-Gītā, frequently quoted by Vivekananda and made popular by the Bengali translation with elaborate commentary by Bankim

> Chandra, taught them to look upon this body as a mere transient thing—a tattered garment to be put off by the soul for a new one-and to perform one's duty in a detached spirit, without looking for its result or reward, laying down life or killing others, if need be, with equanimity—for every man is merely the agent of God and doing His work.[28]

4.32 Many such messages were given by Vivekananda only three years prior to the partition of Bengal, and they were still fresh in the memories of the people. Aurobindo himself was inspired by Vivekananda's words, and he took the editor of the *Indian Patriot* to task "for forgetting the teachings of Vivekananda..... What does he think was the cause of the great awakening in Bengal?"[29]

4.33 To the religious symbols which had assumed importance prior to Aurobindo's joining the anti-partition uprising, Aurobindo himself made a significant addition in the form of the "Kurukṣetra Batterfield". He presented this symbol on the title-page of his weekly journal *Karmayogin.* Although Tilak had already appealed to all Indians to consider the entire country as the new Kurukṣetra battlefield for Swarāj, a pictorial presentation of the Kurukṣetra Battlefield on the title-page of Aurobindo's weekly paper had a special appeal. The Kṛṣṇa-figure giving the Karma-Yoga message to Arjuna provided an explanation as to why the journal itself was called *The Karmayogin.* Ursula King attaches great importance to Aurobindo's contribution in popularizing the Kurukṣetra picture as a religious symbol carrying a political message:

> This motif (a picture of Krishna at Kurukshetra) decorates the title page of Aurobindo's weekly review 'Karmayogin', published at the height of his political activity in Calcutta between 1909-10

> and continued for some time, after his departure for Pondicherry, by Sister Nivedita. As the title explicitly states, the *Karmayogin* was 'A Weekly Review of National Religion, Literature, Science, Philosophy, etc....'. Above the title is the picture of Krishna and Arjuna in a chariot, surrounded by Sanskrit quotations from the Bhagavd-Gītā referring, for example, to verses ii.50 ('Yoga is wisdom in work') and iii.30 ('Offer to me all thy works and rest thy mind on the Supreme'). Religious and political nationalism are closely intertwined in this review which preaches a new Karmayoga through the very effective vehicle of the ideal Karmayogin symbol.[30]

4.34 The activist message symbolized by thc Kurukṣetra-title-page was explicitly and repeatedly stated by Aurobindo in the columns of his weekly journal *The Karmayogin.* A specimen of what he wrote is given below:

> The recurrent cry of Śrī Kṛṣṇa to Arjuna insists on the struggle: 'Fight and overthrow thy opponents!', 'Remember me and fight!'... The charioteer of Kurukshetra driving the car of Arjuna over that field of ruin is the image and description of Karmayoga; for the body is the chariot and the senses are the horses of the driving and it is through bloodshed and mire-sunk ways of the world that Śrī Kṛṣṇa pilots the soul of man to Vaikuṇṭḥa.[31]

4.35 The appeal of the religious symbols turned out to be highly effective because the poetic and literary revolution in Bengal went hand-in-hand with Aurobindo's spiritual fervour. Since Rabindranath Tagore was the greatest of all the patriotic poets in Bengali, Majumdar summarizes his simultaneous revolution in spiritualism and poetry, jointly serving the cause of nationalism:

> If Aurobindo was the high priest, Rabindranath was the great poet of the swadeshī movement. What Aurobindo achieved in the realm of thought by his fearless writings, Rabindranath conveyed to the masses by his songs, incomparable in diction and inimitable in the melody of its tune...
>
> The idea which had inspired Bankim Chandra to write the Bande Mātaram hymn, was expressed through the medium of charming poems and songs by Rabindranath. But Rabindranath did a great deal more. He sang the glories of ancient India and its culture and brought vividly before us the portraits of Shivājī and Guru Govind Singh as nation-builders, and of Banda as a symbol of the stoic heroism. Many of his ballads touch upon the patriotism, chivalry and heroism of the Rājpūts and the struggle of the Marāṭhās and Sikhs for freedom...
>
> Aurobindo and Rabindranath proved that pen is mightier than the sword.... They are entitled to the chief credit for changing the swadeshī into a genuine national movement which swept the whole country.[32]

4.36 Before looking into the various elements that constituted Aurobindo's political activities as a Karmayogin, it may be appropriate to see how Aurobindo's entry into the Swedeshi movement has been perceived by Majumdar, the author of the *History of the Freedom Movement in India:*

> The chief traits of the new cult were enunciated, with something like a spiritual fervour, by Aurobindo Ghose who came to Bengal as the high priest of new nationalism shortly after the inauguration of the Swadeshi movement. These were:

(i) The elevation of patriotism into a religion, and transformation of religion into patriotism by conceiving the motherland not only as mother but as Supreme God whose service is the only way to salvation; and

(ii) Belief in God as the leader of the movement, in complete freedom as the goal, and passive resistance as the method".[33]

These together with other details are presented in the next section.

Political Activities as a Karmayogin

4.37 Even before Aurobindo came to Bengal from Baroda, to work whole-heartedly for the nationalist cause, the Congress was practically sub-divided (though not formally) into two groups, the Moderates and the Extremists. Gopal Krishna Gokhale was the recognized leader of the Moderates. On the Extremists side, three persons were the most prominent, namely, Bal Gangadhar Tilak, Lala Lajpat Rai, and Bipin Chandra Pal, and a popular abbreviated expression for the three together was "Lal-Bal-Pal". The differences between the two groups got accentuated over the issue of how to respond to the partition of Bengal. Boycott, Swadeshi, and national education constituted the core of the Extremists' approach, while the moderates were hesitant to go along with such "revolutionary" ideas that were so different from the policies followed by the Congress since its inception in 1885.

4.38 At the annual session of the Congress held at Banaras in December 1905, the differences between the two groups were somehow patched up because neither of them wanted an open split. (Such a split occurred at Surat in 1907). Since Gokhale, the Moderate leader was Congress President at Banaras, the Extremist group got together, after the Congress session was over, and decided to form what they called a "Nationalist Party" within the Congress but determined to push forward its own radical programme. So, thereafter, the two terms "Extremists" and "Nationalists" practically became synonymous.

4.39 Throughout the year 1906, an acrimonious controversy was carried on by the spokesmen of the two groups, through their respective periodicals, as both looked forward to a decisive trial of strength in the forthcoming session of the Congress at Calcutta scheduled to be held in December 1906. However, public opinion seemed to be going the Extremists' way, and one of the factors responsible for bringing this about was the arrival of Aurobindo and his close association with the Nationalist journal "Bande Mātaram". Majumdar considers Aurobindo's joining the Nationalist movement as significant as the arrival of a "Prophet", and Karan Singh also calls Aurobindo "the Prophet of Indian Nationalism". Here are Majumdar's words:

> Above all, the Extremist party had an accession of immense strength when it was joined by Aurobindo, who proved to be a host in himself. Indeed the entry of this new personality in the Congress arena may be regarded as a major event in Indian politics. Aurobindo's articles in the Bande Mātaram put the Extremist party on a high pedestal all over India. He expounded the high philosophy and national spirit which animated the party, and also laid down its programme of action. But far more valuable to the Extremist party than even his discourses, was his striking personality. Fired with religious fervour, he preached nationalism as a religion, and he, the prophet of this new religion, infused by his precept and

> example, courage and strength into everyone that came in touch with him.[34]

4.40 The difference between the two groups lay in the specification of the political goal to be achieved as well as in the methods to be adopted for achieving it. Considering, first, the goal, the term "Swaraj" used by Tilak was generally accepted, but its interpretation was not the same. The Moderates viewed it as colonial self-government rather than complete independence. A common argument of the Moderates and their sympathizers was that, since Swaraj in any form is bound to be a long way off, the Extremists should accept colonial self-government as an interim goal at least, and retain the right to enlarge it to complete independence in due course of time. However, Aurobindo, voicing the revolutionary spirit of the Nationalists, characterized the "gradualism" of the Moderates as a sign of "fear", and viewed Swaraj as "the direct revelation of God to our people":

> Our ideal is that of swaraj or absolute autonomy free from foreign control.... There are some who fear to use the word 'freedom', but I always use it because it has been the mantra of my life to aspire towards the freedom of my nation...
>
> Swaraj is the direct revelation of God to our people—not mere political freedom but a freedom vast and entire, freedom of the individual, freedom of the community, freedom of the nation, spiritual freedom, social freedom, political freedom....
>
> Social freedom was part of the message of Buddha, Chaitanya, Nanak, Kabir, and the saints of Maharashtra....
>
> Spiritual freedom the ancient Rishis declared to us, ... but without political freedom the soul of man

> is crippled... If political freedom is absent, the community has no great ends to follow.... A slave can never be noble and broad-minded. He cannot forget himself in the service of his fellows.... he cannot be "sarvabhūtahite ratah" or one whose mind is full of the will to do good to others....[35]

It must be mentioned that the Sanskrit phrase "sarvabhūtahite ratah" is from the Gītā.

4.41 Considering, next, the methods to be adopted for achieving the goal, the Moderates believed that considerable progress was possible under the aegies of the British rule itself, because "the weakest links in the chain are our own incapacity and disunity".[36] The Moderates therefore favoured the spread of Western education, a larger share in jobs carrying greater and greater responsibility, removal of evil customs by reforming public opinion if possible and by legislation if necessary, and other peaceful methods of the same type. The Extremists scornfully described the method of petition as mendicancy, and Aurobindo strongly argued why the Moderates' method was bound to be infructuous, for the British administration would never sacrifice its vital interests which the uplift of India necessarily involved. Aurobindo characterized social reform, educational reform, industrial expansion, and all attempts towards the moral improvement of the race "without aiming first and foremost at political freedom", as "the very height of ignorance and futility".[37]

4.42 With a view to deriving political advantage from the revolutionary enthusiasm generated among the people because of the partition of Bengal, the Extremists emphasized the methods of boycott, Swadeshi, national education, and passive resistance. Detailed considerations on these brought to the forefront two related issues, namely, (i) whether the Indian society at that time had the capacity to implement these methods, and (ii) what view to take about the likelihood of violence erupting because of the use of these methods? Needless to say, the attitudes of the Moderates and the Extremists were wide apart, in all these matters. The Moderates strongly felt that it was the best policy at that time to continue the time-honoured method of constitutional agitation. Passive resistance and boycott, according to them, were impracticable, and more in the nature of propaganda than reality. As Gokhale put it:

> We owe it to the best interests of the country to resist this propaganda with all our resources. it means the sure destruction, or at any rate, the indefinite postponement of all these opportunities for slow but peaceful progress which are at present within our reach.[38]

4.43 The Extremists did not try to meet the specific arguments of the Moderates for they too knew that the public at large was not yet ready for radical measures. However, the extremists believed that it was time they should come to regard politics more seriously and as part of their religion, with "the power of faith and will which neither counts obstacles nor measures time".[39] To Aurobindo, any talk of assessing possibilities of success or failure, or of counting losses and gains, as suggested by the Moderates, was a sign of weakness and insincerity. Using the simile of "a demon attacking my mother", he asked: "If a demon sits on the breasts of my mother and is about to drink her blood, shall I sit idle and coldly calculate whether I have the strength enough to fight it? My only duty is to rush to the rescue of my mother". "In a similar spirit", he observed, "the Indians should approach the political question—their prime duty was to save the

Motherland. It was for them to rush headlong to achieve this goal without pausing to think of its probable success or failure".[40]

4.44 To Aurobindo, boycott was a part of passive resistance. The first principle of passive resistance, according to him, was to make administration under existing conditions impossible by an organised refusal to do anything which would help either British commerce in the exploitation of the country or British officialdom in the administration of it. Such boycott he wanted to apply to educational institutions as well because of their anti-national character and discouragement of patriotism. His plan, if accepted by Congress, would ask all countrymen to:

> Refuse to send children to Government schools or to schools aided and controlled by the Government... Refuse also to have any resort to the alien courts of justice... Refuse similarly to go to the executive for help or advice or protection,... and ultimately, refuse to pay taxes.[41]

4.45 Aurobindo knew that even to think of any programme of passive resistance presupposed strength and fearlessness or what in the Hindu tradition were referred to as Kṣatriya-like qualities. To carry on a fight for independence, he said, we have to be guided by Kṣatriya-morality rather than Brahmin-morality, and also avoid any confusion between the two: "Politics is the ideal of the Kṣatriya, and the morality of the Kṣatriya ought to govern our political actions. To impose in politics the Brahmanical duty of saintly sufferance is to preach varṇa-saṁkara (or confusion)".[42]

4.46 While appealing for public cooperation, the Extremists made it clear that sacrifice would be an important element in the quest for freedom. They turned to the religious concept of yajña (sacrifice) and related it to the political plane. Just as offerings put into the sacrificial fire bear fruit only if they are pure and dedicated to the Deity with full faith and devotion, Aurobindo wanted his countrymen to be ready to sacrifice their all—even lives—in the struggle for freedom:

> Liberty is the fruit we seek from the sacrifice, and the Motherland, the Goddess to whom we offer it; into the seven leaping tongues of the fire of the yajña we must offer all that we are and all that we have, feeding the fire even with our blood and lives and happiness of our nearest and dearest; for the Motherland is a Goddess who loves not a maimed and imperfect sacrifice, the freedom was never won from the gods by a grudging giver.[43]

4.47 Although the religious nature of the sacrifice was intended to provide justification for the people to "offer all that they have" in the cause of freedom, Aurobindo also justified the "battle" itself, and the use of "any and every means of self-preservation".[44] For this purpose, Aurobindo made extensive use of the Gītā. The national struggle was another Kurukṣetra, a righteous war against the British imperialists. Aurobindo exhorted all Indians to draw from the Gītā the inspiration to fight, and thus to fulfil their dharma in the battle for freedom: "The Gītā is the best answer to those who shrink from battle as a sin and aggression as a lowering of morality.[45]

> To shrink from bloodshed and violence under such circumstances is a weakness deserving as severe a rebuke as Śrī Kṛṣṇa addressed to Arjuna when he shrank from the colossal civil slaughter on the field of Kurukṣetra. Liberty is the life-breath of a nation, and when the life is attacked, when it is sought to suppress all chances of breathing by violent

> pressure, any and every means of self-preservation becomes right and justifiable—just as it is lawful for a man who is being strangled to rid himself of the pressure on throat by any means in his power.[46]

4.48 Aurobindo also helped organize, through his younger brother, Barindra, "secret societies with revolutionary intentions" for what are sometimes referred to as "terrorist activities." Ironically, members of these societies often carried with themselves copies of the Bhagavad-Gītā and selected writings of Vivekananda. Lizelle Raymond has described Barindra's role in this context in the following words:

> Barindra's work in Bengal was the organization in the villages—even the most remote—of a chain of Samitis, or youth organizations, which would meet under all kinds of pretexts, but with the real aim of providing a civic and political education and opening the eyes of the young to the 'affairs of the nation'... In smoky little grain shops, on the terraced roofs of private houses, young men would meet to hear about the lives of *Mazzini* and Garibaldi, to read exhortations from Swami Vivekananda, to listen to the warlike incidents of the Mahābhārata and to comments on the Bhagavad-Gītā. The number of samitis increased daily.[47]

4.49 V. Subramaniam considers "the expectation of immediate results" as a serious weakness of the violent revolutionaries in India. Militarily, the British administration was too strong to be shaken up by stray incidents of bomb-throwing. Aurobindo himself realized by 1910 the limitations of violent methods of political action, in the circumstances then prevailing in the country. In Karan Singh's words:

> Terrorist outrages were on the increase in 1909 as

> the Government had succeeded in stifling the Nationalist party, the one political body which offered a legal and peaceful outlet for the people's resentment. Government repression was also on the increase. In the *Karmayogin* Sri Aurobindo commented on the shooting and assassinations, and laid the blame squarely on the Government's repressive policy. Finally he came to the conclusion that as the Nationalists were powerless to stem the rising tide of terrorism sweeping over Bengal, they could only suspend their own strictly lawful and peaceful activities and let the Government deal as best as it could with the situation that its own policies had inexorably created. Thus on February 5, 1910, he wrote in the *Karmayogin:* 'We advise our fellow Nationalists also to stand back and give an unhampered course for a while to Anglo-Indian statesmanship in its endeavours to grapple with this hydra-headed evil.[48]

4.50 Aurobindo's political activities as a karmayogin were marked by spiritualism, but the fine balance of political and spiritual elements could not be indefinitely maintained. When the spiritual element in Aurobindo's thinking became predominant, the importance that he had attached to current political problems abruptly receded. Karan Singh has analysed how the rising tide of spiritualism swept aside Aurobindo's interest in political activities:

> Aurobindo's whole concept of political action and theory was based on his spiritual vision, which did not desert him even in the midst of the most extreme and turbulent political controversies of the day. Then came the Surat session and his meeting with Lele, which marked a considerable advance in his spiritual practices and experiences. Soon after came his year of enforced seclusion at

Alipur, where it seems that the spiritual tendencies and powers latent in his psyche rose with a dramatic upsurge to the surface. It is in the very nature of the spiritual call that it is imperative and overriding, and if it develops inevitably dominates the mind of the seeker to the virtual exclusion of other activities.[49]

Importance of Lokasamgraha in "Essays on the Gita"

4.51 Aurobindo's *Essays on the Gītā* belongs to the Pondicherry phase. These essays present a new interpretation of the Gītā, based on new ideas associated with Purushottama, Prakriti, and Sat-Chit-Ananda. For example, to begin with "Purushottama", Aurobindo attaches special importance to the fifteenth chapter of the Gītā which speaks of "Three Purushas" namely, the Kshara, the Akshara and the Purushottama:

> The idea of the Purushottama has been prepared, alluded to, adumbrated, assumed even from the beginning, but it is only now in the fifteenth chapter that it is expressly stated and the distinction illuminated by a name....
>
> The Purushottama is the Lord in the Kshara (the mutable). He is in the heart of every creature and is manifested in his countless Vibhūtis. The Kshara, the personal, the Purusha self-subjected to Prakriti, is only one aspect of the Purushottama.
>
> Another aspect of the Purushottama is the Akshara, the impersonal, the inactive, the immutable self of all...
>
> The Purushottama is both Akshara and Kshara, and yet he is "other"—the third—because he is more and greater than either of these opposites....

> The seventeenth verse of the fifteenth chapter is the keyword of the Gītā's reconciliation of these two—Kshara and Akshara—apparently opposite aspects of our existence. The Gītā uses the expression "anya" meaning "the other", and says: But other than these two is that highest spirit called the supreme Self who enters the three worlds and upbears them, the imperishable Lord.

4.52 A practically significant implication (in terms of continued action) which results from viewing the Purushottama as "greater than the Akshara", has been stressed by Aurobindo in the following words:

> When pursued through the Akshara alone, any attempt at liberation would become the seeking of the Indefinable, the Actionless, a thing hard for our nature embodied as we are here in Matter.... The Purushottama is the supreme Lord, Parameshwara, no aloof and unrelated Indefinable, but the origin and father and mother and first foundation and eternal abode of self and cosmos and Master of all existence and enjoyer of askesis and sacrifice.... The Purushottama is the cosmic spirit in Time and it is he that gives the command to the divine action of the liberated human spirit.[51]

4.53 The doctrine of three Purushas (rather than two) has been further extended by Aurobindo, on the authority of the seventh chapter of the Gītā, in such a way as to include the doctrine of two Prakritis (rather than one):

> The opening verses of the seventh chapter initiate ideas that occupy all the rest of the book.... The Gītā makes the deep and momentous distinction which is the practical basis of all its Yoga, the distinction between the two Natures, the phenomenal Nature and the spiritual Nature....

> The phenomenal Nature, called "aparā prakriti" or "lower nature" in the fifth verse, is the Sānkhya Prakriti of the three guṇas—sattva, rajas, tamas.
>
> The spiritual Nature is designated by Śrī Kṛṣṇa, in the same verse, as "parā prakritirme" or "My supreme nature" ... And this "I" here is the Purushottama, the supreme Being, the supreme soul, the transcendent and universal spirit. The original and eternal nature of the Spirit and its transcendent and originating Shakti is what is meant by the Parā Prakriti. For speaking first of the origin of the world from the point of view of the active power of his Nature, Kṛṣṇa asseverates, 'This is the womb of all beings', etad yonīnī bhūtāni. (VII.6) And in the next line of the couplet, again stating the same fact from the point of view of the originating Soul, he continues, 'I am the birth of the whole world and so too its dissolution; there is nothing else supreme beyond Me. (VII. 6-7) Here then the supreme Soul, Purushottama, and the supreme Nature, Parā Prakriti, are identified: they are put as two ways of looking at one and the same reality... The Sprit is the supreme Being in his infinite consciousness and the supreme Nature is the infinity of power or will of being of the Spirit.[52]

4.54 Aurobindo's views on Parā Prakriti as the infinite timeless conscious power of the self-existent Being, out of which all existence in the cosmos are manifested and come out of timelessness into Time, represent a synthesis of the Vedāntic concept of Sat-Chit-Ananda and the Tāntric concept of the Divine Mother or Shakti. In Aurobindo's harmonizing approach, "Chit" or consciousness is referred to as "chit-shakti" or consciousness-force, and the importance attached thereto is highlighted by Joan Price:

> Perhaps one of the most outstanding features of Sri Aurobindo's philosophy is the importance he places upon chit-shakti, the Divine Mother of the original Tāntric philosophy. ... By this affirmation of Consciousness with Force, Śrī Aurobindo avoids absolute idealism....
>
> Chit-Shakti is the Mother Force (feminine principle)... Because of the "Time" movement of the Consciousness-Force, the timeless eternal co-exists with the multiplicity of forms which are subject to time.... Chit-Shakti is beyond the three guṇas of the lower prakriti; it stands above the world and links the creation to the ever unmanifest.... It creates all these beings and contains and enters, supports and conducts all these million processes and forces, embodies the powers of these and makes them living and near to us.[53]

4.55 According to Aurobindo's interpretation, the main message of the Gītā, founded upon the concepts of Purushottama and Parā Prakriti, is irrevocably linked with action performed for purposes of lokasaṁgraha. Aurobindo summarizes this message as a call from Śrī Kṛṣṇa to Arjuna in the following words:

> I am the eternal worker within you and I ask of you works. I demand of you not a passive consent to a mechanical movement of Nature from which in your self you are wholly separated, indifferent and aloof, but action complete and divine, done as the willing and understanding instrument of the Divine, done for God in you and others and for the good of the world. This action I propose to you, first no doubt as a means of perfection in the supreme spiritual Nature, but as a part too of that perfection. Action is part of the integral knowledge of God and of his greater mysterious truth and of

an entire living in the Divine; action can and should be continued even after perfection and freedom are won.[54]

4.56 Although the Lokasaṁgraha-oriented action founded upon Purushottama and Parā Prakriti constitutes an important part of Aurobindo's interpretation of the Gītā, it is necessary to look into some of his other ideas as well. For example, Aurobindo explains why, in his opinion, the famous verse of the second chapter "Thou hast a right to action, but none to the fruits of action" is "only a preliminary word governing the first state of the disciple when he begins ascending the hill of Yoga:"

> For the Gītā goes on to affirm emphatically that the man is not the doer of the action; it is Prakriti, it is Nature, it is the great Force with its three modes of action that works through him, and he must learn to see that it is not he who does the work. Therefore the "right to action" is an idea which is only valid so long as we are still under the illusion of being the doer; it must necessarily disappear from the mind like the claim to the fruit, as soon as we cease to be to our own consciousness the doer of our works. All pragmatic egoism, whether of the claim to fruits or of the right to action, is then at an end.[55]

4.57 When Aurobindo characterizes "the call to action as a right" only a preliminary teaching of the Gītā, it does not imply that he is encouraging inaction. In fact, he attaches great importance to the activism of the Gītā which so strongly modifies the quietistic tendencies of the Sānkhya as well as of the old metaphysical Vedānta. Aurobindo quotes Śrī Kṛṣṇa's warning given in the third chapter of the Gītā, to the effect that none can stand even for a moment without doing work because everyone is made to do action helplessly by the modes born of Prakriti. He compares this teaching of the Gītā with that of the Tāntric Shaktas:

> The strong perception of the great cosmic action and the eternal activity and power of the cosmic energy, which was so much emphasized afterwards by the teaching of the Tāntric Shaktas who even made Prakriti or Shakti superior to Purusha, is a very remarkable feature of the Gītā. Although here an undertone, it is still strong enough, coupled with what we might call the theistic and devotional elements of its thoughts, to bring in that activism which so strongly modifies in its scheme of Yoga the quietistic tendencies of the old metaphysical Vedānta. Man embodied in the natural world cannot cease from action, not for a moment, not for a second; his very existence here is an action; the whole universe is an act of God, mere living even is His movement.[56]

4.58 Recognising that action cannot be avoided, Aurobindo discusses the relative importance of the "the call of social duty" and "divine obligation in response to the call of God". Among those who emphasized the significance of duty, Aurobindo includes Bankim Chandra Chatterji, while among those who gave precedence to God's work, he refers to Buddha. Duty, according to Aurobindo, is a relative term depending on one's position in the society. If there is a conflict between one's duty and moral conscience, says Aurobindo, the latter commands unconditional obedience. The Gītā, as interpreted by Aurobindo, calls us to ascend to this higher plane, which is a 'supreme poise', leaving behind the mainly practical, and the purely ethical. This ascent leads to the 'Brahmanic consciousness'. The attainment of this consciousness is, according to Aurobindo, the meaning of rising beyond the three guṇas, or of becoming triguṇātīta. Aurobindo points to the carama śloka of the Gītā (XVIII.66) and says that the call to abandon all duties and take refuge in the Supreme alone, negates the importance of duties which society and custom demand from an individual. He writes:

> If that (refuge in the Supreme) can only be attained by renouncing works and life and all duties and the call is strong within us, then into the bonfire they must go, and there is no help for it. The call of God is imperative and cannot be weighted against any other considerations.[57]

Thomas sees in this statement a great personal meaning for Aurobindo. He abandoned what he considered as his dharma at one time and went to Pondicherry in obedience to a divine call to "take refuge in the Supreme alone".[58]

4.59 However the call of God and the call of social duty need not pull in different directions. Confusion can be avoided, either if both the calls pull in the same direction, or if one surrenders to the call of God and devotes oneself whole-heartedly to the action enjoined thereby. To act with a right will, fixed in the One, aware of the one self in all and acting out of its equal serenity, not running about in different directions under the thousand impulses of one's superficial mental self—this is what the Gītā calls the Buddhi-yoga. Aurobindo describes the process by which buddhi can be firmly fixed in the calm self-knowledge of the Purusha, mentioning also the need to take refuge in the Lord:

> It is the upward and inward orientation of the intelligent will that we must resolutely choose with a settled concentration and perseverance... This cannot be done perfectly by the act of the intelligence itself, by a merely mental discipline;

> it can only be done by Yoga with something which is higher than itself and in which calm and self-mastery are inherent. And this Yoga can only arrive at its success by devoting, by consecrating, by giving up the whole self to the Divine, "to Me, "says Krishna; for the Liberator is within us, but it is not our mind, nor our intelligence, nor our personal will, —they are only instruments. It is the Lord in whom, as we are told in the end, we have utterly to take refuge. And for that we must at first make him the object of our whole being and keep in soul-contact with him. This is the sense of the phrase "he must sit firm in Yoga, wholly given up to Me". (II.61)[59]

4.60 After describing how the Yoga of the intelligent will culminates in the Brahmic status, Aurobindo devotes a good deal of attention to yajña and the "eternal connecting truth of God and the world and works", which also helps him explain the special significance of Purushottama. Aurobindo's contention is that, if the sacrifice were to be offered to the "impersonal Brahman", then there is a risk that work may not receive the attention it deserves. On the other hand, if the sacrifice is offered to Purushottama, then there is a positive sanction for continuance in works, and the nature of the action also matters, with the result that the concept of Lokasaṁgraha comes to the forefront. This comparison between the sacrifice offered to the impersonal Brahman and that offered to Purushottama, is brought out in two successive paragraphs:

> The impersonal Brahman has no activity and no desires, no object to be gained, no dependence for anything on all this world of creatures; it exists for itself, in its own self-delight, in its own immutable eternal being. We may have to do works

> without desire as a means in order to reach this impersonal self-existence and self-delight, but, that movement once executed, the object of works is finished; the sacrifice is no longer needed. Works may even then continue because nature continues,.... but then, works may well be whittled down and reduced to a minimum,.... and the nature of the works also does not matter....
>
> But the Gītā insists that the nature of the action does matter and that there is a positive sanction for continuance in works, not only that one quite negative and mechanical reason, the objective compulsion of Nature. There is still, after the ego has been conquered, a divine Lord and enjoyer of the sacrifice, and there is still an object in the sacrifice... Therefore, through the Impersonal, we have to arrive at the Purushottama, and he in his divine greatness possesses both the Akshara and the Kshara. He manifests himself in the movement and in all the action of cosmic Nature; to him even after liberation the sacrifice of works in Nature continues to be offered.[60]

4.61 Aurobindo believes that, for understanding the basis of the Gītā philosophy of divine works, the Lokasaṁgraha— related verses of the third chapter are probably the most important. He translates Lokasaṁgraha as the holding together of the peoples. In his view, "this great march of the peoples towards a far-off divine ideal has to be held together, prevented from falling into the bewilderment, confusion and utter discord of the understanding which would lead to dissolution and destruction and to which the world moving forward in the night or dark twilight of ignorance would be too easily prone if it were not held together, conducted, kept to the great lines of its discipline by the illumination, by the strength, by the rule and example, by the visible standard and the invisible influence of its Best. The best, the individuals who are in advance of the general line and above the general level of the collectivity, are the natural leaders of mankind, for it is they who can point to the race both the way they must follow and the standard or ideal they have to keep to or to attain. But the divinised man is the Best in no ordinary sense of the word and his influence, his example must have a power which that of no ordinarily superior man can exercise. What example then shall he give? What rule or standard shall he uphold?"[61]

4.62 In order to indicate more perfectly his meaning, the divine Teacher, the Avatāra gives his own example, his own standard. Aurobindo says that the giving of the example of God himself to the liberated man is profoundly significant:

> The liberated man is he who has exalted himself into the divine nature and according to that divine nature must be his actions. But what is the divine nature? It is not entirely and solely that of the Akshara, the immobile, inactive, impersonal self; for that by itself would lead the liberated man to actionless immobility. It is not characteristically that of the Kshara, the multitudinous, the personal, the Purusha self-subjected to Prakriti; for that by itself would lead him back into subjection to his personality and to the lower nature and its qualities. It is the nature of the Purushottama who holds both these together and by his supreme divinity reconciles them in a divine reconciliation which is the highest secret of his being, rahasyam hyetad uttamaṁ.[62]

4.63 Aurobindo attaches great importance to bhakti, "the love and adoration of the Purushottama", its role being to "rear the spirit towards some greatest highest perfection"— founded on the base of "equality, desirelessness and freedom of spirit".[63] Referring to the characteristics of the bhakta, as given in chapter XII of the Gītā, Aurobindo writes:

> Several formulas of this fundamental equal consciousness are given here. First, an absence of egoism, of I-ness and myness, nirmamo nirahaṁkāraḥ. The bhakta of the Purushottama is one who has a universal heart and mind which has broken down all the narrow walls of the ego. A universal love dwells in his heart, a universal compassion flows from it like an encompassing sea. He will have friendship and pity for all beings and hate for no living thing: for he is patient, long-suffering, enduring, a well of forgiveness. A desireless content is his, a tranquil equality to pleasure and pain, suffering and happiness, the steadfast control of self and the firm unshakable will and resolution of the Yogin and a love and devotion which gives up the whole mind and reason to the Lord, to the Master of his consciousness and knowledge. Or, simply, he will be one who is freed from the troubled agitated lower nature and from its waves of joy and fear and anxiety and resentment and desire, a spirit of calm by whom the world is not afflicted or troubled, nor is he afflicted or troubled by the world, a soul of peace with whom all are at peace.[64]

4.64 Harmonizing Karma, Bhakti and Jñāna, Aurobindo summarizes "the Message of the Gītā as being a call centred on "Lokasaṁgraha":

> All becomes here by the power of the Spirit; all do their works by the immanence of God in things and his presence in the heart of every creature. The Creator of the worlds is not limited by his creations; the Lord of works is not bound by his

> works; the divine Will is not attached to its labour; for it is omnipotent, all possessing and all-blissful. But still the Lord looks down on his creations from his transcendence; he descends as the Avatara; he is here in you; he rules from within all things in the steps of their nature. And you too must do works in him after the way and in the steps of the divine nature untouched by limitation, attachment or bondage. Act for the best good of all, act for the maintenance of the march of the world, for the support or the leading of its peoples. The action asked of you is the action of the liberated Yogin; it is the spontaneous output of a free God-held energy, it is an equal-minded movement, it is a selfless and desireless labour.[65]

4.65 Aurobindo is very particular about the spiritual attainment of any person who, according to his understanding of the Gītā, can really do acts for Lokasaṁgraha. As Betai summarizes Aurobindo's views on this topic, acts for real Lokasaṁgraha can be done only by a *muktātmā* or a liberated soul who has no egoism and who has gone beyond the three guṇas.[66] Aurobindo uses the term 'divine activity' for such acts. A *mumukṣu* or one who is still struggling to attain spiritual heights can, at the most, perform sāttvika karma but not the full karma-yoga of Aurobindo's interpretation. Aurobindo does not deny the practical importance of sāttvika karma, but he insists that the teaching of the Gītā goes beyond disinterested performance of duty. He clarifies this by means of giving examples of *muktāmā's:* "The Gītā teaching means the following of the divine life. The abandonment of all Dharmas, Sarvadharmān, to take refuge in the supreme alone, and the divine activity of a Buddha, a Ramkrishna, a Vivekananda is perfectly in consonance with this teaching".[67]

Social Aspects of Integral Yoga, Supermind, and Spiritual Evolution

4.66 The ideas contained in *Essays on the Gītā* were extended by Aurobindo, in the light of his own Sādhanā, culminating in the formulation of his theory of Spiritual Evolution, in which the concept of Supermind has a crucial role. He also developed a new technique, called integral Yoga, or Pūrṇa Yoga, by means of which the Yogī rises to the Supramental plane and then descends back to the material plane to help others achieve a similar Spiritual Evolution as quickly as possible. Aurobindo wrote volumes to explain these and related ideas. For purposes of the present study, a selective approach has been adopted, with a view to showing that the Integral yoga of Aurobindo has important social implications, because Aurobindo had specifically stated the main objectives of his "quest for the truth" to include "the application of our ideas to the problems of man's social and collective life".[68]

Spiritual Evolution

4.67 In an attempt to give a brief and simple account of Aurobindo's theory of Spiritual Evolution, the Vedāntic concept of Brahman as the Omnipresent Reality can be viewed as the foundation. Accordingly, all this, both spirit and matter, is Brahman. Aurobindo accepts the three attributes of the Omni-present Reality denoted by Sat-Chit-Ananda, but he brings in the Tāntric principle of Shakti to modify Chit as Chit-Shakti. The nature of the Reality is thus the transcendent Absolute manifesting itself as a universal Conscious-Force and creating individual multiplicities out of self-delight. And this is the reality that humanity is—the cause and aim of growth and creativity, as Aurobindo puts it:

> As the poet, artist or musician, when he creates, does really nothing but develop some potentiality in his unmanifested self into a form of manifestation, and as the thinker, statesman, mechanist only bring out into shape of things that which lay hidden in themselves, was themselves, is still themselves when it is cast into form, so is it with the world and the eternal.[69]

4.68 All creation or becoming, according to Aurobindo, is this self-manifestation. The Infinite Being emerges in the appearance of the finite soul, the Infinite Consciousness emerges in the appearance of a limited consciousness. Mind, Life and Body are an inferior consciousness and a partial expression. Aurobindo uses the term "Involution" to denote the emergence of Matter out of Spirit, and the process leading the Matter back to its source of origin—the spirit—is the "Spiritual Evolution" Aurobindo views it as a continuation of the "Biological Evolution" which has seen the emergence of Life out of Matter, and a Mind out of Life. Whereas the Biological Evolution was a slow, natural process, Aurobindo believes that the Spiritual Evolution could be expedited by human effort. The special feature of Aurobindo's theory of Spiritual Evolution is the anticipated emergence of Supermind out of Mind. As Karan Singh puts it:

> The advent of the human race (in which Mind has a dominating role) is by no means the final phase of evolution. In fact it is an intermediate stage, and mankind is now poised on the threshold of the next leap forward in the evolutionary process. This step is the evolution of mind to Supermind, the luminous realm of Truth-Consciousness, which will be a development even more profound than the preceding step from animal to human consciousness.[70]

Integral Yoga

4.69 Aurobindo used the term "Integral Yoga" or "Purna Yoga" to denote the technique by which one can ascend to the Supramental plane and then descend back to the material plane with a view to helping others.

Social Implications

4.70 Embree draws attention to Aurobindo's rejection of the jagat-mithya doctrine and of the popular myth of yuga-to-yuga decline in spirituality—

> Aurobindo envisages that the achievement of the state of Divine Life would lead to an enriched order of humanity.[71]

4.71 Joan Price also views the Supermen playing the important role of trying to transform the values of the entire world, and of acting as a free force with respect for truth and peace in society.[72]

Auroville

4.72 A practical demonstration of how a community might follow Aurobindo's ideals can be seen in Auroville — a few miles from the Aurobindo Ashram in Pondicherry.

Summary of Aurobindo's Contribution to Practical Vedanta

4.73 (a) He rejected the jagat-mithya doctrine of Shankaracharya.

(b) He rejected the Karma-samnyasa message of Shankaracharya.

(c) His "Auroville" project contributed to the process of making Vedanta universal.

(d) His book "Essays on the Gita" was a very valuable

addition to Gita-literature.

Notes

1. Karan Singh, Prophet of Indian Nationalism. George Allen and Unwin, London, 1963, p. 155.
2. R.C. Majumdar, History of the Freedom Movement in India, op. cit., vol. I, p. 461.
3. Ibid., pp. 243 and 330.
4. Ibid., p. 333.
5. Ibid., p. 333.
6. Ibid., p. 423.
7. Karan Singh, Prophet of Indian Nationalism, op cit., p. 42.
8. D.S. Sarma, The Renaissance of Hinduism, op. cit., pp. 308-9.
9. Sri Aurobindo Birth Centenary Library (30 volumes), vol. 22, p. 121.
10. Karan Singh, Prophet of Indian Nationalism, op. cit., p. 138.
11. Ibid., p. 136.
12. Ibid., p. 143.
13. T.V. Parvate, Bal Gangadhar Tilak, op. cit., pp. 529-30.
14. Ibid., p. 530.
15. Karan Singh, Prophet of Indian Nationalism, op. cit., pp. 143-4.
16. D.S. sarma, The Renaissance of Hindiusm, op. cit., p. 340.
17. Joan Price, An Introduction to Sri Aurobindo's Philosophy. Pondicherry, second edition, 1982, p. 14.
18. Ibid., pp. 18-9.
19. Karan Singh, Prophet of Indian Nationalism, op. cit., pp. 155-6.
20. R.C. Majumdar, History of the Freedom Movement in India, op. cit., vol. II, pp. 92 and 186 7.
21. Ibid., p. 24.
22. Ibid., pp. 23-4.

23. Ibid., pp. 166-7.
24. Ibid., p. 24.
25. D.S. Sarma, The Renaissance of Hinduism, op. cit., p. 310.
26. R.C. Majumdar, Swami Vivekananda: An Historical Review, op. cit., p. 115.
27. Ibid., p. 120.
28. R.C. Majumdar, History of the Freedom Movement in India, op. cit., vol. I, p. 447.
29. Sri Aurobindo, On Nationalism. (First Series). Pondicherry, 1965, p. 73.
30. Ursula King, "Who is the Ideal Karmayogin? The Meaning of a Hindu Religious Symbol." In Religion, Vol. X, Spring 1980, p. 50.
31. Ibid., p. 51.
32. R.C. Majumdar, History of the Freedom Movement in India, op. cit., vol. II, pp. 141-3.
33. Ibid., pp. 140-1.
34. Ibid., pp. 230-4.
35. Ibid., p. 191, and Sri Aurobindo, On Nationalism, op, cit., p. 63.
36. R.C. Majumdar, History of the Freedom Movement in India, op. cit., vol. II, p. 180.
37. Ibid., p. 176.
38. Ibid., p. 180.
39. Ibid., p. 186.
40. Ibid., p. 187.
41. Ibid., p. 178.
42. Sri Aurobindo, The Doctrine of Passive Resistance. Pondicherry, 1952, pp. 80-1.
43. Ibid., pp. 77-8.
44. Ibid., p. 29.
45. Ibid., p. 81.
46. Ibid., p. 29.

47. Karan Singh, Prophet of Indian Nationalism, op. cit., pp. 58-9.
48. Ibid., pp. 143.
49. Ibid., p. 145.
50. Sri Aurobindo, Essays on the Gita (Second Series). Arya Publishing House, Calcutta, 1949, pp. 222-7.
51. Ibid., p. 224-5.
52. Ibid., p. 4-9.
53. Joan Price, An Introduction to Sri Aurobindo's Philosophy, op. cit. pp. 26-7.
54. Sri Aurobindo, Essays on the Gita (Second Series), op. cit., p. 407.
55. Sri Aurobindo, Essays on the Gita (First Series). Arya Publishing House, Calcutta, 1949, p. 45.
56. Ibid., p. 134.
57 Ibid., p. 30.
58. P.M. Thomas, Twentieth Century Indian Interpretations of Bhagavad Gita, op. cit., p. 108.
59. Sri Aurobindo, Essays on the Gita (First Series), op. cit., p. 126.
60. Ibid., p. 162-5.
61. Ibid., p. 171-2.
62. Ibid., p. 173.
63. Sri Aurobindo, Essays on the Gita (Second Series), op. cit., pp. 179-80.
64. Ibid., p. 180.
65. Ibid., p. 408.
66. R.S. Betai, Gita and Gandhiji, Gujarat Vidyapith, Ahmedabad, 1970, pp. 70-2.
67. Ibid., p. 65.
68. S. Radhakrishnan and C.A. Moore (eds.), A Sourcebook in Indian Philosophy. Princeton Univ. Press, 1957, p. 577.
69. Joan Price, An Introduction to Sri Aurobindo's Philosophy, op. cit., p. 29.

70. Karan Singh, Prophet of Indian Nationalism, op. cit., p. 67.
71. Ainslie T. Embree (ed.), The Hindu Tradition, op. cit., pp. 334-5.
72. Joan Price, An Introduction to Sri Aurobindo's Philosophy, op. cit., pp. 125 and 134.

CHAPTER 5

Tagore's Mission to Make Vedanta Universal

A Brief Life-sketch

5.1 Biographers of Rabindranath Tagore usually begin with his famous grandfather, Dwarkanath, who was called a "Prince" when he visited England. Side by side with his substantial business activities, he supported the social reformer, Rammohun Roy.

5.2 Tagore's father, Debendranath, was called "Maharshi", in recognition of his spiritual achievements. Vivekananda had called on him, seeking advice (before he met his Master, Ramakrishna Paramahansa).

5.3 Rabindranath was born on 6th May, 1861. His mother died when he was a child, so his upbringing devolved much on servants, He did not like the way children were taught in schools, therefore his education (at home) was through private tutors. His biographer Thompson, gives a picturesque account of how Rabindranath received his education—

"His real education came, not from the desultory and experimental alternation of tutor and school, with a background of time spent with servants, but from the whole circumstances and environment of his life. The family house Jorsanko is a vast, rambling congeries of mansions and rooms, representing the whims of many generations. These run round a central courtyard, and look out upon crowded Calcutta. In the poet's youth, he could watch the strange, alien life of the poor who inhabited a cluster of miserable huts before the great house; and perhaps the dominant picture of his "Reminiscences" is that of a dreaming, interested child, standing with face pressed against the veranda railings. He could watch, too, the folk who came to bathe in the tank; and in these early days his mind was already storing many a vignette, many a swiftly-taken glimpse of habit or idiosyncrasy. Within doors was a life so varied and busy that it was abundant compensation for the outside fair that he missed, except as spectator. Here every movement found echoes, and the political and literary and religious disturbances rippled against these banks."[1]

5.4 Rabindranath's brothers (who were themselves writers/artists) spotted in the young boy a keen interest in verse-writing, and they encouraged him to start writing when he was quite young. To quote Thompson again—

> "Music and drama were the air he breathed. He has told us of the way his eldest brother entranced the household with the poetical opulence of his "Dream-Journey", and of the way his fourth brother improvised melody after melody. The women were hardly less gifted, and were certainly not less eager."[2]

5.5 Rabindranath wrote in his "Reminiscences" about his feeling oneness with nature during his visit to the countryside:

> "Every morning, as a I awoke, I somehow felt the day coming to me like a new gilt-edged letter with some unheard-of news awaiting me on the opening of the envelope."[3]

And Thompson added:

> "Past the garden (where Rabindranath was staying) flowed the Ganges. Bengal by the Ganges is a land of luxuriant vegetation, of fields of an incredible lushness and greenness, of pools where black-and-white kingfishers dart and hawk, of great white—headed kites, sitting on telegraph wires and poles, of stretching sandbanks climbing out of the lazy stream to sun their broad backs, of drowsy, drifting sails and of that mighty, worshipped river. This is the Bengal which Rabindranath knows and has celebrated in countless passages, his life one with its life of steady flow and sudden storm and flood. He knows its rain-swollen currents, its dreadful roar and tussle of cloud and lightning and thunder, its exquisite peace and stillness, its vast spaces. He is a river-poet, first and last. The Himalayas were the very soul of his father's passionate delight. But to the son they have been very little. In this respect, he differs not only from his father, but from his master, Kalidasa, a mountain - poet."[4]

5.6 In his "Reminiscences", Rabindranath has left some desultory notes on his first appearances in print. These occurred before he was fifteen. Thompson explains how his brother promoted his literary activity—

> "His brother Jyotirindra launched many projects, among them a line of patriotic (i.e. Bengali-owned and run) steamers, and a monthly, the "Bharati". The latter enterprise had the boy-poet as one of the crew, and for long enough it was his medium

> of expression, so much so that his first fifteen years of literary activity might be called the Bharati-period."[5]

5.7 Rabindranath felt unhappy to read the recent history of Bengal— how the British were able to establish their military superiority. From this consideration, he admired the Sikhs. Thinking of all this, he composed songs and published them under the title "Bhanu Singh", Thompson draws attention to the high honor which these songs brought to him—

> "Rabindranath tells with glee how Dr. Nishikanta Chatterji was awarded a German Ph.D. for a thesis on Bengali lyric poetry, in which "Bhanu Singh" was given high honor as one of the ancient glories of his land's literature."[6]

5.8 Thompson notes that Rabindranath was only sixteen when his talent as a writer of prose came to light—

> "His "Letters of a Visitor to Europe" are fresh and free from pose. His prose-writing skill was displayed in these letters. Then there was a famous assault on Michael Dutt's 'Meghnadbadh'. It is vigorous and acute. Rabindranath has always been the most independent critic of literature in Bengal, and one of the very few whose opinions have reason behind them."[7]

5.9 Further diversification in his literary career took place with the publication of a novel "Karuna", and a blank verse tragedy "Rudrachandra". This "gloomy" period reached its climax in his lyrical drama "Bhagna-Hridaya", about which Rabindranath wrote in his "Reminiscences"—

> "When I began to write "Bhagna-Hridaya", I was eighteen. Curiously, everyone around me seemed to be eighteen likewise; and we all flitted about in the same baseless, substance-less world of

> imagination, where even the most intense joys and sorrows seemed like the joys and sorrows of dreamland. This period of my life was one of utter disorderliness."[8]

5.10 Luckily, the "disorderly" years were followed by a period of intellectual ferment and literary experiment. Thomson saw clear signs of Rabindranath's transition—

> "A break in his mood was provided by two musical comedies: "Balmiki Pratibha" and "Kal Mrigaya". To the musical comedies he gave a rapture which he tells us has never gone to the making of any other work of his. When "Balmiki Pratibha" was written, his house was a fountain of song."[9]

5.11 A short period of social interaction followed. His activities drew him first into comradeship and co-operation with Bankim Chandra Chatterji, the novelist, and then, when Bankim's reactionary religious views became pronounced and aggressive, into conflict with him. Rabindranath gave expression to his reformatory views in 1887 when he gave a lecture on Hindu Marriage. Then he published "Kari O Komal", which represents the high-water mark of his early lyrical achievement.

5.12 The age of thirty marks Rabindranath's entry into "worldly life." The first phase of his transition was "Travels", the second phase being "managerial responsibilities". In Thompson's words—

> "Leaving Ghazipur, he determined to travel across India in a bullock-cart, on the Grand Trunk Road to Peshawar. He planned to be a spectator of life's pilgrimage, using watchful eyes. But his father intervened with the suggestion that he should go to Shelidah and manage the family estates. At first, he was a little afraid, but at last he consented"[10]

5.13 Rabindranath spent about ten years as "Manager". Two aspects of this phase are brought out in "Chhinnapatra". The first was: his desire to do something to help the poor villagers. In his own words—

> "My work as Zamindar took me on long distances from one village to another. In this way, I saw all aspects of village life. Slowly but surely I began to understand the sorrow and the poverty of the villagers, and I grew restless to do something about it."[11]

The second aspect was: non-cooperation from the villagers themselves. Again, in his own words—

> "I had built a road from our estate office up to Kushtia. I told the villagers who lived close to road, 'The upkeep of this road is your responsibility.' They replied, 'Must we look after the road so that gentle folk from Kushtia can come and go with ease?' I was deeply disappointed."[12]

5.14 In the early years of the twentieth century, Rabindranath became associated with anti-partition movement. He traced it to a divisive decision taken by the British—

> "The moment Lord Curzon's order was issued that Bengal would be divided, there arose from east to west one single cry that all Bengalis are one. When the pain of division became intolerable, we thought we would find redress if we made an appeal to the king. We did not know then that there were other ways, too, open to us."[13]

Stirred by these developments, he plunged into the Swadeshi Movement, and contributed several patriotic songs to it. He even took part in street processions. But he was shocked when the movement degenerated and broke into violence.[14]

5.15 Although his "worldly activities" ran into difficulties, his literary activities moved up to great heights. The year 1901 saw the revival of the monthly "Bangadarshan", under the editorship of Rabindranath. His novel "Gora", which appeared a few years later, was acclaimed as 'the greatest novel in Bengali.' In 1908, a collected edition of his prose moved towards completion. He wrote a series of symbolical dramas. His religious poetry, expressing Vedantic ideas into melodious Bengali, rose to great heights. The original Bengali version of Gitanjali appeared in 1909.

5.16 As soon as the English version of Gitanjali came out, his fame spread over America and Europe. In 1913, he was crowned before the whole world with the Nobel prize for literature.

5.17 Gitanjali gave the message of peace and freedom.[15]

Where the mind is without fear and the head is held high;

Where knowledge is free;

Where the world has not been broken up into fragments by narrow domestic walls;

Where the mind is led forward by thee into ever-widening thought and action;

Into that heaven of freedom, my father, let my country awake.

5.18 Although Europe read Gitanjali, it headed towards World War I. Rabindranath was surprised to discover that some powerful sections in Europe were even suspicious of his message of peace, because he spoke out against militant nationalism.

5.19 At this point, we take a look into Rabindranath's great contribution in the field of education. In 1901, he founded the Shantiniketan, beginning with five students only. The initial period was difficult, as he wrote to C.F. Andrews, a great admirer of Tagore—

> "I sold all my books, my copyrights, everything I had, in order to carry on with the school. I cannot really tell you what a struggle it was, and what difficulties I had to go through. At first, the object in view was purely patriotic, but later on it grew more spiritual.... Because the growth of the school was the growth of my life and not that of a mere carrying out of my doctrines, its ideals changed with its maturity like a ripening fruit that not only grows in its bulk and deepens in its color, but undergoes change in the very quality of its inner pulp."[16]

5.20 With the War of 1914-18 in the West and the political conflicts in India, Rabindranath was in no doubt about the need for global cooperation. On 22 December 1918, he called a special meeting of students, teachers and well-wishers of the school at Shantiniketan, to explain his ideas about creating an institution for East-West fellowship and the study of cultures. The name Vishva-Bharati dates from that time and also its motto 'yatra vishvam bhavati ekanidam", taken from the Vedas, meaning "where the world meets in one nest". During 1920-21, he went to Europe and America to raise funds and to enlist support for the institution. With professor Sylvain Levi of Sorbonne University accepting his invitation to come as a visiting professor, the institution got off to a brilliant start.

5.21 In 1923, the Lecture Association of Peking invited him to China. Rabindranath gave lectures in the cities of Shanghai and Peking as well as in five of the country's twenty-four provincial capitals. From China, he went to Japan. The first international student at Shantiniketan had earlier come from Japan— a Sanskrit student named Hori San.

5.22 On his return form China and Japan, Rabindranath stayed home barely two months before he was travelling again. This time he went to South America. The most memorable part of this trip was his visit to Argentina, where he was received by the famous writer and activist, Victoria Ocampo. This is what she wrote about this event:

> "In September 1924 it was announced that Tagore would pass through Buenos Aires on his way to Peru. This was great news for those of us who knew his poems, in English, French, and Spanish. So we anxiously awaited his arrival which for us would be the great event of the year."[17]

5.23 During his visit to USA, Rabindranath gave his message through lectures. However, during his visit to Ceylon, students of Vishva-Bharati staged his dramas. He also visited Persia and Iraq.

5.24 In the course of "The Nobel Prize Acceptance Speech", Rabindranath told the distinguished gathering of scholars from all over the world—

> "I want to assure you that the prize, which you have awarded to me was not wasted upon myself. I have used this money for establishing and maintaining the university which I have started. I invite you to come and join hands with us and not to leave this institution merely to us. Let your students and learned men come to us and help us make this university a common institution for the East and the West. May we all together make it a true representative of the undivided Humanity of the world."[18]

5.25 We mentioned earlier that Japanese scholars joined hands with Rabindranath in developing Shantiniketan. But the situation changed in the thirties. The Japanese military machine invaded

China, and even Japanese scholars supported this. In 1938, Rabinndranath appealed to his friend, Yone Noguchi, to reconsider the matter calmly—

> "Please take the risk and speak against Japan's aggression, as you had done against Italy's aggression. Please view this conflict as a temporary digression from the long-term trend. Let us hope, the Japanese and Chinese people will soon join hands together, in wiping off memories of a bitter past. True Asian Humanity will be reborn. Poets will raise their song and will be unashamed to declare, fearlessly, their faith in a human destiny which cannot admit of a scientific mass production of fratricide."[19]

Summary of Tagore's Contribution to Practical Vedanta

5.26 (a) During the first forty years of the 20th century, he was a major contributor to the cause of world peace (i.e. to Practical Vedanta).

(b) His Nobel-Prize-winning book "Gitanjali" was a very valuable addition to world's Vedantic literature.

(c) He established Shanti-Niketan and Vishva Bharati University to continue doing the work that he had started.

(d) He tried his best to help the poor.

Notes

1. Edward John Thompson, Rabindranath Tagore, His Life and Work. Oxford University Press, 1921, p. 7.
2. Ibid., pp. 7-8.
3. Ibid., p 8
4. Ibid., pp. 8-9.

5. Ibid., pp. 9-10.
6. Ibid., p. 11.
7. Ibid., p. 12.
8. Ibid., p. 13.
9. Ibid., p. 14.
10. Ibid., p. 20.
11. Uma Das Gupta (ed.), Rabindranath Tagore: My Life in My Words. Penguin Books, 2010, p. 99.
12. Ibid., p. 109.
13. Ibid., p. 13.
14. Ibid., p. 148.
15. Rabindranath Tagore, Gitanjali, KBS/Visa-Bharati, eighth reprint, 2005, p. 35.
16. Uma Das Gupta (ed.), Rabindranath Tagore, op. cit., pp. 137-8.
17. Ibid., p. 227.
18. Rabindranath Tagore, Gitanjali, op. cit., pp. 295-300.
19. Uma Das Gupta (ed.), Rabindranath Tagore, op. cit., pp. 295-8.

CHAPTER 6

Gandhi's Multidimensional Contributions

A Brief Life-sketch

6.1 Mohandas Karamchand Gandhi (or Gandhi for short) was born at Porbandar (Gujarat) on 2 October 1869. His father (Karamchand) was the Prime Minister of the small princely state of Porbandar, and later, also of two more neighbouring states of Rajkot and Vankaner. Gandhi's mother had a long-lasting influence on his life, and about the things that remained fresh in his memory, Gandhi wrote:

> The outstanding impression my mother had left on my memory is that of saintliness. She was deeply religious. She would not think of taking her meals without daily prayers. Going to Haveli— the Vaishnava temple—was one of her daily duties.... To keep two or three consecutive fasts was nothing to her....[1]

6.2 Gandhi's schooling till High School was mainly at Rajkot. Two plays—The Filial Love of Śravaṇa, and the Devotion to Truth of Harish Chandra—which Gandhi witnessed during his boyhood left an indelible impression in his mind. The reason why he called his autobiography as "The story of my Experiments with Truth" can be traced back to the ideal which the legendary Harish Chandra upheld under all circumstances: As Gandhi himself says:

> To follow truth and to go through all the ordeals Harish Chandra went through was the one ideal it inspired in me. I literally believed in the story of Harish Chandra. The thought of it all often made me weep. My common sense tells me today that Harish Chandra could not have been an historical character. Still both Harish Chandra and Śravaṇa are living realities for me, and I am sure I should be moved as before, if I were to read these plays again today.[2]

6.3 Among other influences of a religious nature, which started in Gandhi's early life and which are highlighted by him in his autobiography, "toleration for all branches of Hinduism and sister religions" is attributed to his father's close and friendly ties with Shiva worshippers as well as Jain monks.[3] Chanting God's name—or Rāmanāma—was taught to Gandhi by his nurse, Rambhā, and his father's illness provided to him an opportunity to listen to the Rāmāyaṇa. Sarma summarized (in 1944) Gandhi's recollections in the following words:

> When he was a child, his nurse taught him Rāmanāma (uttering God's name) to cure his fear of ghosts and spirits. The seed sown by that good woman was not lost, for Rāmanāma is still looked upon by Gandhiji as an infallible remedy for all the ills of life. The boy also listened to the reading of the Rāmāyaṇa of Tulsīdās in the presence of his father during his illness. Naturally he was profoundly impressed and has come to regard Tulsīdās's book even today as the greatest book in

all devotional literature. Also at this time a Gujarati stanza gripped his mind and heart, especially its concluding lines (which can be translated as):

"But the truly noble know all men as one,

And return with gladness good for evil done."

Its precept that one should return good for evil became thenceforth the guiding principle of his life.[4]

6.4 At the age of eighteen Gandhi went to England to study law, but only after he had taken tree solemn oaths—to obtain clearance from his mother for going abroad—that he would not touch wine, woman and meat during his stay in England. Gandhi has described how a strong pressure was put on him by "a friend and well-wisher" to break the vows regarding meat and wine, and also how "peer pressure put him on the track of "close companionship and marriage with an English girl, as so many Indian boys used to do". But, says Gandhi: "Daily I would pray to God for protection and get it. Not that I had any idea of God. It was faith that was at work—faith of which the seed had been sown by the good nurse Rambhā...

"Who dare harm whom God protects?"[6]

6.5 Gandhi's first reading of the Bhagavad-Gītā took place in England, through the translation by Edwin Arnold, entitled "The Song Celestial" and this opened his eyes in new directions. On one side, he became anxious to know more and more about his religion of birth—Hinduism—and on the other side he read the scriptures of other religions. Especially remarkable was the very first impression of the Gītā, of the second chapter in particular and there too of the Sthitaprajña-section. He read again and again verses II.62-63 which came to him in the following translation by Arnold:

> If one
> Ponders on subjects of the sense, there springs
> Attraction; from attraction grows desire;
> Desire flames to fierce passion, passion breeds
> Recklessness; then the memory—all betrayed—
> Lets noble purpose go, and saps the mind,
> Till purpose, mind, and man are all undone.

Gandhi wrote in his autobiography:

> The verses in the second chapter... made a deep impression on my mind and they still ring in my ears. The book struck me as one of priceless worth. The impression has ever since been growing on me with the result that I regard it today as the book par excellence for the knowledge of Truth. It has afforded me an invaluable help in my moments of gloom.[7]

6.6 Gandhi returned to India with a Law degree in 1891, to find that his saintly mother, whose memory kept him pure in England all these years, had passed away and that his brother had kept the news from him to save him from pain and sorrow in a foreign land. After he returned home, he tried to set up legal practice in Bombay. But he found it impossible to make both ends meet. So he went back to Rajkot to live with his brother and try his luck in the local court there. But he had a very unpleasant experience with the British Political Agent in whose court he had to appear. Consequently he was in a state of profound depression, when a job offer came from Dada Abdulla and Co., a firm in Porbandar which had business in South Africa. He was asked whether he would go to South Africa to instruct the Company's Counsel in a big case. Gandhi accepted this job offer and sailed for South Africa in April, 1893.

6.7 The twenty-one years (1893-1914) that Gandhi spent in South Africa are the most important from the viewpoint of the development of his personality—how he decided to spend all his time for social causes, how religious influences—and particularly the Gītā—moulded his philosophy of life, and how he developed a new technique of social action—Satyāgraha. Accordingly, a separate section attempts to indicate the main elements of Gandhi's experiments with Satyāgraha in South Africa.

6.8 When Gandhi arrived in India from South Africa in the beginning of 1915, he had already attained considerable fame but it remained to be seen how and with which "group" he would make common cause. His "political guru" Gokhale advised him to take a year, seeing personally what was going on in different parts of the country, and then make the appropriate institutional connections. The conflict between the Moderates and the Extremists was still on but due to Gokhale's death and widespread dissatisfaction with the British, the Extremists led by Tilak moved to the forefront. On the issue of obtaining mass participation by common people in the activities of the Congress, Tilak and Gandhi broadly agreed. Tilak's new interpretation of the Gītā was the topic of the day, because he had explained how Gītā's Karma-yoga could be applied to the freedom fight. Tilak gave to Gandhi the Gujarati translation of his book—*Gītā-Rahasya,* originally written in Marathi during his long political imprisonment. Gandhi too had formulated his own views in South Africa, based on his unique interpretation of the Gītā. On the need for applying the Gītā to the political problems of the country, Tilak and Gandhi were equally enthusiastic. However, Gandhi's insistence on viewing truth and non-violence as the basis of all social and political activities, was considered entirely unrealistic by Tilak. Such differences between the two leaders began to be voiced in 1919.

6.9 The Tilak-Gandhi transition can be said to have begun with the 'Satyāgraha Pledge' that was taken throughout the country in April 1919, and completed in August 1920. In fact, the date fixed for starting the All-India non-cooperation movement under Gandhi's leadership—1 August 1920—happened to coincide with the date of Tilak passing away from this world. However, during the preceding four years, Gandhi had established the Satyāgraha Ashram near Ahmedabad, and had attracted thereto persons like Vinoba—who was then a college student and was moved by the "eye-opening" speech of Gandhi at Banaras University. Jawaharlal Nehru, too, a young lawyer at that time, felt the arrival of Gandhi "like a powerful current of fresh air", as he later wrote in 1946:

> And then Gandhi came. He was like a powerful current of fresh air that made us stretch ourselves and take deep breaths; like a beam of light that pierced the darkness and removed the scales from our eyes; like a whirlwind that upset many things, but most of all the working of people's minds. He did not descend from the top; he seemed to emerge from the millions of India, speaking their language and incessantly drawing attention to them and their appalling condition. Get off the backs of these peasants and workers, he told us, all you who live by their exploitation; get rid of the system that produces this poverty and misery. Political freedom took new shape then and acquired a new content. Much that he said we only partially accepted or sometimes did not accept at all. But all this was secondary. The essence of his

> teaching was fearlessness and truth, and action allied to these, always keeping the welfare of the masses in view.[8]

6.10 Before venturing to present to the country, the new technique of Satyāgraha, it was necessary to see how the experiment conducted in South Africa would work out under Indian conditions which were obviously far more complex than those in South Africa. A separate section is therefore devoted to summarizing the main elements of 'small-scale applications of Satyāgraha in India during 1915-18'.

6.11 The Gandhian era in Indian politics began in 1919 and after twenty-eight years the goal of independence was achieved. However, for Gandhi himself, the experiments with Truth and Non-violence were always the first priority. When he found that, due to lack of training in the technique of Satyāgraha, mob violence had crept into the movement, he called it a 'Himalayan blunder' and called off the agitation. His long imprisonment on many occasions enabled him to write his own commentary (in Gujarati) on the Gītā, as he explained in the introduction thereto:

> During my incarceration, I was able to study the Gītā more fully. I went reverently through the Gujarati translation of the Lokamānya's great work...
>
> It has been my endeavour, as also that of some companions, to reduce to practice the teaching of the Gītā as I have understood it. The Gītā has become for us a spiritual reference book. I am aware that we ever fail to act in perfect accord with the teaching. The failure is not due to want of effort, but is in spite of it. Even through the failures we seem to see rays of hope. The accompanying rendering contains the meaning of

> the Gītā message which this little band is trying to enforce in its daily conduct.
>
> My desire to leave to Gujaratis, through the mother tongue, whatever knowledge I may possess,.... does not mean any disrespect to other renderings. They have their own place. But I am not aware of the claim made by the translators of enforcing their meaning of the Gītā in their own lives. At the back of my reading there is the claim of an endeavour to enforce the meaning in my own conduct for an unbroken period of forty years.

6.12 Panikkar has summarized Gandhi's ideas as to how the non-violent fight for independence from a foreign rule had close links with the Gītā doctrine of swadharma:

> It was the Mahatma's conviction that foreign rule, i.e. the imposition of an alien way of life and thought, was not merely sinful because it was an attack on the Dharma of the ruled but it was even more against the Dharma of the ruler. That is why all through the twenty-eight years of his fight against British rule and even when he denounced that rule as satanic, he claimed to be a true friend of the British, as they now accept him to have been. The very denunciation of British rule to be satanic is the clue to his approach and can in its full significance be understood only in terms of the Gītā doctrine of Swadharma, or the law of one's own nature.[10]

6.13 Parallel to the 'agitational' element in the Satyāgraha campaigns against the foreign rule, there was the 'internal growth' element to which Gandhi gave the meaningful name: Constructive Programme. Gandhi attached the greatest importance to the various activities which were included in the constructive programme. As of 1940, the importance of the following items was highlighted by Gandhi under this programme:

(i) Hindu-Muslim or communal unity
(ii) Removal of untouchability
(iii) Prohibition
(iv) Khādī
(v) Other village industries
(vi) Village sanitation
(vii) New or basic education
(viii) Adult Education
(ix) Uplift of women
(x) Education in hygiene and health
(xi) Propagation of rashtrabhasha (national language)
(xii) Cultivating love of one's own language
(xiii) Working for economic equality

6.14 To give an idea of the comprehensive view of the Indian situation which Gandhi had for purposes of bringing about an all-round development of the Indian society along non-violent lines, it is necessary to present the following list of organizations connected with the constructive programme, as prepared by V.K.R.V Rao:

(i) Sevāgrām Āśrama
(ii) Kasturba Hospital
(iii) Nai Talim Sangh
(iv) Khadı Research Institute
(v) Gandhi Sevā Sangh
(vi) Mahilā Āśrama
(vii) Bajajwadi
(viii) Shikshā Maṇḍala
(ix) Gandhi Gyān Mandir
(x) Village Industries Research Institute

(xi) Magan Sāngrahālaya
(xii) Rashtra Bhāshā Prachār Samiti
(xiii) Leprosy Foundation
(xiv) Grām Sevā Maṇḍala
(xv) Go Sevā Sangh
(xvi) Maharogi Sevā Maṇḍala
(xvii) Paramdhām Āśrama
(xvii) Mātri Sevā Sangh[12]

6.15 Within six months of India's independence, Gandhi faced the assassin's bullet, on 30 January 1948, with the words 'He Rāma'. The closing days of Gandhi's life witnessed 'the worst trials and tribulations' as Betai puts it.[13] India's independence on 15th August 1947 was won at the cost of the country's partition which led to intercommunal disturbances on an unprecedented scale. Gandhi tried his best to restore peace and harmony, but could achieve only partial success. Faced with violence in so many places at the same time, he even expressed his agony in words like the following:

> There was a time when people immediately carried out whatever escaped from my lips. Truly, I was then the commander of a non-violent army. But today mine is a cry in the wilderness....
>
> In this age perhaps I am the only believer in non-violence. I pray to God to give me enough strength so that at least I, if none else, may be able to practise non-violence....[14]

Betai remarks:

> It is remarkable that absolute devotion to God, total surrender to His will, directing all one's activities and one's very self towards becoming an instrument in the hands of God— these were the most remarkable features of Gandhiji's utterings

in these last days. And he had read just this in the Gītā."[15]

Experiment with Satyagraha in South Africa

6.16 Gandhi's technique of waging "non-violent fights" for social and political causes took a concrete shape in South Africa during the years 1906-14, and his own spiritual, moral and mental preparedness for making such a "new experiment" can be traced back to the years 1903-6. Prior to that, in 1894, he had helped the Indian community in the Natal province of South Africa to set up the socio-political organization called "The Natal Indian Congress". The word "Congress" helped create a feeling of close relationship with the Indian National Congress which had started functioning in India in 1885. During the initial years of its existence, the Natal Indian Congress circulated pamphlets to draw attention of the authorities and the general public to the discriminatory treatment which the Indian community and particularly the "indentured" and "ex-indentured" labourers were receiving from the white population of South Africa. The indentured labourers were those Indians who had gone to Natal on an agreement to serve for five years, in the sugarcane, tea and coffee estates. These labourers were practically "slaves" of their employers for the period of their agreement. They were contemptuously called "coolies". Even after the expiry of five years, the ex-indentured labourers were subjected to special taxation and other restrictions if they wanted to go from one place to another in an attempt to find means of living. The success which the ex-indentured labourers had started achieving in the trading and other occupations aroused the jealously of European colonists whose real intentions were to force "unwanted" groups of Indians back to

India, by subjecting them to intolerable restrictions.

6.17 At the start of the twentieth century, when the Transvaal-part of South Africa also came under the British administration, the Asiatic department of Transvaal Government wanted all the Indians to obtain a "certificate" which would show, in particular, their photographs and finger-prints. Sarma describes how, in Gandhi's opinion, the draft Ordinance of the Transvaal Government amounted to treating Indians like "criminal tribes":

> When he (Gandhi) read the various sections of the draft Ordinance reeking with hatred to Indians, he shuddered. He saw that, if the Ordinance was passed and meekly accepted, it would spell absolute ruin for the Indians in South Africa. He said, it was better to die than to submit to such a law. Even the laws to which the indentured labourers were subject were a mere flea-bite compared to the drastic rules and penalties proposed for all free Indians, rich or poor, educated or uneducated. Gandhiji thought the Ordinance could only be compared to some of the drastic laws directed against criminal tribes in India and would not suffer in comparison. Under its provisions even women and children had to be registered.[16]

6.18 With a view to determining the Indian community's response to the discriminatory legislation, the Transvaal Indian Association called, in September 1906, a public meeting which was attended by three thousand men. On the advice of Gandhi, fully supported by leading members of the community, a resolution was drafted, stating that "we declare our solemn determination not to submit to the Ordinance, if it became law, and to suffer all penalties attaching to such non-submission". Sarma adds:

> Gandhi made a speech which will go down into history. He explained the consequences of taking a solemn oath, he announced that he himself was taking the oath and would not violate it, even if all others did and left him and he had to face the wrath of the Government alone, and asked every man in the hall to come to a decision for himself individually. Others also spoke to the same effect including the President. And at last all present, standing with upraised hands, took an oath with God as witness not to submit to the Ordinance if it became law. Thus was Satyāgraha born on the 11th September, 1906.[17]

6.19 But how did Gandhi, a coolie barrister as he was called, feel that, in 1906, he had the spiritual courage as well as moral and material support of the Indian community so as to recommend to them the breaking of a law, howsoever unjust it might be? Sarma attributes this to the taking of "significant steps" by Gandhi during the years 1903-6, which marked the adoption of a new philosophy of life:

> The first step was his intense study of the Bhagavad-Gītā which from 1903 became his infallible guide in conduct... It was in the company of his Theosophist friends that he read Pātañjali's Yoga-sūtras and the Bhagavad-Gītā in the original. These two books gripped his mind, and he wanted to put into practice the Gītā teaching—that one should be in the world, but not of it. He wanted to practise *aprarigraha* (not having any possessions) and *samabhāva* (treating all as equals). So he deliberately allowed his Life Insurance policy to lapse and wrote to his brother giving him all his savings up to that moment and telling him that all his future savings, if any, would be utilized for the benefit of the community.

> The second step was the launching of a weekly journal called 'Indian Opinion', in 1904, financed by himself and practically edited by himself....
>
> The third step was the nursing of the poor Indians at the time of the plague epidemic...
>
> The fourth step was founding of the Phoenix Settlement near Durban.... It was agreed that all the people in this settlement would maintain themselves by manual labour on the farm and draw the same living wage...[18]

6.20 Now to the conduct of the Satyāgraha itself, the first phase of which started in September 1906. The Transvaal legislation making it obligatory for Indians to obtain a "certificate" by 31 July 1907 was called by the Indian community as "the Black Act" and they had decided not to submit to it and to suffer the consequences thereof, but not to resort to violence. In the beginning, this movement was described as "Passive Resistance". However, Gandhi saw that the English term "Passive Resistance" was misleading because it did not correctly indicate the nature of the Indian movement. Passive resistance was supposed to be the weapon of the weak, who would use methods of violence, if any when they could use them. This term could not therefore be applied to the Indian movement, which had renounced all violence in thought as well as deed and which aimed at conquering untruth by truth, hatred by love, and violence by non-violence. Gandhi therefore offered a prize, through his journal 'Indian Opinion', for the person who would invent the most suitable Indian expression, in place of 'Passive Resistance'. Maganlal Gandhi suggested the word "Sadāgraha", and Gandhi himself modified it to Satyāgraha".

6.21 With a view to obtaining the Indian population's

compliance with the "Black Act", the Transvaal Government opened many offices for receiving applications and for issuing "certificates". However, volunteers of the Indian community dissuaded the would-be applicants by picketing, so much so that only 500 certificates could be issued, as against a target of 13,000. On the last day of registration, that is, 31 July 1907, a mass meeting of the Indian community was called at Pretoria, the capital of the Transvaal. The Government sent one of their officers to this meeting, to admonish the leaders not to break their heads against a stone wall. However, this type of warning only strengthened the resolve of the people who were determined not to be cowed down by threats, nor even by punishment.

6.22 Soon the Government sent a warning to Gandhi and to other leading members of the Indian community that they must either register themselves under the Act or leave the country or face arrest. Accordingly, Gandhi was arrested and sentenced to two months' imprisonment. This was his first experience of jail life. Within a weak, more than a hundred Satyāgrahī prisoners joined Gandhi. With more and more Indians ready to go to jail, the Government offered a compromise, saying that if a majority of Indians registered voluntarily, and not by compulsion, the Black Act would be repealed. This compromise was accepted by the leaders of the Indian community, and all the Satyāgrahī prisoners were freed.

6.23 Gandhi had a hard time convincing a small section of the Indian community, composed of some Paṭhāns, about the reasonableness of the compromise agreement with the Government. Among these Paṭhāns, some mischief-monger spread a rumour that Gandhi had taken a bribe from the Government. One of the Paṭhāns became so angry with Gandhi that he struck him on his head with a heavy cudgel. Gandhi fainted and fell down. A British clergyman took him to his house and arranged for medical care. Gandhi issued a statement that he did not want the assailant to be prosecuted, but the police took its own course and got him sentenced to three months' imprisonment. In the meantime, the misunderstanding underlying this incident was removed and the Indian community was again united in its whole-hearted support to Gandhi over the issue of voluntary registration.

6.24. Now it was the turn of the Transvaal Government to repeal the Black Act, but General Smuts, the head of the Government, refused to honour the word that he had given at the time of the compromise. Gandhi, who had risked his life in making his countrymen register themselves voluntarily, was shocked, at this breach of faith. How could he face the Indian community after this, he asked himself. He addressed a letter to General Smuts, but there was no reply. He then consulted the other leaders of the community and announced that, unless the Government acted by a specific date (16 August 1908) the certificates collected by the Indians voluntarily would be burnt, and "they would humbly and firmly take the consequences".

6.25 General Smuts called this message of the Indians an ultimatum sent to the Government by people who had no idea of its power. But the Indians too were determined to meet the challenge, as Sarma describes:

> A public meeting was announced to be held two hours after the time limit, for the purpose of the ceremony of making a bonfire of the certificates... On the mosque ground of Johannesburg every inch of available place was filled by Indians of all classes. An iron cauldron of the largest size available

in the market was brought and set up on a platform in the grounds for the burning of the certificates. As the meeting was about to commence, a volunteer who had been posted at the Telegraph Office arrived on a cycle with a telegram from the Government announcing their inability to change their minds. The telegram was read to the audience, who received it with cheers, and who re-confirmed their determination to continue the Satyāgraha struggle

6.26 The second phase of the Satyāgraha began in 1909 and many arrests were made. Gandhi spent three months in jail along with his son. When the jails became overcrowded with the Satyāgrahī prisoners, the Government tried the method of deporting them to India. But many of them were born and brought up in South Africa, and there was an outcry in India and England against their deportation. The prison authorities then opened road-side camps where prisoners had no protection against cold. Two young prisoners died because of these hardships. Still the community did not falter. The more cruel the Government, the firmer the resolve of the Satyāgrahīs. In one of the prisons, the Satyāgrahīs had to go on a hunger-strike for seven days to obtain the minimum facilities required for human subsistence.

6.27 During the latter part of 1909, a deputation of the South African Indians, including Gandhi, went to England to plead for their just cause. They received a sympathetic hearing by Lord Ampthill, a former Governor of Madras, who tried to persuade General Smuts to repeal the Black Act, but the latter refused to change his policy. Lord Ampthill thereupon said that he had nothing but congratulations to offer to those who were so willing to suffer for principle and to carry on such a righteous struggle with such clean weapons.

6.28 During the third phase of the Satyāgraha, the problem of maintaining the families of the poor Satyāgrahī prisoners called for attention. What was needed was a large farming area in the Transvaal where these families could live together as members of a cooperative establishment, and maintain themselves by their own labour. The Phoenix settlement which Gandhi had started in 1906, was in Natal, nearly three hundred miles away. Luckily for the poor Indian community, a German architect and a friend of Gandhi, Kallenbach, who had a big farm of eleven hundred acres in the Transvaal region, lent the use of his farm for the Satyāgrahī families without any rent. Gandhi called this "Tolstoy Farm", in recognition of what he had learnt from Tolstoy's writings about the importance of the concept of "bread-labour".

6.29 This phase of the non-violent struggle of the Indians in South Africa thus continued till 1912 when Gokhale, a prominent Indian leader held in high esteem by the British Government, accepted Gandhi's request and decided to visit South Africa. Both Indians and Europeans living in South Africa vied with one another in welcoming and honouring the great Indian statesman. Gokhale had long discussions with the ministers, and before leaving South Africa, he told Gandhi, "Everything has been settled. The Black Act will be repealed. The racial bar will be removed from the immigration law. The tax on the ex-indentured labourers will be abolished".

6.30 But nothing came out of the assurance given by the ministers to Gokhale. General Smuts announced that, as the Europeans in Natal objected to the repeal of the tax, the Government could not pass any legislation. Gandhi informed Gokhale, who expressed deep pain but saw no further use of his intervention. The only course left was for the Indians in South Africa to intensify the fight.

6.31 In March 1913, another intolerable grievance cropped up for the Indian community, necessitating the participation of Indian women also in the nonviolent struggle. The Cape Supreme Court decided in a case that all marriages that were not celebrated according to Christian rites and registered by the Registrar of Marriages were outside the pale of legal marriages in South Africa. Thus according to this judgment, all Hindu, Muslim and Zoroastrian marriages were illegal, and therefore the married women of these communities and their children lost their legitimacy. Gandhi wrote to the Government but got no reply. He therefore invited the Indian women to come into line with men to offer Satyāgraha. Even women with babies in arms came forward to take part in the struggle. Kasturba Gandhi was among the women who were arrested and imprisoned, in this, the fourth, phase of the Satyāgraha.

6.32 The arrest of women and their imprisonment with hard labour aroused much sympathy in India and England. The Satyāgraha in South Africa entered its fifth phase when indentured labourers in Natal also started going on strike. Their employers retaliated by cutting off their light and water supply, driving them out of their quarters and even whipping them. Hundreds of them came to Gandhi and offered to do whatever he would advice.

6.33 Faced with five thousand indentured labourers who were thrown out of their quarters, the only solution that Gandhi could devise was to start a journey on foot to the Tolstoy Farm. This was the sixth phase of the Satyāgraha and it called for detailed planning and organization because the marchers, covering twenty miles a day for eight days, had to be provided with bread and sugar, and rules for sanitation and discipline had to be be observed throughout the eight-day march. A large European bakery agreed to supply bread because its owner knew that the Satyāgrahī marchers were only seeking the minimum of justice through their unity and self-suffering.

6.34 As the marchers completed nearly half of their journey, observes Sarma, the Government felt more and more confused. It was the firmness of the Indians coupled with their peacefulness that distressed General Smuts. If they had taken to rioting or violence of any kind, they could have been easily shot down. But something had to be done before they reached their destination. Gandhi was arrested and sentenced to nine months' imprisonment. His friends Polak and Kallenbach were also arrested. The march of the indentured labourers of Natal was also stopped, and the Government made plans to deport them back to Natal by special trains.

6.35 The Satyāgraha entered its seventh phase when the indentured labourers of Natal, who were deported and treated as convicts, refused to work in mines. They were then whipped, kicked and maltreated in various ways. The strike now spread to all the mining centres, and the men came out in thousands. The Government adopted a policy of blood and iron. Mounted policemen chased the strikers, brought them back and forced them to work. When the strikers resisted, fire was opened on them, killing some and wounding others. These atrocities were all reported by cablegrams to Gokhale, and the news spread throughout India. The Viceroy, Lord Hardinge spoke in favour of the Satyāgrahīs, and at Gokhale's request, Andrews and Pearson offered to intervene.

6.36 Upset by the attitude of the Viceroy of India, the South African government decided to get out of the awkward situation by appointing a commission to inquire into the grievances of Indians and make recommendations. An interim recommendation of the commission was to release Gandhi, Pollak and Kallenbach. Gandhi and Andrews saw General Smuts, and when a provisional agreement for redressing all the grievances of Indians was reached, the Satyāgraha was suspended. After some time, the commission recommended compliance with all the demands of the Satyāgrahīs, and the necessary legislation was enacted by the South African Government in June 1914. Thus ended, successfully, Gandhi's first experiment with Satyāgraha, which passed through seven phases and lasted eight years.

6.37 In Spratt's opinion, thc Satyāgraha in South Africa could be called a 'model', not only because it was the first use of the new technique but also because it stayed very close to the 'principles': "It was conducted against very heavy odds by poor and ignorant people—the majority indeed were illiterate—but there was hardly an instance of breach of the principles..."[20]

6.38 Perhaps the greatest testimony of Gandhi's success as a Satyāgrahī was the change of heart that was apparently brought about in the "so-called opponent", viz. General Smuts. Verma quotes how Smuts became deeply conscious of the virtues of sincerity, unselfishness and humanism that he found in Gandhi, Smuts wrote:

> However often we may differ from him, we are conscious all the time of his sincerity, his unselfishness, and above all of his fundamental and universal humanity. He always acts as a great human, with deep sympathy for men of all classes and all races and especially for the under-dog.[21]

Small-scale Applications of Satyagraha in India during 1915-18

6.39 The feasibility of applying the Satyāgraha technique to Indian conditions was tested by Gandhi, mainly on five occasions during the years 1915-18. The most well-known of these was the Champaran Satyāgraha of 1917. However, there were two occasions prior to Champaran when Gandhi had prepared the concerned groups of people to be ready to offer Satyāgraha if the issues were not settled through negotiations. Although the need to actually use the Satyāgraha weapon did not arise in either of these two cases, because the problems were solved prior to reaching that stage, Gandhi still considers the first of these two occasions as "heralding the advent of Satyāgraha in India."[22] In view of this, a brief account of two of the five "tests" of Satyāgraha, conducted by Gandhi during the years 1915-18, namely the first and the third, is given below.

6.40 The first occasion was in 1915, on the issue of the customs barrier at Viramgam, between British India and the Kathiawad States, due to which all the railway passengers travelling on that route had to suffer hardships. Motilal, a voluntary social worker of that area and tailor by profession requested Gandhi to do something to end the trouble. Gandhi asked him, "Are you ready to go to jail?" "We are ready to march to the gallows", was the firm reply of Motilal. Gandhi went to Rajkot, collected all the necessary information about the customs barrier at Viramgam and opened correspondence with the Government. He also dropped a hint in his speeches at various places that the people should be prepared, if necessary, to offer Satyāgraha at Viramgam.

6.41 Gandhi's speeches were duly reported to the

Government of Bombay, by the police (C.I.D.). When Gandhi saw the Governor of Bombay, he was told that the Government of India was responsible for the customs barrier and that he should turn to them for relief. Gandhi then met the Viceroy, Lord Chelmsford, and placed the facts before him. The Viceroy was astonished, for he knew nothing about the matter. He at once called for the papers and within a few days thereafter the customs cordon was removed.

6.42 Prior to the favourable decision of the Viceroy, Gandhi was asking the people of Kathiawad States to be ready to pursue the matter, without fear but peacefully. In general the attitude of the Government to public grievances was extremely unsympathetic in those days. Therefore getting ready for a showdown with the Government was not a small thing. Although in the end Satyāgraha was not actually offered, the imminent possibility of its being offered was probably an important factor in obtaining redress. Gandhi therefore regarded the Viramgam Customs Case as "heralding the advent of Satyāgraha in India".[23]

6.43 As already pointed out, the main test of the Satyāgraha technique took place in connection with the Champaran struggle of 1917 when Gandhi had to actually offer Satyāgraha on behalf of the poor farmers who were being exploited by indigo planters. For the last hundred years, every Champaran tenant was bound by law to plant three out of every twenty parts of his land with indigo for his landlord. This system was known as 'tīnkaṭhiā', and it worked as a great hardship for thousands of poor farmers. At the Congress session of December 1916, Gandhi was requested to go to Champaran and to do something to relieve the distress of the people.

6.44 Gandhi thought it necessary to make an unbiased

inquiry into the grievances of the Champaran farmers. For this, he thought it was his duty, before starting the inquiry, to know the planters' side of the case. He interviewed both the Secretary of the Planters' Association and the Commissioner of the Tirhut Division. Both of them resented his 'intrusion', as they called it, and said that an outsider like him had no business to come between the planters and their tenants, and advised him to leave the place at once.

6.45 Gandhi ignored the advice of the Secretary and the Commissioner and went to Motihāri, the headquarters of the Champaran district. A legal notice was then served on him, ordering him to leave Champaran. Gandhi refused to leave till his inquiry on behalf of the riots was finished. He then received a summons to take his trial the next day for disobeying the order.

6.46 The news of the summons served on Gandhi spread like wild fire, and huge crowds gathered together in Motihāri and followed Gandhi wherever he went. The people had now lost all fear of the authorities. They yielded obedience to Gandhi and not to the police. The officials did not know how to proceed with the case. The Government pleader pressed the magistrate to postpone it, but Gandhi requested him not to do so, as he wanted to plead guilty.

6.47 In the Court of the Magistrate, Gandhi read a statement in which he said, he had come to Champaran on a pressing invitation from the ryots, who had some grievances against the indigo planters. He had come to study the situation and, if possible, to assist the Administration in doing justice. He had no other motive. He could not believe that his coming would in any way disturb public peace or cause loss of life. As a law-abiding citizen his instinct was to obey the order of the Magistrate. But his sense of duty to those who had invited him compelled him to stay. Amidst this conflict of duties he would throw the responsibility of removing him on the Administration. Therefore he decided to submit without protest to the penalty of disobedience.

6.48 Gandhi's statement concluded with the words: "I have disregarded the order served on me, not for want of respect for the lawful authority, but in obedience to the higher law of our being, the voice of conscience".[24]

6.49 About twenty-five years after Gandhi had made this famous statement before the Champaran magistrate, he recalled the wider political significance thereof and told Louis Fischer: "That day in Champaran became a red-letter day in my life. This was my first act of civil disobedience against the British. It became the method by which India could be made free".[25]

6.50 The Champaran magistrate was taken by surprise to hear Gandhi's statement and he did not know what to do, because the apparently simple matter had grown into such a big issue as to call for a political decision by the Lieutenant-Governor. The only thing that the magistrate could do was to postpone judgment. Gandhi wired the details of the situation to the Viceroy, to Madan Mohan Malviya and to other friends. The result was that, before Gandhi could appear before the court to receive the sentence, the magistrate wrote to him that the Lieutenant-Governor had ordered the case to be withdrawn.

6.51 The Collector then wrote to Gandhi that he might conduct the proposed inquiry and that all the necessary help would be given to him by the Government officials. The planters were much displeased, but Gandhi's inquiry went on. At his suggestion, the Lieutenant-Governor appointed a committee to go into the whole question. The committee's findings were in favour of the ryots. A bill to abolish the 'tīnkaṭhiā' system was introduced. It was fiercely opposed by the planters, but owing to the firmness of the Lieutenant-Governor, the century-old burden on the poor farmers was removed. This was the first occasion in India on which Satyāgraha, actually offered, brought relief to the people. After this and two more 'tests', Gandhi offered to apply the Satyāgraha-technique to All-India political problems, from 1919 onwards.

Mass Scale Applications of Satyagraha in India During 1919-48

6.52 For purposes of applying Satyāgraha against the foreign rule in India, Gandhi attached great importance to the technique of non-violent non-cooperation by the masses. This implied chiefly the withdrawal of cooperation from a government that, in the non-cooperators' view, was extremely unjust, oppressive or corrupt. The purpose of non-cooperation was to put so much pressure upon the government that the act of governance itself might become impossible. As Gandhi put it:

> I believe, and every body must grant, that no government can exist for a single moment without the cooperation of the people, willing or forced, and if people suddenly withdraw their cooperation in every detail, the government will come to a standstill... Cooperation with a just government is a duty; non-cooperation with an unjust government is equally a duty.[26]

6.53 In September 1920, Gandhi moved the resolution on non-cooperation at the special session of the Indian National Congress. Lala Lajpat Rai, a close colleague of the late B.G. Tilak, presided over this session.

However, Bipin Chandra Pal, another close colleague of Tilak, supported by C.R. Das, opposed Gandhi's move, and put forward an amendment to the effect that a mission should be sent to England to lay India's grievances before the British Prime Minister and explain the temper of the Indian people. After a long discussion among the Congress delegates—numbering nearly three thousand—Gandhi won by a majority of two to one. By this resolution the Congress adopted the policy of progressive non-violent non-cooperation until the atrocities committed in the Punjab were acknowledged and corrective action taken to set them right and a policy of leading the country to Swarāj was announced.

6.54 A seven-point scheme of non-coopcration was specified, indicating what the countrymen were advised to do to put into effect the Congress resolution, namely:

(i) Surrender of titles, honorary offices and nominated seats in Local Bodies.

(ii) Refusal to attend Government levies, durbars and other official and semi-official functions.

(iii) Gradual withdrawal of children from schools and colleges owned or aided by Government, and the establishment of national schools.

(iv) Gradual boycott of British courts by lawyers and litigants and the establishment of private arbitration courts.

(v) Refusal on the part of the military, clerical and labouring classes to offer themselves as recruits for services in Mesopotamia.

(vi) Withdrawal by candidates of their candidature from the so-called 'Reformed Councils' and refusal on the part of voters to vote for any candidate thereto

(vii) Boycott of foreign goods.[27]

6.55 Nehru believes that the full impact of the comprehensive scheme of withdrawal of cooperation went so deep as to shake up the very foundations of the British rule in India:

> Realising that the main props of British rule were fear, prestige, the cooperation, willing or unwilling, of the people, and certain classes whose vested interests were centred in British rule, Gandhi attacked these foundations. Titles were to be given up and though the title-holders responded to this only in small measure, the popular respect for these British-given titles disappeared and they became symbols of degradation. New standards and values were set up and the pomp and splendour of the viceregal court and the princes, which used to impress so much, suddenly appeared supremely ridiculous and vulgar and rather shameful, surrounded as they were by the poverty and misery of the people. Rich men were not so anxious to flaunt their riches; outwardly at least many of them adopted simpler ways, and in their dress, became almost indistinguishable from humbler folk.[28]

6.56 The last item in the seven-point scheme of non-cooperation was 'boycott of foreign goods'. Although, on paper, it sounded like what the Nationalist Party had preached at the time of Bengal partition nearly fifteen years earlier, the actual events of the 1920's proved to be far more revolutionary. Khādī—the hand-spun and hand-woven cloth—became a symbol of Swadeshi. On this issue, too, there was an initial opposition to Gandhi's ideas by some of the leaders, but soon the impact of Khādī on the society—and particularly the villages—was so great as to dispel all doubts. Gandhi pleaded the cause of Khādī in repeated statements like the following:

> Khādī is a controversial subject. Many people think that in advocating Khādī I am sailing against a head wind and am sure to sink the ship of Swarāj and that I am taking the country to the dark ages. But the proof of the pudding is in the eating. For me nation-wide spinning is a yajña. It is the symbol of unity of Indian humanity, of its economic freedom and equality and, therefore, ultimately, in the poetic expression of Jawaharlal Nehru, "the livery of India's freedom".[29]

6.57 Nehru found in Khādī and other Swadeshi activities, a practical programme of uniting the urban and rural areas, and of enabling educated people like himself to establish bonds of sympathy with the poorest of the villages:

> Gandhi sent us to the villages, and the countryside hummed with the activity of innumerable messengers of the new gospel of action. The peasant was shaken up and he began to emerge from his quiescent shell. The effect on us was different but equally far-reaching, for we saw, for the first time as it were, the villager in the intimacy of his mud-hut, and with the dark shadow of hunger always pursuing him. We learnt our Indian economics more from these visits than from books and learned discourses. The emotional experience we had already undergone was emphasized and confirmed and henceforward there could be no going back for us to our old life or our old standards, howsoever much views might change subsequently.[30]

6.58 While non-violent non-cooperation as one type of Satyāgraha was tried by Gandhi in the 1920's, he adopted in 1930 the second type of Satyāgraha, namely, Civil Disobedience. Iyer has tried to clarify the subtle difference between these two types of Satyāgraha:

> Non-cooperation was conceived in a much wider context as an instrument of social action...
>
> Civil disobedience is more difficult than non-cooperation because it presupposes the habit of willing obedience of laws without fear of their sanctions....
>
> Gandhi's emphasis was on Ahiṁsā in non-cooperation and on Tapas in civil disobedience, although both concepts contained elements of self-suffering and non-violence.
>
> Non-cooperation made fewer spiritual demands on its users.... Civil Disobedience called for a spirit of Tapas or self-suffering, which in practice only a few were capable of exemplifying....[31]

6.59 Gandhi himself, while tracing the expression 'civil disobedience' to Thoreau, explained how the Indian experiment was wider in terms of application and stricter in regard to the emphasis on non-violence:

> Civil disobedience is civil breach of unmoral statutory enactments....
>
> The expression was, as far as I am aware, coined by Thoreau to signify his own resistance to the laws of a slave State. He has left a masterly treatise on the duty of Civil Disobedience. But Thoreau was not perhaps an out and out champion of non-violence. Probably, also, Thoreau limited his breach of statutory laws to the revenue law, i.e., payment of taxes, whereas the term Civil Disobedience as practised in India covered a breach of any statutory and unmoral law. It signified the resister's outlawry in a civil, i.e., non-violent manner. He invoked the

sanctions of the law and cheerfully suffered imprisonment. It is a branch of Satyāgraha.[32]

6.60 In 1930, Gandhi picked up the issue of breaking the "Salt Tax Law" because this hurt the poorest of the Indians relatively more deeply. He envisaged a twenty-four-day march from his Ashram to the sea coast— known as the Dāṇḍī March— so that he could explain the idea personally to hundreds of thousands of people and the message of civil disobedience could thus spread all over the country. Before starting the march, he addressed thousands of people who had gathered near Ahmedabad to receive his message: "Our case is strong, our means the purest and God is with us. There is no defeat for the Satyāgrahīs till they give up truth. I pray for the success of the battle which begins tomorrow."[33]

6.61 The twenty-four-day march by seventy-nine volunteers generated unprecedented enthusiasm and big support for the cause which Gandhi represented. The marchers reached Dāṇḍi on 5 April 1930, and next morning, Gandhi broke the salt law by picking up the salt from the sea-shore without paying tax, and added: "Now that the technical or ceremonial breach of the salt law has been committed, it is now open to anyone who would take the risk of the prosecution under the salt law to manufacture salt, wherever he wishes and whenever it is convenient".[34]

Sarma summarizes the events that followed:

> This was the signal for huge demonstrations with tens of thousands of men and women in all the important towns of India. The whole country was ablaze with the fire of Civil Disobedience. The salt law was broken in many places. And there were picketings of foreign cloth shops and drinking booths by Satyāgrahī women. All these were, of

course, followed by arrests on a vast scale.[35]

6.62 In order to make the mass-scale Satyāgraha movements as effective as possible, Gandhi carried on his "mass education" through writings, speeches, personal advice, and continuous field level training of volunteers by local leaders. For example, he made it clear time and again that the following psychological and sociological conditions must be fulfilled to bring the Satyāgraha movements as close as possible to the moral standards envisaged in his idealistic formulation:

(i) The Satyāgrahī is not to harbour any hatred in his heart against the opponent because in the long run hatred is a waste of energy.

(ii) The issue for which Satyāgraha is launched should be a true and substantial one, i.e., the cause must always be legitimate and just.

(iii) The Satyāgrahī must be prepared to undergo all kinds of humiliations, persecutions and sufferings. In the end he must be ready to lay down his life. Hence Satyāgraha can be practised only by the stout in heart.[36]

6.63 Prior to the launching of the Civil Disobedience campaign of 1930, Gandhi also laid down the following "Important Rules for the Satyāgrahī"—the ideal image of whom was drawn so as to be like the Sthitaprajña of the Gītā"

(i) A Satyāgrahī will harbour no anger.

(ii) He will suffer the anger of the opponent.

(iii) In so doing he will put up with assaults from the opponent, never retaliate; but he will not submit, out of fear of punishment or the like, to any order given in anger.

(iv) When any person in authority seeks to arrest a civil resister, he will voluntarily submit to the arrest.

(v) If a Satyāgrahī has any property in his possession as a trustee, he will defend it, even at the cost of his life.

(vi) A Satyāgrahī will neither swear nor curse.

(vii) A Satyāgrahī will never insult his opponent.[37]

6.64 Nehru has described how the Congress organization, in response to Gandhi's call, condemned terroristic activities, and appealed to the countrymen to willingly accept pain and suffering inflicted by the British administration through imprisonment and other repressive measures:

> Gandhi brought about a complete change in the Congress organization....
>
> Action was to be the basis, and more specifically, action using peaceful methods. Thus far the alternatives had been just talking and passing resolutions, or terroristic activity. Both of these were set aside and terrorism was especially condemned as opposed to the basic policy of the Congress. A new technique of action was evolved which, though perfectly peaceful, yet implied non-submission to what was considered wrong and, as a consequence, a willing acceptance of the pain and suffering involved in this. Gandhi was an odd kind of pacifist, for he was an activist full of dynamic energy. There was no submission in him to fate or anything that he considered evil; he was full of resistance, though this was peaceful and courteous

6.65 The 1930's and 1940's also saw increasing attention paid by Gandhi as well as the Congress to tackle the problem of untouchability and of inter-communal harmony. Whenever the situation became critical, Gandhi staked his life, by announcing "fasts" till the leaders of the various groups would get together and agree to "reasonable solutions". Nehru has highlighted how the fight was simultaneously on two fronts—"against the foreign rule" and "against our own social evils":

> The call of action was twofold. There was, of course, the action involved in challenging and resisting foreign rule; there was also the action which led us to fight our own social evils. Apart from the fundamental objective of the Congress— the freedom of India—and the method of peaceful action, the principal planks of the Congress were national unity, which involved the solution of the minority problems, and the raising of the depressed classes and the ending of the curse of untouchability.[39]

6.66 Regarding the efforts made by Gandhi to establish inter-communal harmony during the last six months of his life, M.M. Verma writes:

> Perhaps, even Gandhi did not realize the great heights to which he had attained in his last phase....
>
> 15 August 1947 saw Gandhi trying to quell riots in Calcutta. He spent the day in fasting and prayer, and while India woke into freedom, Gandhi was peaceless....[40]

And similar views have been expressed by Louis Fisher:

> The fact that Gandhi's fast restored Calcutta to its senses and peace, the fact that his presence reduced the mass killing in Delhi to occasional outbursts, the fact that his fleeting visit to Dr. Zakir Hussain's Okhla Academy gave it immunity to violence, the fact that hardened bandits laid their arms at his feet, the fact that Hindus would listen to Koran verses and that Moslems would not object to hearing the holy words of Islam from the mouth of a Hindu—all this remains to inspire or haunt those whose actions would suggest that they have

forgotten it. It is the seed of conscience and the source of hope.[41]

Adopting the Gita-Ideals in Thought, Word and Deed

6.67 A practical application of the Karma-yoga teaching of the Gītā, as Gandhi interpreted it, meant the voluntary acceptance and enthusiastic fulfillment of the duties that naturally came one's way—Swadharma. He believed that if pursued with a sense of detachment and unselfishness, a life of Karma-yoga could lead to the attainment of *moksha.* A life of dedicated service to one's kind in the spirit of the Gītā, believed Gandhi, would not generate an attitude of aggressive or self-righteous altruism; rather it would lead to a progressive expansion of the human self till it came to comprehend the whole of mankind. The Gītā further insisted on cultivating an attitude of equanimity. A state of perfection, in the terminology of the Gītā, was represented in the personality of a Sthitaprajña or a Bhakta or a Trigunatita. This also meant, in Gandhi' words, an ideal Satyāgrahī".[42] As he put it, "For me the road to salvation lies through incessant toil in the service of my country and humanity. I want to identify myself with every thing that lives. I want to live at peace with both friend and foe. So my patriotism is for me a stage on my journey to the land of eternal freedom and peace".[43]

6.68 When Gandhi was in South Africa, there were, besides the Gītā, two other strong infuences on his philosophy of life, namely Ruskin and Tolstoy. Ruskin's "Unto this last" impressed Gandhi so much that he translated it into Gujarati under the title "Sarvodaya". Gandhi listed three main ideas put forth by Ruskin:

(i) The good of the individual is contained in the good of all

(ii) A lawyer's work has the same value as the barber's, as all have the same right of earning their livelihood from their work

(iii) A life of labour, i.e. the life of the tiller of the soil and the handicraftsman is the life worth living.[44]

To Tolstoy, Gandhi gave credit for enunciating convincingly the "Bread Labour Law", namely that "God created man to work for his food and said that those who ate without working were thieves".[45]

6.69 After Gandhi returned to India and made a deeper study of the Gītā, in consultation with his Ashrama-residents and particularly Vinoba, the ideas underlying "Sarvodaya" were found to be included in the comprehensive Gītā-ideals of sarvabhūtahitaṁ', 'Swadharma', and 'yajña'. As V.P. Verma also states: "Literally Sarvodaya means the good of all living beings and thus it has almost the same meaning as the concept of sarvabhūtahita advocated in the Bhagavad-Gītā. Similarly, Gandhi's interpretation of 'yajña' included 'bread-labour' as well as the need to do it in a spirit of service".[46] As Gandhi put it: "The Gītā says that anybody who eats without performing yajña, in Tolstoy's language 'bread-labour', is a thief, and he eats sin. But body-labour becomes yajña only when it is undertaken in a spirit of service, not of indulgence as it may easily become when it is done only to develop the animal in man".[47]

6.70 Betai is of opinion that, with the passage of time, as Gandhi explained the meaning of the Gītā-ideals more and more to the nation, the comprehensive nature of these ideals became clearer to him as well.

> The Gītā grips his mind as his guide in matters of religion and conduct and the same is destined to become in later life his guide for all matters

spiritual. Of course, the reading of the spiritual works of different religions continues. 'Unto This Last' of Ruskin leaves a permanent impression on his mind, but, as it becomes clear in the years that follow, the influence of Hinduism is enhanced and the influence of the Gītā grows deeper and deeper. Gandhiji is now a man of his own natural heritage, environment, cultural background and religious as also spiritual leanings and here the Gītā is his guide.[48]

6.71 Gandhi's technique of Satyāgraha, which began on a rather modest scale in South Africa in 1906, gradually became an All-India movement, affecting hundreds of millions of people. Since the Indian society was deeply divided because of differences in religions, castes, languages, political ideologies, etc., it was an extremely difficult task to present a united front in the non-violent agītātion against the British Rule. Furthermore, Gandhi's move was not only against the foreign administration but also against evil customs and traditions that had plagued the Indian society for centuries. Orthodox sections of the society, interpreting religious books in their own way, opposed social reforms. The foreign administrators, following the policy of 'Divide and Rule', exploited inter-religious and inter-caste differences and adopted policies which came in the way of Indian unity. Gandhi's followers had to undergo suffering in the form of imprisonment, police violence and repression. To sustain a non-violent movement under such circumstances, Gandhi had to present a series of programs, and not be dis-heartened by set-backs and difficulties. Only a true Karmayogin following the Gītā-ideals in thought, word and deed could carry on the non-violent fight on so many fronts for so many years. That is why Gandhi compared an ideal Satyāgrahī with the Sthitaprajña—the term used in the Gītā for a Karmayogin who is able to maintain steady wisdom under the most difficult circumstances. In fact, the Sthitaprajña verses of the Gītā (II. 54-72) constituted part of the evening prayer which Gandhi conducted as a public function everyday.

6.72 Many of the common people of India were poor and illiterate but the long cultural tradition had so moulded their thinking that they instinctively placed their confidence in a person whose image was like that of a saint—a person trying to do good to the society or "Sarvabhūtahite rataḥ" in the language of the Gītā, and having no selfish designs (*niṣkāma*), and willing to undergo suffering (tapasyā) for a just cause. The Indian tradition is full of stories showing the victory of dharma over adharma, of truth over falsehood, of the devas over asuras —in fact, victory of unarmed monkeys over armed demons. In the Mahābhārata, Śrī Kṛṣṇa gave the choice to Arjuna and Duryodhana—either take all the army of Yādavas or take Śrī Kṛṣṇa himself who would guide but not fight. Arjuna immediately chose Śrī Kṛṣṇa and not his army. Only in a society where such stories had become a part of non-formal education and cultural tradition, could Gandhi talk convincingly that 'There is no such thing as defeat in non-violence; the end of violence is surest defeat'.[49]

6.73 The cause of ending foreign rule appeared to the Indian society to be intrinsically just, although some people thought the country was not fully prepared for independence right away. From the practical point of view, it was necessary to focus attention on what can be called 'secondary causes'. For example, the first All-India Satyāgraha of 1919 was directed against two Bills which would have given the British authorities emergency powers, and which according to the draft

Satyāgraha pledge, were characterised as "unjust, subversive of the principle of liberty and justice and destructive of the elementary right of individuals".[50] The fact that Gandhi lived in an Ashram wholly devoted to the cause of doing good to the society helped in establishing his credentials as a selfless worker who sought no personal gains. Furthermore, the Ashram rules and regulations, enjoining spiritual discipline and tapasyā on all its members, made it clear that Gandhi was willing to undergo suffering for a just cause. The essence of the non-violent agitation was to make people willing to undergo similar tapasyā. As Sarma puts it:

> Gandhi drafts a brief appeal to the nation to observe a twenty-four hours' fast and a complete all-India hartal, to regard the day to be fixed by the leaders as a day of national humiliation and prayer and to hold meetings on that day in all cities, towns and villages throughout India and pass resolutions praying for the withdrawal of the hateful Act. The date that was fixed at first was 30 March 1919, but it was subsequently changed to 6 April. The appeal went home to the hearts of the people and, though the notice was short, there was a complete suspension of work throughout India on that date, and in all big cities monster meetings such as were never witnessed within living memory were held.[51]

6.74 Similarly, for the Satyāgraha campaign of 1930, Gandhi chose a 'secondary cause' represented by 'Tax on Salt', the burden of which fell relatively more heavily on the poor. And the technique for arousing countrywide awareness included a twenty-four-day march, from the Satyāgraha Ashram to Dāṇḍi on the sea-coast. Furthermore, Gandhi's spirit of sacrifice for a just cause was reflected in his declaration that he would not come back to his Ashram till Swarāj was won. Even a leader like Motilal Nehru (father of Jawaharlal Nehru) saw in Gandhi's march a parallel to the epic of Rāmāyaṇa and said: "Like the historic march of Ramachandra to Lanka, the march of Gandhi would be memorable, and the places he passes through would be sacred".[52]

6.75 Sarma has given further details as to how Gandhi utilized the Dāṇḍi-march to explain the non-violent way of carrying on the fight:

> There were 79 volunteers to march with Gandhi and the distance to be covered was 223 miles. Thousands of men, women and children stood as spectators on either side of the road... Gandhiji preached his gospel of non-violence to the assembled crowds.... At Borsad he said, "The British rule in India has brought about moral, material, cultural and spiritual ruination of this great country. I regard this rule as a curse. I am out to destroy this system of government. ... Sedition has become my religion. Ours is a non-violent battle. We are not out to kill anybody, but it is our dharma to see that the curse of this government is blotted." At Bhatgam he turned the searchlight inwards and severely castigated the people for the luxuries they provided for him and his followers and said, "To live above the means befitting a poor country is to live on stolen food. Nor did I bargain to set out on this march for living above our means."[53]

6.76 Gandhi knew that unless something concrete was offered to the poor people to reduce the pangs of hunger, mere exhortation for making sacrifice and for observing non-violence would sound hollow. Therefore, the 'Constructive Programme'. which included work-opportunities (howsoever inefficient in the strict economic sense)—in hand-spinning, hand weaving, and other village industries—became the backbone of the entire movement. As M.M. Verma puts it:

> The constructive programme carried Gandhi's message to the Indian peasants and created among them consciousness of their rights. It provided an opportunity to the rank and file to do some work for social reconstruction. It produced common bonds of fraternity....
>
> Constructive activities are not only an evidence of the sincerity of Satyāgrahīs but they also show to the masses, as mere words cannot, the potentiality of Satyāgraha for ending all exploitation and elevating their status. Constructive work also goes a long way to convince the opponent of the non-violent intentions of Satyāgrahīs....
>
> Constructive work has to be quiet, solid and substantial. It is a direct personal service of the masses—suffering for them, organizing them, educating them in the ways of non-violence and thus bringing about a peaceful atmosphere of solemn determination. Constructive work is thus collective purification effort through service. It is mass effort and mass education.[54]

6.77 Removal of untouchability was another important element of Gandhi's constructive programme. He coined a new term "Harijan"—meaning "God's men"—for the so-called 'untouchables' in the Hindu society. Some Harijan leaders fell into the trap of the British policy of 'Divide and Rule' and expressed support for 'separate electorate for the Harijans'. Gandhi warned them that such an arrangement would perpetuate the evil custom of untouchability. He even announced that he would give up his life—by fasting unto death—unless the Harijans are considered equal citizens like everybody else and their representation assured by a system of reservation, within a joint electorate system. On the seventh day of Gandhi's fast, the proposal for separate electorate for Harijans was dropped by mutual agreement, enabling Gandhi to issue the following statement:

> The hand of God has been visible in the glorious manifestation throughout the length and breadth of India during the past seven days. The cables received from many parts of the world blessing the fast have sustained me through the agony of body and soul that I passed through during the seven days, but the cause was worth going through that agony. The sacrificial fire once lit shall not be put out as long as there is the slightest trace of untouchability still left in Hinduism.[55]

6.78 Orthodox Hindus tried to justify untouchability by interpreting some of the old books in their own way. The situation was similar to the arguments put forward by the Suttee-advocates who had opposed Rammohun Roy's suttee-abolition efforts in the 1820's Faced with such claims on behalf of the protagonists of untouchability on religious grounds, Gandhi adopted a similar course as Rammohun Roy had done more than a century ago, namely, to take the help of the Bhagavad-Gītā. Betai summarizes the success achieved by Gandhi on the untouchability-front, through the authoritative support of the Gītā:

> The Gītā told him that all men are equal, all men deserve the supreme blessings of God, the Gītā bars no one from divine attainment that he called self-realization. This spirit that he derived from the Gītā made him a life-time servant of and upholder of the rights of the untouchables in particular and the down-trodden of the society in general. He rightly opined that untouchability is a blot on

Hindu society and religion and he prided in calling himself a Bhangi. Eradication of untouchability is one of the greatest work of Gandhiji and for this he derived justification from the Gītā.

6.79 'Uplift of women' constitutes another important plank in Gandhi's constructive programme. The fact that the Gītā makes no distinction between man and woman strengthened Gandhi's belief in the need to provide equal opportunities to women. He always wanted India's womanhood to rise to realise its due status, work and duty in society. He wanted women to have due education. He wanted them to become real partners in the lives of their husbands and family; he wanted women to play a leading role in the Satyāgraha movements and in the reconstruction of the country. So many of his activities were guided by these ideas.[56]

6.80 Another important cause for which Gandhi fasted several times, and ultimately faced the assassin's bullet, was interreligious harmony, in general, and Hindu-Muslim unity in particular. In his prayer meetings, verses from various scriptures—including the Gītā and Koran—were recited. Louis Fischer attaches great significance to 'the fact that Hindus would listen to Koran verses and that Moslems would not object to hearing holy words of Islam from the mouth of a Hindu'.[57] Gandhi's argument was that, even after the partition of the country, Muslims in the 'secular state of India' should feel safe and equal to all other citizens. He helped restore communal harmony in Calcutta by undertaking a fast in September 1947 till the city's leaders pledged to keep peace. In January 1948, just a couple of weeks before his assassination, Gandhi's fast in Delhi helped restore intercommunal goodwill—and this was acknowledged by Pakistani Minister Zafrullah Khan who said that 'a new and tremendous wave of feeling and desire for friendship between the two Dominions is sweeping the subcontinent in response to the fast'.[58]

6.81 J.H. Holmes wrote to Gandhi, 'I count these last months to be crown and climax of your unparalleled career. You were never so great as in these dark hours'.[59] Betai attributes this capability to face all calamities—like the Sthitaprajña of the Gītā—to Gandhi's adherence to the Gītā as a child adheres to its mother. Betai summarizes some of the happenings of the closing days of Gandhi's life:

> In those days he invoked the help of the Gītā again and again... So fearless was he that when Lady Mountbatten came to congratulate him when he was saved from the bomb-explosion on 20 January 1948, he could reply in perfect equanimity of spirit and perfect fearlessness: "On this occasion, I have shown no bravery. If somebody fired at me point-blank and I faced bullet with a smile, repeating the name of Rama in my heart, I should indeed be deserving of congratulations".[60]

And indeed this is what happened when Nathuram Godse fired at him on 30 January 1948. And this proved to be the final evidence in support of the statement that Gandhi tried to live by the Gītā-ideals—as he interpreted them—in thought, word and deed. As Sarma puts it:

> There is perfect harmony between Gandhiji's life and his teaching. In fact, his whole life is an embodiment of his teaching. His greatest contribution to the thought of our age is contained in the word 'Satyāgraha', which he invented. If his writings are an exposition of this new dharma, he is himself an incarnation of it. He is not only the author of Satyāgrha but also an ideal Satyāgrahī. Therefore his character, as revealed by his actions, is as important for us as his writings.[61]

6.82 Ursula king has summarised what might be called the general assessment of the people in regard to Gandhi's effort to be an ideal Karmayogin:

> The ideal Karmayogin is for Gandhi the person who chooses the way of selfless action and sacrifice as path to God. The central importance of this message for Gandhi and the way it presupposes a substantial reinterpretation of the Bhagavad-Gītā has been commented in detail by Agehananda Bharati and will not be further discussed here. It may be mentioned, however, that a further development has taken place in that today Gandhi himself is often seen as the ideal Karmayogin. The newly understood Karmayoga taught by the Krishna of the Bhagavad-Gītā has found concrete and permanent historical expression in the person and work of Gandhi. Hindu religious teaching today makes use of the ideal Karmayogin symbol by applying it both to the classical Krishna and the contemporary Gandhi. Not only Hindus but others, too, refer to Gandhi as Karmayogin; for example, in a recent study of mysticism and contemporary spirituality, a western author describes Gandhi as a 'true mystic of action, a true karmayogin'. This shows the wide diffusion of the Karmayogin ideal and implies an even further transformation of its meaning. One may also note that no other representative of modern Hinduism illustrates the originality as well as the dilemma of the Karmayogin symbol more strikingly than Gandhi does.[62]

Summary of Gandhi's Contribution to Practical Vedanta

6.83 (a) He moulded Gita's use for the freedom struggle, into a Vedantic act, by introducing

Ahimsa.

(b) He supported demands for human rights, provided they are non-violent.

(c) He set an example for the whole world, how the military might of an Empire can be successfully challenged by non-violence. United Nations declared 2nd October as International Day of Non-violence.

(d) He gave the Vedantic message that world peace can not be established through wars.

(e) He demonstrated that struggle against discrimination can be successfully conducted by non-violent means, in all countries. Leaders like Martin Luther King were inspired by him.

(f) He declared that untouchability is inconsistent with Vedanta. He risked his life for this cause, facing stiff resistance from orthodox people.

(g) He demonstrated that women can play an important role in non-violent struggles for just causes.

(h) He helped in advocating and convincing people that anti-poverty programs deserve whole-hearted support.

(j) He helped in securing for India, a respectful view from world leaders.

(k) He helped in securing for Hinduism, a respectful view from other religious leaders.

(m) He sacrified his life for promoting inter-religious harmony.

(n) He supported vegetarianism, not only on health grounds, but also as a spiritual practice.

(p) His Gita-commentary was a very valuable addition to Gita-literature.

Notes

1. M.K. Gandhi, The Story of My Experiements with Truth. Beacon Press, Boston, 1957, p. 4.
2. Ibid., p. 7.
3. Ibid., p. 33.
4. D.S. Sarma, The Renaissance of Hinduism, op. cit., p. 408.
5. M.K. Gandhi, The Story of My Experiments with Truth, op. cit., pp. 63-6.
6. Ibid., pp. 70-2.
7. Ibid., p. 67.
8. Jawaharlal Nehru, The Discovery of India. Oxford Univ. Press, New Delhi, 1983 (third impression), p. 358.
9. Mahadev Desai, The Gospel of Selfles Action or The Gita according to Gandhi. Navajivan, Ahmedabad, 1977, pp. 125-7.
10. K.M. Panikkar, The Foundations of New India, op. cit., 44.
11. M.M. Verma, Gandhi's Technique of Mass Mobilization. R.K. Gupta, New Delhi, 1990, p. 124.
12. Ibid., p. 124.
13. R.S. Betai, Gita and Gandhiji, op. cit., p. 154.
14. Ibid., p. 155.
15. Ibid., p. 156.
16. D.S. Sarma, The Renaissance of Hinduism, op. cit., p. 440.
17. Ibid., pp. 440-1.
18. Ibid., pp. 436-7.
19. Ibid., p. 449.
20. Raghavan Iyer, The Moral and Political Thought of Mahatma Gandhi. Oxford Univ. Press, New York, 1978, p. 326.
21. V.P. Verma, The Political Philosophy of Mahatma Gandhi and Sarvodaya. Laxmi Narain, Agra, 1959, p. 59
22. D.S. Sarma, The Renaissance of Hinduism, op. cit., p. 477.
23. Ibid., p. 477.
24. Ibid., p. 480.

25. Ibid., p. 480.
26. Raghavan Iyer, The Moral and Political Thought of Mahatma Gandhi, op. cit., p. 282.
27. D.S. Sarma, The Renaissance of Hinduism, op. cit., p. 502.
28. Jawaharlal Nehru, The Discovery of India, op. cit., p. 361.
29. Shriman Narayan (ed.), The Selected Works of Mahatma Gandhi. (Six volumes), Navajivan, Ahmedabad, 1968, vol. IV, pp. 344-6.
30. Jawaharlal Nehru, The Discovery of India, op. cit., pp. 361-2.
31. Raghavan Iyer, The Moral and Political Thought of Mahatma Gandhi, op. cit., pp. 275-83.
32. Ibid., p. 275.
33. D.S. Sarma, The Renaissance of Hinduism, op. cit., p. 532.
34. Ibid., p. 533.
35. Ibid., p. 533.
36. V.P. Verma, The Political Philosophy of Mahatma Gandhi and Sarvodaya, op. cit., p. 160.
37. Ibid., p. 161.
38. Jawaharlal Nehru, The Discovery of India, op. cit., p. 360.
39. Ibid., p. 361.
40. M.M. Verma, Gandhi's Technique of Mass Mobilization, op. cit., pp. 205-7.
41. Ibid., p. 207.
42. Harijan, 7th April 1946, quoted by V.P. Verma, The Political Philosophy of Mahatma Gandhi and Sarvodaya, op. cit., p. 31.
43. Quoted by V.P. Verma, The Political Philosophy of Mahatma Gandhi and Sarvodaya, op. cit., p. 72.
44. Shriman Narayan (ed.), The Selected Works of Mahatma Gandhi, op. cit., vol. IV, p. 39.
45. V.P. Verma, The Political Philosophy of Mahatma Gandhi and Sarvodaya, op. cit., p. 83.
46. Ibid., p. 89.
47. Young India, 20th Sept. 1928, quoted by R.S. Betai, Gita and

Gandhiji, op. cit., p. 249.

48. R.S. Betai, Gita and Gandhiji, op. cit., p. 150.
49. Raghavan Iyer, The Moral and Political Thought of Mahatma Gandhi, op. cit., p. 194.
50. D.S. Sarma, The Renaissance of Hinduism, op. cit., p. 488.
51. Ibid., p. 489.
52. Ibid., p. 532.
53. Ibid., p. 532-3.
54. M.M. Verma, Gandhi's Technique of Mass Mobilization, op. cit., pp. 125-6.
55. D.S. Sarma, The Renaissance of Hinduism, op. cit., p. 546.
56. R.S. Betai, Gita and Gandhiji, op. cit., p. 196.
57. M.M. Verma, Gandhi's Technique of Mass Mobilization, op. cit., p. 207.
58. Ibid., p. 207.
59. Ibid., p. 207.
60. R.S. Betai, Gita and Gandhiji, op. cit., pp. 3 and 155.
61. D.S. Sarma, The Renaissance of Hinduism, op. cit., p. 406.
62. Ursula King, "Who is the Ideal Karmayogin?", op. cit., p. 52.

CHAPTER 7

Nehru's Role in Making the Abolition of Untouchability a Part of India's Constitution

A Brief Life-sketch

7.1 In his Autobiography, Jawaharlal Nehru began with the year 1716, when his ancestors, who were Kashmiri Brahmins, moved to Delhi, at the invitation of the then Moghul Emperor, Farrukhsiar. The family's connection with the Delhi Durbar lasted for five generations, but came to a disastrous end in 1857. The family then moved to Agra. It is an interesting coincidence that Jawaharlal's father, Motilal was born on 6th may 1861, that is, exactly the same date when Rabindranath Tagore was born.

7.2 Motilal's achievements were noteworthy. He topped the list of all the candidates that appeared at the High Court Lawyer's examination, and was awarded a gold medal. He moved the family from Agra to Allahabad where he established himself as a successful lawyer. His rise in the legal profession was recognized by the British Administration—they invited him to the grand function at New Delhi, which became, in 1911, the Capital of India. The Indian National Congress, which had started in 1885, did not attract him—he thought that the politicians just talked and talked, without doing anything.

7.3 Jawaharlal was born at Allahabad on 14th November 1889. His mother's name was Swarup Rani. The family had one son (Jawaharlal) and three daughters. About his childhood, he recalled how his parents created a playful atmosphere—

> "Full of the spirit of play and fond of good living in every way, my father found no difficulty in spending what he earned. And gradually our ways became more and more westernized...
>
> "At night, I enjoyed listening to stories from the ancient Hindu scriptures, particularly the Ramayana and the Mahabharata, that my mother and aunt used to tell in a very interesting way."[1]

7.4 Jawaharlal received his education in England, at famous schools and colleges. He did his schooling from Harrow, and obtained his Law degree from Cambridge. Although he was not physically present in India, he could not draw his attention away from his country. When he was about to complete his schooling, he got news of big events happening in India. Bengal seemed to be in an uproar, and Tilak's name was often splashed from Poona. Subsequently, when he was at Cambridge, he got news of Tilak's jail sentence.

7.5 It was Motilal's earnest hope that his son, after returning from England, would start preparing himself to take over the family's legal profession, and also contribute to a happy generational growth of the family. And for the first six years, things seemed to move accordingly. Jawaharlal returned to Allahabad in 1912, and started legal practice. In 1916, he married Kamala, who gave birth to Indira in 1917.

7.6 But Jawaharlal started feeling uneasy, as he wrote in his Autobiography—

> "The early months after my return were pleasant. I was glad to be back home and to pick up old threads. But gradually, the life I led, in common with most others of my kind, began to lose all its freshness and I felt that I was being engulfed in a dull routine of a pointless and futile existence. Fortunately my home atmosphere was fairly congenial and that was some help, but it was not enough. There were not even worthwhile amusements or diversions, On the whole, the atmosphere was not intellectually stimulating and a sense of the utter insipidity of life grew upon me."[2]

7.7 'To do useful work for a social cause'—this is what Jawaharlal was booking for. Luckily, Gandhi's arrival on the political scene provided the magical touch, as Jawaharlal wrote in "Discovery of India"—

> "And then Gandhi came. He was like a powerful current of fresh air that made us stretch ourselves and take deep breaths, like a beam of light that pierced the darkness and removed the scales from our eyes; like a whirlwind that upset many things, but most of all the working of people's minds. He did not descend from the top, he seemed to emerge from the millions of India, speaking their language and incessantly drawing attention to them and their appalling condition. Get off the backs of these peasants and workers, he told us, all you who live by their exploitation; get rid of the system that produces this poverty and misery. Political freedom took new shape then and

acquired a new content. The essence of his teaching was fearlessness and truth, and action allied to these, always keeping the welfare of the masses in view."[3]

7.8 To Jawaharlal, Gandhi's advice to see first-hand the miserable condition of the villagers, proved to be an eye-opener, and it strengthened his resolve to work with him. But Motilal wanted to assess the relative merits of various approaches, so he attended the specially convened session of Congress in Calcutta, in September 1920. That proved to be the turning point, as Judith Brown explains—

> "The days of the Calcutta Congress were Motilal's personal turning point. He had arrived in Calcutta apparently determined to oppose Gandhi's program, but ended supporting Gandhi. Jawaharlal portrayed his father as coming through a time of grappling with the personal implications for himself of aligning with Gandhi, as well as weighing the worth of Gandhi's strategy in the context of the sense of national humiliation following the Punjab tragedy and its political aftermath, and then coming to a final and considered decision. However, other considerations almost certainly played a part. One was the certainty that if he continued to oppose Gandhi, he would split his family. Another was the clear evidence that in his own province political opinion was flowing in favor of non-cooperation, and that he would lose local credibility if he continued to oppose it."[4]

7.9 Motilal's conversion to Gandhi's program led to big changes in the Nehru-family's life-style. To quote Judith Brown again—

> "Motilal was nothing if not thorough. In his own

life he immediately set about making big changes. He resigned his membership of the existing provincial legislature and announced that he would not stand for election in the next legislature. He wound up his legal practice, and also began the process of dismantling the elaborate life-style he had created for himself and his family. Foreign clothes were disposed of or burnt, the wine cellar was done away with, and from now on, only one kitchen provided for the family's simpler needs. Father and son had found a new unity of purpose and style, and both adopted the sartorial symbolism of hand-made Indian dress and what became known as a Gandhi cap. Their political and social world had been turned upside down by the Mahatma."[5]

Subsequently, Motilal donated his large house to Congress, which became Swaraj Bhawan.

7.10 In an effort to weaken the nonviolent struggle (Satyagraha in Gandhi's terminology), the British administration adopted a policy of putting the Satyagrahis is jail, in large numbers. Jawaharlal's first experience of prison came in 1921. He was released in March 1922, but re-imprisoned two months later. Judith Brown draws attention to how the jail hurt Jawaharlal, but he viewed it as an honorable way of serving the country—

> "During his trial, Jawaharlal said he went to prison willingly and joyfully. To serve in India's battle for freedom was a great honor.... Nevertheless, prison was a daunting prospect physically for a man like him, brought up in comfort. Perhaps even more daunting psychologically, because prison was assumed to be a place for criminals."[6]

7.11 In 1928, Jawaharlal faced bravely, terrible acts of

"physical violence and beating" perpetrated by the British police sergeants—

> "Indian politicians boycotted and opposed the Simon Commission. Jawaharlal threw himself into the organisation of this opposition, and was beaten by the police in the course of a non-violent demonstration in Lucknow. He managed to restrain himself from responding, but was deeply shaken by his first real experience of physical violence and what seemed to him the hatred of the British police sergeants who did most of the beating."[7]

7.12 In his Autobiography, Jawaharlal draws special attention to the years 1930-31, calling them 'wonder years'. Ten great events tooks place—

- (i) Lahore Congress
- (ii) Observing 26 January 1930 as 'Independence Day'
- (iii) Dandi March (Salt Satyagraha)
- (iv) Kamala's imprisonment and noteworthy role of other women too
- (v) Reiterating the 'Pledge of Independence' on 26 January 1931
- (vi) Motilal's death
- (vii) Jawaharlal's meeting with Indian Jews
- (viii) Jawaharlal's meeting with Indian Christians
- (ix) Kamala's speech on Women's Rights
- (x) Honor given to Gandhi in England.

In the next ten paragraphs, we will explain briefly why each of these events was so important.

7.13 Lahore Congress

It was in Punjab that the massacre of Jallianwala Bagh in 1919 had proved to be the turning point in the politics of India. Now, after eleven years, a major step in regard to the freedom struggle was taken at Lahore Congress, namely, a declaration that India wanted Independence, not Dominion status. Jawaharlal wrote in his Autobiography—

> "The Lahore Congress remains fresh in my memory—a vivid patch. That is natural, for I played a leading role there, as President of the Congress."[8]

7.14 Observing 26th January 1930 as Independence Day.

The Pledge taken on that day is a unique Declaration of Independence, in the whole world, because there was a commitment not to use violence—

> "We believe that it is the inalienable right of the Indian people, as of any other people, to have freedom and to enjoy the fruits of their toil and have the necessities of life, so that they may have full opportunities of growth. We believe also that if any government deprives a people of these rights and oppresses them, the people have a further right to alter it or to abolish it. The British Government in India has not only deprived the Indian people of their freedom but has based itself on the exploitation of the masses, and has ruined India economically, politically, culturally, and spiritually. We believe, therefore, that India must sever the British connection and attain Purna Swaraj or complete independence. We recognize, however, that the most effective way of gaining our freedom is not through violence. We are convinced that if we can but withdraw our voluntary help and stop payment of taxes without doing violence, even under provocation, the end of this inhuman rule is assured."[9]

7.15 Dandi March (Salt Satyagraha)

In March 1930, Gandhi picked up the issue of breaking the "Salt Tax Law" because this hurt the poorest of the Indians relatively more deeply. The twenty-four-day march (covering a distance of 223 miles) by seventy-nine volunteers generated unprecedented enthusiasm and big support for the cause which Gandhi represented. The marchers reached Dandi on 5th April, 1930, and next morning, Gandhi broke the salt law. The whole country was ablaze with the fire of Civil Disobedience.

The success of this satyagraha turned American public opinion in favor of India's independence.

7.16 Noteworthy Role of Women

Salt Satyagrahis were brutally attacked by the police. Large numbers of women volunteers, facing lathi charge, provided first-aid to the wounded. They also organized boycott of liquor and imported cloth. Jawaharlal's mother and wife played a leading role. When Kamala was arrested, a pressman asked her for a message—and Kamala said, "I am happy beyond measure and proud to follow in the footsteps of my husband."[10]

7.17 Reiterating the pledge on 26 January, 1931.

We mentioned in para 7.14 that the Pledge of Independence was first taken on 26 January 1930. Emboldened by the successful Satyagraha of 1930, the Pledge was reiterated on 26th January 1931. Patriotic feelings in the country were further strengthened by declaring "Vande Mataram" (composed by Bankim Chandra Chatterji) as the national song. In recognition of the importance of these events, when India became a Republic, 26th January was designated "Republic Day".

7.18 Motilal's Death

In the midst of great events, Jawaharlal suffered the shock of his father's death on 6th February 1931. He wrote in his Autobiography—

> "Many thousands of messages of sympathy came to my mother and to me. Lord and Lady Irwin also sent my mother a courteous message. This tremendous volume of goodwill and sympathy took away somewhat the sting from our sorrow, but it was, above all, the wonderfully soothing and healing presence of Gandhiji that helped my mother and all of us to face that crisis in our lives."[11]

7.19 Jawaharlal's meeting with Indian Jews

So many events, happening one after another, taxed Jawaharlal's energy very heavily, so his doctors urged him to take some rest and go for a change. Jawaharlal decided to go to South India. In Cochin he visited the quarter of the 'White Jews', and attended services held in their synagogue. He wrote in his Autobiography—

> "This community is very ancient and very unique. I had long desired to meet them. They told me that the part of Cochin they lived in, resembled ancient Jerusalem."[12]

7.20 Jawharlal's Meeting with Indian Christians

> "Along the backwaters of Malabar," wrote Jawaharlal, "I went to the towns inhabited chiefly by Christians. Few people realize that Christianity came to India as early as the first century. Although their religious head is in Syria, they are 100% Indians".[13]

7.21 Kamala's Speech on Women's Rights

Jawaharlal gave an interesting account of this event—

> "Kamala and I went to Hyderabad, especially to pay a visit to Mrs. Sarojini Naidu and her two daughters. During our stay with them, a small gathering of 'purdahnashin' (i.e. veiled) women

> assembled at their house and wanted Kamala to give them a message Kamala spoke of women's struggle for freedom against man-made laws and customs (a favorite topic of hers) and urged the women not to be too submissive to their menfolk."[14]

7.22 Honor given to Gandhi in London

In 1931, Gandhi went to London to attend Round Table Conference. The King of United Kingdom invited him. However, there was a message from Buchingham Palace, saying 'There is a dress code for visitors to the Palace.' Gandhi replied, 'I represent poor people of India, who are scantily dressed.' Back came the reply from the Palace, 'You are welcome, irrespective of your dress.' After his meeting with the King, he was asked by a pressman whether he had felt under-dressed. His widely reported comment, expressed with typical Gandhian wit, was, 'The King had enough on for both of us.'[15]

7.23 Death of Wife and Mother in the thirties

Kamala's death occurred on 28th February 1936. Judith Brown narrates how it affected Jawaharlal—

> "Kamala's health problems were causing much worry to Jawaharlal. She was moved to a sanatorium in Switzerland. Jawaharlal was mostly in jail, but the British administration released him so that he could be with his wife. Jawaharlal was with her when the end came. Jawaharlal told Gandhiji how devastated he felt.[16]

7.24 A successful campaigner

Jawaharlal's capability to convince people to vote for Congress came to light during 1936-37. To quote Judith Bown again—

> "He travelled like a hurricane, using a hectic schedule, using every conceivable form of transport

from plane, train and car, to elephant, camel, horse, bicycle, and varieties of river boats. He addressed vast crowds, and was successful in achieving victory for Congress. Considering all these capabilities, Gandhi publicly proclaimed that Jawaharlal was his heir."[17]

7.25 Books

Jawaharlal utilized his jail sentences to write books, and thus made a very useful contribution to the world's literature, as Sonia Gandhi explained—

> "Jawaharlal Nehru's three classics—Glimpses of World History. An Autobiography, and The Discovery of India—remain essential reading for any one who wishes to understand the ideas and personalities that have shaped India through the ages, and moulded the character and special genius of her people. Though written more than fifty years ago these books address issues that remain vitally relevant today."[18]

7.26 Jawaharlal's speech on 15th August 1947

Jawaharlal's speech (when power was transferred from England to India) has been acclaimed a masterpiece. It is a fairly long speech, but we have space for just a few lines (It is unthinkable to omit it completely)—

> "Long years ago, we made a tryst with destiny, and now the time comes when we shall redeem our pledge, not wholly or in full measure, but very substantially.... We are citizens of a great country, on the verge of bold advance, and we have to live up to that high standard. All of us, to whatever religion we may belong, are equally the children of India with equal rights, privileges and obligations. We cannot encourage communalism or narrow-mindedness, for no nation can be great

whose people are narrow in thought or in action...."[19]

Summary of Nehru's Contribution to Practical Vedanta

7.27 (a) He played a very important role in making the abolition of untouchability, a part of India's constitution. His Law Minister Ambedkar was the Chairman of the Drafting Committee.

(b) Not only abolishing untouchability, he played a very important role in giving to India a secular, democratic constitution in which all citizens have equal rights.

(c) He, supported by Sardar Patel, achieved political unity for India.

(d) He helped in settling several international disputes, thus making a contribution to world peace.

(e) His books were a very valuable addition to the literature on religious and cultural history of India.

Notes

1. Jawaharlal Nehru, An Autobiography. Penguin Books India, 2004, pp. 5-9.
2. Ibid., p. 31.
3. Jawaharlal Nehru, The Discovery of India, op. cit., p. 358.
4. Judith M. Brown, Nehru: A Political Life. Yale University Press, 2003, pp. 58-9.
5. Ibid., p. 59.
6. Ibid., p. 70.
7. Ibid., p. 88.
8. Jawaharlal Nehru, An Autobiography, op. cit., p. 212.

9. Ibid., pp. 637-8.
10. Ibid., p. 253.
11. Ibid., p. 260.
12. Ibid., p. 286.
13. Ibid., pp. 286-7.
14. Ibid., p. 287.
15. Internet
16. Judith M. Brown, Nehru: A Political Life, op. cit., pp. 120-1.
17. Ibid., pp. 127-8.
18. Jawaharlal Nehru, An Autobiography, op. cit., p. (xi)
19. Internet.

CHAPTER 8

Radhakrishnan's Scholarly Support to Practical Vedanta

A Brief Life-sketch

8.1 Sarvepalli Radhakrishnan (or Radhakrishnan for short) was born on 5th September 1888, at Tiruttani, near Madras. His father was Servepalli Veeraswami, and his mother's name was Sitamma. They were both Brahmins.

8.2 Radhakrishnan's schooling started at Tiruttani. In recognition of his brilliance, he was awarded a scholarship to go to Luthean Mission School in Tirupati, for his high school. Thereafter he started college at Vellore, but transferred to Madras Christian College. He chose Philosophy as his major, and obtained his M.A. In partial fulfilment for his M.A. degree, he wrote his thesis entitled "The Ethics of the Vedanta and its Metaphysical Presuppositions."

8.3 His thesis marked him out as a rising star. Professor A.G. Hogg was highly impressed and he wrote, "This thesis which he prepared in the second year of his study for this degree shows a remarkable understanding of the main aspects of the philosophical problems, a capacity for handling easily a complex argument, besides more than the average mastery of good English."[1]

8.4 This thesis was published in the American journal, The International Ethical Quarterly, in July 1911. Tilak's famous 'Gitā-Rahasya' recognizes the high quality of Rdhakrishnan's contribution.

8.5 Radhakrishnan's teaching career (which attained great heights later) began in 1909, at the age of 21. His first job was as Assistant Lecturer at Madras Presidency College. Because of his remarkable teaching skills, he rose to the high rank of Professor at the same college.

8.6 The year 1921 proved to be a time of great achievements. Radhakrishnan published Volume I of his famous book "Indian Philosophy". Immediately thereafter, Calcutta University honoured him, about which Professor J.N. Mohanty of Temple University, Philadelphia wrote enthusiastically—

> "The publication of his book in the Muirhead Library of Philosophy series, shot the young scholar to international fame. Sir Asutosh Mukherjee appointed him to the prized King George V Professorship in Philosophy at the University of Calcutta. The Department of Philosophy in Calcutta had such stalwarts as Hiralal Haldar, K.C. Bhattacharya, and S.N. Dasgupta. It created a stir that a young and relatively unknown scholar from the south was placed above them. But soon this young man proved his worth and endeared himself to all by his gentle and courteous manner."[2]

8.7 In 1926, Radhakrishnan was invited by Manchester College, Oxford, to deliver "Upton Lectures", which were published in 1927 in the form of a book entitled "The Hindu View of Life". Since Hinduism is not an organized religion, and it has no founder, it was not properly understood in the West, at that time. Radhakrishnan's book helped in filling this gap.

8.8 "An Idealist View of Life" was another famous look of Radhakrishnan, based on his lectures in UK in the years 1929 and 1930. These lectures were delivered by him at the University of Manchester and University College, London, under the auspices of Hibbert Trustees.

8.9 In India, Radhakrishnan's rank in relation to universities, rose from Professorship to Vice-chancellorship. His first appointment in that capacity was at Andhra University in 1931. This university needed a forward—looking leader. The Honors-courses and Post-Graduate teaching in Humanities and Languages were modernized by Radhakrishnan, and Science and Technology Departments were practically developed from scratch. By the time he left in 1936, he had transformed the University into a robust and well-recognized institution.

8.10 In this paragraph, we depart from a chronological presentation, because we want to maintain continuity in regard to Radhakrishnan's role as Vice-Chancellor—he became Vice-Chancellor of Banaras Hindu University (BHU) in 1939. The period of his stay there coincided with revolutionary political upheaval in the whole country, under the leadership of Mahatma Gandhi, and university students could not stay aloof. The British Governor of Uttar Pradesh wanted to punish the students of BHU for having participated in the freedom struggle, and even threatened to close the university. Radhakrishnan went to Lucknow (where the Governor was stationed), to protest. The Governor was initially unsympathetic, but ultimately, he had to soften his stand. In the midst of all these disturbances,

Radhakrishnan strengthened the Science and Technology Departments at BHU, as he had earlier done at Andhra University.

8.11 Now we pick up the chronological thread of events, and refer to the year 1936, which marked the high point of Radhakrishnan's academic achievement at the international level. In Mohanty's words—

> "He received offers from several universities, all crowned by his appointment, concurrently with his responsibilities in India, to the Spalding Professorship in Eastern Religion and Ethics at the University of Oxford."[3]

8.12 Radhakrishnan's writings are too well known to be listed here. But we do want to draw attention to the following books:

(i) The Philosophy of Rabindranath Tagore

(ii) Manatma Gandhi: Essays and Reflections on His Life and Work, Presented to him on his 70th Birthday.

(iii) Mahtma Gandhi: His Message for Mankind.

8.13 Radhakrishnan's book "The Bhagavad-Gita", written in 1948, was dedicated to Mahatma Gandhi. In the latter part of this chapter, we shall quote from this book.

8.14 During the eighteen years (1949-1967), Radhakrishnan served the nation in three positions—

(a) Ambassador to the Soviet Union (3 years)

(b) Vice-President of India (10 years)

(c) President of India (5 years)

Much of what Radhakrishnan did in these 18 years, is recorded in "official documents". But glimpses of some notable happenings have been made public (and are available on internet), of which we mention a few, briefly, in the next three paragraphs.

8.15 In 1949, Radhakrishnan was appointed Ambassador to the Soviet Union. The appointment raised many eyebrows because people wondered what kind of impression Radhakrishnan, a philosopher, would generate on Stalin, the communist. But such misgivings were laid to rest within one year. In 1950, Radhakrishnan was called to the Kremlin to meet Stalin, who asked him (through an interpreter) to say something from ancient Indian history which may be relevant today. Radhakrishnan said, "We had Ashoka, the emperor who, after a bloody victory, renounced war and became the most active promoter of peace. Who knows we might see a similar transformation today." Stalin smiled and replied, "Yes, miracles do happen sometimes. I was in a theological seminary for five years." Subsequently, on April 5, 1952, a few days before Radhakrishnan's departure for India, Stalin called on him, Radhakrishnan has recorded that, since Stalin looked very unwell, he expressed good wishes for his health and long life. Stalin was deeply moved. He held Radhakrishnan's hand and said, "You are the first person to treat me as a human being and not as a monster. You are leaving us and I am sad. I want you to live long. I have not long to live." Stalin died six month later. But his regard for Radhakrishnan laid the foundation for close relationship between India and the Soviet Union.[4]

8.16 In 1952, on his return from the Soviet Union, Radhakrishnan was elected the Vice-President of India. In that position, one of his main functions was to preside over the Rajya Sabha sessions, and he did that in a dignified manner, Often during heated debates, he would intervene with shlokas from the Mahabharata or quotations from the Bible, to cool down the charged atmosphere. As Nehru observed, "By the way in which Dr. Radhakrishnan conducted the proceedings of the Rajya Sabha, he made the meetings of the House look like family gatherings."[5] It was during this time that Radhakrishnan was honored with the Bharat Ratna award, and the international community also honored him by releasing, in USA, the book entitled, "The Philosophy of Dr. Sarvepalli Radhakrishnan." In 1957, he was re-elected as the Vice-President of India.

8.17 Radhakrishnan was elected President of India in 1962. There was a strong demand from the people to celebrate his birthday (5th September) in a big way, Radhakrishnan suggested that his birthday should be celebrated as Teacher's Day. Nehru welcomed this suggestion and observed, "Dr Radhakrishnan has served his country in many capacities. But above all, he is a great teacher from whom all of us have learnt much and will continue to learn. It is India's peculiar privilege to have a great philosopher, a great educationist and a great humanist as her President. That in itself shows the kind of men we honor and respect."[6]

Summary of Radhakrishnan's Contribution to Practical Vedanta

8.18 (a) His books and lectures were a very valuable addition to Vedantic literature.

(b) He helped in bridging the gap between Eastern and Western academicians in the field of religion and philosophy, thus promoting the cause of inter-religious harmony.

(c) He continued the scholarly process, started by Tilak and Aurobindo, of pointing out methodological errors in Shankaracharya's Gita-commentary. An interesting example of how he did this is given below, with reference to shloka 6.3—

Shloka 6.3, when correctly interpreted, has two messages—

1. There are two stages of Lokasamgraha—

   Stage 1 is "duty-bound Lokasamgraha".

   Stage 2 is "spontaneous Lokasamgraha".

   The subtle difference between these two can be understood by means of—

   (i) Paid nurse looking after a baby (usually her duty will be for 8 hours per day).

   (ii) Mother taking care of her own baby (she does it naturally and joyfully for 24 hours per day).

2. The second message of shloka 6.3 is that "karma-samnyasa" is ruled out

   The messages which Shankaracharya derived from shloka 6.3 are the opposite of these two, and therefore can not be accepted.

Notes

1. Internet.
2. S. Radhakrishnan, Indian Philosophy, Volume one, Second edition. Oxford University Press, 2008, p. (xvii).
3. Ibid., p. (xvii).
4. Internet.
5. Internet.
6. Internet.

CHAPTER 9

"Living Vedanta: Will Tuttle and The World Peace Diet"

Will Tuttle, Ph.D., author of The World Peace Diet, called by some "the most important book of the 21st century," is a recipient of the Courage of Conscience Award and the Empty Cages Prize for his decades of spiritual and vegan leadership. Beginning his spiritual journey after college with a pilgrimage on foot in which he explored the self-inquiry used by Ramana Maharshi, he later became a Zen monk and studied many spiritual traditions. He earned a doctorate in philosophy of education at the University of California, Berkeley, in 1988, and since 1990 has travelled internationally promoting the message that veganism is a spiritual revolution with the potential to transform our world to a peaceable, sustainable and compassionate place for all beings. From a March 2015 interview with Susan Pitcairn.

Dr. Will Tuttle

9.1 In ancient India there was a well-established tradition of including animals in the sphere of moral concern. We see this clearly in the ancient Vedantic tradition as well as in the later reforming traditions of 2500 years ago, in the teachings of both Shakyamuni Buddha as well as Mahavir. These Buddhist and Jain traditions developed and rejuvenated the ancient philosophy of *ahimsa*, and specifically promoted the ethic of not owning, killing, or eating animals.

9.2 A modern articulation of ahimsa is veganism and vegan living. The word ahimsa means non-harming, and other ways of saying this are loving kindness, compassion and caring. The sense of deep interrelatedness that the idea of ahimsa expresses is also the foundation of justice, fairness, forgiveness, and of morality generally. It is clear that ahimsa is a primary teaching of all the world's religions. For example, what Jesus taught, in essence, was kindness. Theistic religions have typically emphasized that God is merciful and we are called therefore to be merciful as well, though these religions, as products of herding cultures, predictably tend to exclude animals from the field of moral concern. This central teaching of kindness is also found in non-theistic religions such as Buddhism, Jainism, Taoism, and Confucianism, where it is often more explicitly inclusive of animals.

9.3 This ethic of compassion is foundational and universal, and veganism makes it practical. In vegan living we refrain from owning animals as property, and from harming, killing or eating them. We don't steal their milk, their eggs, their lives, or their purposes. We understand that animals are capable of suffering and that their suffering is significant to them, and in today's world of widespread animal agriculture and abuse, this perennial wisdom of ahimsa is more relevant and urgent than ever.

9.4 Because the common foundation for both spirituality and veganism is ahimsa, vegan ahimsa, as the core of spiritual living, is based upon both ancient teachings as well as upon our modern sensibilities, awareness, rationality, and scientific evidence. It is undeniable that there are now millions of vegans in the world, many raised vegan successfully from birth. This way of eating and living has also been going on for thousands of years and yet, as far as we know, it is somewhat new to have large numbers of people conscientiously choosing a vegan way of living motivated primarily by compassion for animals. In the past it was often because people simply couldn't afford to eat animal-sourced foods, or it was for reasons of personal purity, health, or tradition. Today we see an inspiring movement of people consciously choosing to make an effort to embody the ancient principle of ahimsa, and including animals in their moral concern, even when their culture and upbringing exclude animals.

9.5 It is fascinating to look carefully and discover that we humans are physiologically designed to have optimal health on an organic plant-based diet. Our bodies are not designed to assimilate meat fibres, and we are certainly not designed to digest casein, the main protein in milk. We naturally lack the digestive enzyme rennin, which calves use to digest the casein in their mothers' milk. Additionally, about 75% of us are lactose intolerant as adults, which is normal after the age of weaning. No other species takes the milk of another species, and compared to our long evolution, this is only a recent practice for humans, going back at most about ten thousand years, when we started confining wild sheep, goats, and cows for food.

9.6 Our resourceful bodies will handle meat, dairy and eggs, as best they can, of course, but it's easier for all of us to get the nutrients we need from plant-based sources. It's well understood now that people who eat a well-balanced whole-foods plant-based diet have the best health in general. They have the lowest risk for heart disease, kidney and liver disease, diabetes, obesity, arthritis, and cancer, in addition to other common conditions.

9.7 Even the conservative American Dietetic Association

has recognized that humans in all stages of life—infancy, childhood, adulthood, pregnancy, lactating, and old age—will do fine on well-planned plant-based diets. A recent large-scale study by Kaiser Permanente, the largest health-care provider in the U.S., concluded, "Healthy eating may be best achieved with a plant-based diet, which we define as a regimen that encourages whole, plant-based foods and discourages meats, dairy products, and eggs as well as all refined and processed foods. Physicians should consider recommending a plant-based diet to all their patients, especially those with high blood pressure, diabetes, cardiovascular disease, or obesity."

(http://www.ncbi.nlm.nih.gov/pmc/articles/PMC3662288/)

9.8 We are also learning that such a diet greatly benefits our environment. That's because plant based agriculture is far more efficient. As soon as we bring animals into the equation, we have to feed them. They convert the plants they eat, most of which we could be eating, into acidifying animal protein, saturated fat, and cholesterol, as well as enormous amounts of toxic sewage, and nitrous oxide and methane gas, which are destablizing our climate. The World Bank estimates are that livestock production contributes more to greenhouse gas production than any sector, over fifty percent of the total.

9.9 It is clear that the major ecosystem destruction occurring on our Earth today involving oceans, rain forests, acquifers and water quality, as well as habitat loss, species extinction, and soil erosion, are all attributable primarily to animal agriculture. We are losing about an acre of rain forest every second. Within ten years we could lose the Amazon forest, 91% of which is being razed to graze livestock or to grow crops like soybeans to feed them. This is dangerous not only because rain forests are the lungs of our Earth, converting carbon dioxide to oxygen, but also because the loss of forested areas contributes to regional droughts, climate destabilization, and the destruction of genetic diversity.

9.10 Animal agriculture is also devastating our economy. The large-scale government subsidies of the meat and dairy industries, paid for with taxes, hide the true costs of their products, which would be much higher without subsidies, tax breaks, and other incentives. These subsidies make animal foods more affordable to the general population and yet, as we eat more meat and dairy we are getting more sick, which also consumes more of our health care spending and has harmful economic impacts on virtually everyone, increasing health care costs and the prices of everything. This cluster of economic problems is especially serious in the United States, but it is spreading globally. Ranchers, animal agriculturalists and the chemical, fertilizer, pharmaceutical, and biotechnology industries all work together and they are well connected with large financial institutions, and in many ways these forces determine government policies today more than do the votes and input from citizens. Living a vegan lifestyle, though, is a powerful antidote to all this, especially as we educate and inform our fellow citizens, because today we vote primarily with our wallets.

9.11 India is a telling example of how biotechnology companies like Monsanto aggressively invade societies and farming communities, causing devastation to farmers and ecosystems, and triggering personal and cultural tragedies. One example is the recent flood of farmer suicides due to the seemingly hopeless indebtedness they are forced into, caused by buying Monsanto's expensive genetically-engineered seed. Growing more livestock feed and eating more animal-sourced foods is also causing increased obesity and diabetes in India. As Western financial and cultural pressures promote excessive meat and dairy consumption, grains and vegetables are increasingly being displaced from Indian people's diets. Amazingly, three out of four urban Indians are considered obese today, and diabetes is skyrocketing.

9.12 How does all this fit with the ancient Indian traditions, including Vedanta?

We don't know for sure how India's traditions of treating animals emerged, but it is clear that what is happening in India and elsewhere today is devastating to the animals used for food, leather, and other uses, as well as to ecosystems, wildlife, and water quality, and it is clear that many conditions in India have been rapidly worsening in recent years due to Western influence. Animals used for food—in India or anywhere—are inevitably abused in some fashion.

9.13 For example, I have a friend who is a Jain who went to India recently and spent time talking with people who use cows in the traditional way, and have only one or two cows who seem to be part of the family. He said that when asked two questions these people would become uncomfortable.

9.14 The first question was, "*What do you do with the male calves who are born?*" Usually they would say, "We send them off to market." This is of course a euphemism for slaughter, often requiring a painful journey to another state. Occasionally they may be castrated and used as oxen in the fields, and a few may be kept intact to regularly impregnate the cows so they will keep producing milk.

9.15 The other question that made these farmers uncomfortable was, "*What do you do with your cows when their milk production declines?*" Usually there was one of two reasons. Either they would euphemistically say that they send them off to market, or they would say they let them go to wander in the countryside. However, because of this widespread practice, there are countless half-starved cows who are wandering the Indian landscape eating plastic, garbage, and scraps, and who suffer enormously in their perpetually hungry, miserable lives.

9.16 Mahatma Gandhi said long ago that he refused to eat dairy products because he knew how cows were abused, how farmers with just one or two cows would for example, poke a stick in their vagina to make them produce more milk and things like that. He knew there has always been cruelty in animal agriculture. It's inherent in owning animals as property, because as owners, we are always taking something from them. This includes stealing not just their milk, but also their inherent sovereignty, as well as their power, dignity and purpose.

9.17 Maybe there was a time in the past when people were far more enlightened and there was some kind of a mutual agreement with cows or other animals for this milk relationship with humans. We don't know. But certainly today, understanding how these animals are abused and that there are no nutrients in milk or meat that we need in order to be healthy, we simply don't need to eat animal products.

Happily, we also do not need animal products to create delicious meals. Traditional Indian dishes using ghee or yogurt can be prepared instead with things like coconut milk, cashew cheese, and nut butters. There are also thousands of excellent vegan recipes online from all the world's cuisines, as well as a wealth of cookbooks, videos, booklets, and handouts that teach people how to eat plant-based in a way that prevents and can reverse many diseases. My wife Madeleine has produced one such handout at: *http://www.worldpeacediet.org/intuitivecooking.pdf.*

9.18 I have been a vegan for over 35 years and am far healthier than the average population. This is true for millions of other vegans as well. I have not needed to go to a doctor for decades and enjoy running long distances up and down hills. Many plant-based physicians have successfully treated and reversed chronic disease in their patients with such a plant-based approach. There is abundant information online in videos and essays by doctors like John McDougall, Neal Barnard, Michael Greger, Michael Klaper, Caldwell Esselstyn, Dean Ornish, Joel Fuhrman, and others.

9.19 In terms of world peace, the inefficiency of meat production raises another important issue. Because we are feeding most of the grain we grow to animals—60% in many places and as much as 90% in the United States—right now we could actually feed over twelve billion people if everyone ate a plant-based world peace diet. Yet, a billion of our brothers and sisters are starving or malnourished. By buying and consuming animal products, we are causing long term food insecurity and global hunger, which is a driving force behind war. Interestingly, the original Sanskrit word for war was "*Gavyaa*", which means "the desire for more cows".

9.20 There are also psychological and spiritual ramifications that negatively affect our cultural health. Being taught to eat the flesh and secretions of animals as children desensitizes us to the suffering of the animals involved. This reduces our capacity for awareness, intelligence, and compassion. In addition, the slaughterhouse workers and dairy operators who have to do this work suffer terribly. Slaughterhouse workers, in particular, experience high rates of physical injuries and of abuse, addictions, suicide, and what is referred to as perpetrator-induced traumatic stress disorder.

Objections

9.21 People often ask, "*Isn't there a place for the small farmer to create a balanced ecosystem with a few outdoor chickens, who scratch for bugs, provide manure and eggs, and who seem to have a good life?*" Yes, it is true that hens and other animals can be useful in farming, just as it was useful to have slaves in the American South in the 1840s. But this ownership and theft is a form of violence towards animals, in this case, to birds who have lived freely for millions of years, nesting in the jungles of Southeast Asia without human interference. In the wild, they live in balanced groups with males, females, and chicks together in their forest communities, serving and thriving in their ecological niche. With domestication, these beings are torn out of the living ecosystems and communities they are designed for, and forced into artificial prison settings allowing only females laying eggs, with just one or two roosters at most. The frustration, confusion, and suffering we cause them tend to be invisible to us because we've been taught to look without seeing, viewing chickens merely as producers of something we want.

9.22 Additionally, animal-sourced inputs such as manure and blood meal are not necessary for healthy agricultural systems, as veganic farmers are demonstrating. These farmers eschew animal inputs and chemical fertilizers, and use cover crops, green manures, compost, food forests, and other techniques to successfully produce food and build healthy soil. Veganic farming and gardening is a step beyond organic. Like vegan ways of eating, it has arisen out of the same foundational principles of compassion and respect for all life.

9.23 These principles that inform the attitudes and practices we are talking about here are rooted in *living ahimsa*: dynamic harmlessness and kindness that emerge naturally from our understanding that every being yearns for sovereignty in their life, and for freedom to live according to their inherent nature.

9.24 Another question that comes from some people on a spiritual path concerns karma and reincarnation. It goes something like this: "*What if the souls of these animals have somehow agreed to come to Earth and to serve us in this role?*" Again, this same argument could have been used by slave owners before our societies came to see this as wrong. And even if this was somehow true, it does not give us permission to rape, abuse or kill others.

9.25 We can see that this is a self-serving argument, as are virtually all of the arguments against veganism. We can rationalize many harmful behaviors, especially if we are safely within the established majority with its broadly-accepted official narratives. Those who have power have always created philosophical rationalizations to easily justify their exploitation of others. That's why we have religious traditions such as the idea that God wants us to sacrifice animals and that our reward will be to live in the "land of milk and honey," as in the Old Testament. Or we may have been taught the idea that Krishna gave us cows so that we can drink their milk and so on. Our spiritual test is to liberate others, not to oppress them.

9.26 In India today we can see that cows are mistreated intensely. That's why it's important to question traditions and narratives that lead to abuse. Modern India has the largest number of dairy cows in the world. Huge numbers of spent dairy cows are sent off to the leather industry in Pakistan and states that allow cow slaughter. Workers may break their tails and rub pepper in their eyes to keep them moving, because many are in such poor condition they can barely walk. The cruelty involved is hideous. This little-known situation provides most of the leather in the world, none of which is necessary because today we have good alternatives.

9.27 Opposition to vegan living comes mainly from the fact that many of us are afraid to change and afraid to move beyond comfortable habits and traditions. Perhaps we have a certain self-image, or we are afraid of being seen as different. We may worry about our health, but it has been well documented that we can have equal or better health eating vegan. In some 30 years of travelling and speaking, I have never once heard an argument against veganism or against ending our routine cruelty to animals that had merit.

9.28 The other main source of opposition, of course, is simply self-interest. There are enormous amounts of money involved in animal agriculture and food marketing, as well as in the pharmaceutical and medical industries that profit from our poor health due to our eating animal products.

9.29 Whether we look at it from the point of view of ecological health, physical health, spiritual health, or cultural health, the arguments for adopting a vegan lifestyle are compelling. But the root of the vegan evolution lies in its ethics, in our authentic yearning to minimize our harmfulness to others. Vegan living is the outcome of this yearning for peace, harmony, creativity, freedom, justice, respect, authenticity, love, and greater awareness.

9.30 That's why vegan and Vedantic teachings are intimately connected. The Upanishads are about spiritual awakening, and explore the enlightened understanding that one life lives in all. From that awareness, we see that harming another, whether that being is expressing as a human or as another animal, is harming oneself. That is a foundational teaching and we are called to experience it intuitively to fully understand it.

9.31 It's important to be mindful that accepting the popular idea that "we are one" can also be used to rationalize killing. For example, some of us may say, "I have no problem killing bugs in my garden or eating meat, because I feel at one with them." Ironically, we then tend to avoid information about the animal suffering we're directly causing.

9.32 This convenient limiting of our awareness is easy in a culture like ours that is organized completely around owning and abusing animals. We are part of the confident and unreflective majority. But all this causes a deeper, long-term discomfort in our spiritual being. If we espouse spiritual ideas and nevertheless continue to participate in behaviours we know are abusive and unnecessary, we are not comfortable with ourselves in essential ways. This makes it difficult for us to go deeper into meditation and spiritual realization.

9.33 Another objection is that of survival. Some may say that killing is the way of the world, and that many animals kill others to eat. The truth is that most don't, but either way, it is not a justification for *us* to do so. We don't say it is all right to steal or to rape or to assault someone, just because another person or animal may do that. Some animals will eat their own babies, and some primitive tribes were cannibalistic, but we don't see a man coming home from work, eating his baby for dinner, and saying, "Well, that's what *they* do, so it must be right for me also." We don't go up in trees at night to sleep because some animals do. It's humorous how we pick one behaviour out of countless behaviours that animals have, so we can use it as a justification for our behaviour.

9.34 Perhaps during the ice ages or in extreme climates some people have had to kill animals to survive. It's not however necessary today when food can be shipped and shared all over the world and we have developed greenhouses, permaculture, and other ways to work with varied climates and topography. Even in pretty cold environments we can grow and gather a lot of plant food locally. I once spoke with a Native American woman in a seasonally cold mountainous area in Virginia and she told me that her people's ancestral diet was 99% plant based. Likewise, in the American Southwest the natives relied upon the "three sisters": corn, beans and squash. In any event, whatever happened in the past should not be used to justify our behaviour now. That some people found it necessary to eat meat is not a reason to do so now. Today, it is actually closer to the truth to say that our collective survival is more dependent upon us *not* eating meat and dairy, and not harming animals.

9.35 We are called to live according to our own true nature, which at its heart is joy and compassion. No one as an infant, unconditioned by culture, has the urge to attack and rip apart a squirrel for food, or to suckle from a female of another specifies. This is clearly contrary to our inherent nature.

9.36 Our awareness of our essential wisdom and compassion has, unfortunately, been strongly reduced by the meal rituals of our societies that force us as children to eat animal foods. This has reduced our ability to connect with ourselves authentically, to realize the essential beauty and abundance of the Earth, and to celebrate the fact that we can feed everyone on a fraction of the land and resources we use today.

The Urgency of Change

9.37 This brings us to the urgency of getting the vegan message to as many people as possible, as effectively as we can. The global spread of the Western diet, which is devastatingly heavy in meat, dairy and eggs, has taken a huge toll not only on the environment and on our health, but also on the inner landscape of our awareness and our natural wisdom and compassion. This impedes our social well-being.

9.38 If we effectively communicate the vegan message of compassion, sustainability, freedom, justice, and equality—not only for humans but for animals and everyone—then we will be able to heal our relationship with other species and each other, and create foundations for healthy families, ecosystems, and societies, as well as for our own health. We will be able to reduce obesity, diabetes, cardiovascular disease, cancer, mental stress, and many aspects of social malaise. Without vegan living, the odds of human civilizations surviving are decreasing every passing year. Fortunately, we have the capacity to turn this around quickly if we continue our effort to understand and to fully embody the vegan ahimsa message of radical inclusion and respect and kindness for all.

9.39 The beauty of the vegan message is that when we hear these ideas they resonate with us at a deep level. We all know these things in our bones. We know deep down that what we do to others does come back to us. We all know that our life is meant to be an expression of our unique talents and gifts for the good of all. It is not in our interest to numb our feelings and become shallow and insouciant consumers, exploiting others and ecosystems and reducing our awareness.

9.40 Animal agriculture takes us in this destructive direction. It is based upon dominating and exploiting other living beings in order to get what I want for myself. Both spirituality and rationality bring us to the same conclusion, that we don't *have* to live in this way, which reinforces the delusion of essential separateness. Through vegan living we can create societies based upon equality, justice, sustainability and caring for everyone: for animals, for workers, for each other, for wildlife, and for future generations. Our future potential is calling us to awaken from the cultural trance of reducing beings to mere commodities to be used and eaten.

9.41 What I have tried to do for several decades is to show that veganism is a spiritual path, and also that any spiritual path requires us to embrace vegan living, which is the non-violent ethic of ahimsa. Because of this work some have called me the father of vegan spirituality. Fortunately, the connection between veganism and spirituality has become obvious to ever-increasing numbers of others as well.

9.42 It has been heartening to see brothers and sisters from cultures around the world resonating with this message, and articulating it in unique and creative ways. We are increasingly realizing that this is not merely a personal message. Rather, it is a message from the universal intelligence abiding within us. It guides and elevates us so that we can awaken from delusion, heal our minds, hearts, and relationships, discover our proper place here, and finally unfold our hitherto hidden purpose on this beautiful, abundant, and wounded Earth.

Notes

1. This chapter is written by Dr. Will Tuttle, based on the following book—

Will Tuttle, The World Peace Diet: Eating for Spiritual Health and Social Harmony. Lantern Books, New York, 2005.

2. In 2014, we sent him a copy of our book "Anu-Gita in the Mahabharata", which recommended a Vegan diet more than 2000 years ago. Dr. Tuttle found this book relevant, as he wrote in the following "Endorsement"—

Endorsement - *The Anu-Gita* and *Selections from the Mahabharata* by Satya and Urmila Agarwal.

By Dr. Will Tuttle

"What an inspiring revelation to read the ancient sacred text, *The Anu-Gita*, translated and published by Satya and Urmila Agarwal, in which the sages of India over 2,000 years ago recommended that human beings eat a vegan diet with no meat and animal-sourced foods. The Anu-Gita is part of the great Mahabharata, and Satya and Urmila have also translated and published *Selections from the Mahabharata* that contain a chapter recommending a meatless diet. Anyone interested in a deeper understanding of the roots of vegetarianism and veganism in our world today will find these two books by the Agarwals to be helpful and valuable contributions."

Dr. Will Tuttle, Ph.D., award-winning author of the best-selling The World Peace Diet, *is a pianist, composer, former Zen monk, and cofounder of the Prayer Circle for Animals.*

CHAPTER 10

Suggested Formulation of Practical Vedanta for the 21st Century

10.1 Before we present our suggestions, we want to have a quick look at the first nine chapters of this book. Chapter 1 lists ten points in Shankaracharya's Vedanta, in respect of which the concept of practicality has been developed in the last 120 years. Chapter 2 points out how a march towards practicality was initiated by Vivekananda in 1896, when he delivered four lectures in London saying that they will form a 'basis' of his vision of Practical Vedanta. For us, the word 'Practical' conveys the message that Vedanta will be updated so as to be relevant today. Chapters 3-9 describe how seven scholars and activists, who followed Vivekananda, continued the updating process.

10.2 Our suggested formulation is in respect of the ten points listed in Chapter 1. Point-by-point, we pick up suggestions from chapters 2-9. We consider it necessary to add thereto our own "humble ideas". Keeping in view the convenience of readers, we present two variants—

(a) Formulation at a glance

(b) Formulation in detail

Since many Vedantins in India are not comfortable with English language, we write the suggestions in Sanskrit also — in fact, we first present the Sanskrit version, and then the English one.

10.3 प्रस्ताविता परिभाषा व्यावहारिकवेदान्तस्य — दशांगिका प्रस्तुतिः

प्रथमः प्रकारः —परिभाषा संक्षिप्तरूपेण

I के के मुख्य-मुख्य-मंत्राः ?

महावाक्यानि शाश्वतानि परन्तु जगत्-मिथ्या कदापि न।

II पुरुषार्थानां परिभाषायां किंचित् परिवर्तनम् ?

अधुना पुरुषार्थयोः नवीना भाषा वांछिता।

धर्मः सर्वहितकरः जीवन्मुक्तिः चतुर्थश्च॥

III ज्ञानस्य का परिभाषा ?

ज्ञानं अर्थात् भेदभावनाशः।

आचारो यस्य भेदभावरहितः स हि ज्ञानी।

IV सात्त्विककर्मणः का परिभाषा ?

सात्त्विकं कर्म अर्थात् सर्वभूतहितकरं कर्म।

V जीवनलक्ष्यस्य का परिभाषा ?

जीवनलक्ष्यं जगत्-हितं — आध्यात्मिकं लौकिकं चापि।

VI भिन्नभिन्नयोगात् का उपलब्धिः ?

कर्मभक्तिज्ञानयोगाः समन्विताः श्रीगीतासु।

तथापि जगत्-हिताय कर्मयोगो विशिष्यते॥

व्यावहारिके वेदान्ते तु न हि कर्मसंन्यासः।

VII दीनानां हिताय का विधिः ?

दीनानां हिताय सेवायोगः।

न सेवा दैन्यभावेन नाहंकारमानेच्छया।

हरिरूपदरिद्राय मत्वैवं ज्ञानप्रेरिता॥

VIII मानवाधिकारं प्रति का दृष्टिः ?

मानवाधिकारप्राप्तिकांक्षा समर्थनीया — परन्तु

अहिंसाप्रयोगः अनिवार्यः।

IX विश्वशान्तिं प्रति का दृष्टिः ?

विश्वशान्त्यै परा चेष्टा कर्तव्या।

X के के आधारूपाः ग्रन्थाः ?

प्रस्थानत्रयस्त्वाधारः शंकराचार्यशिक्षायाः।

वर्तमाने वांछनीया शान्तिपर्वानुगीतापि।

पंचशास्त्रोपयोगो ह्याधाररूपेण संज्ञितः॥

10.4 Suggested Formulation of Practical Vedanta for the 21st century—Ten-point Presentation.

First Variant—Formulation at a glance

I What are the main mantras?

Practical Vedanta whole-heartedly respects the Mahavakyas— but Shankaracharya's doctrine of jagat-mithya is ruled out.

II Is there a need for any change in the definition of Purusharthas?

Yes, two Purusharthas are redefined—

(a) Dharma is redefined as service to the world.

(b) Moksha is redefined as jivan-mukti.

III What is the definition of jnana?

Jnana is re-defined as discrimination-free behaviour.

IV What is the definition of sattvika karma?

Sattvika karma is re-defined as karma for jagad-hitam.

V What is the goal of human life?

The goal of human life is to serve the society — covering both spiritual and secular aspects.

VI What is the role of different yogas?

Although Karma-Bhakti-Jnana-Yogas are harmonized in the Gita, still, for purposes of jagad-hitam, Karma-yoga receives top priority.

Karma-samnyasa is ruled out.

VII How to help the poor?

By doing Seva, seeing God in the poor.

VIII What about human rights?

Human rights are supported, but the demand for rights must be made nonviolently.

IX What about World Peace?

All possible efforts should be made to promote the cause of world peace?

X What are the basic texts?

Prasthanatraya (i.e. Upanisads, Brahmasutras, and Bhagavad-Gita) are widened to Pancha-Shastra (by adding ShantiParva and Anu-Gita).

10.5 प्रस्ताविता परिभाषा व्यावहारिकवेदान्तस्य — दशांगिका प्रस्तुतिः

द्वितीयः प्रकारः — परिभाषा विस्तृतरूपेण

I के के मुख्य-मुख्य-मंत्राः ?

1. नासतो सद् जायते
2. एकं सत्। प्रभवः प्रलयः स्थानम्।
3. सर्वं खल्विदं ब्रह्म। अनादिमत्परं ब्रह्म। प्रज्ञानं ब्रह्म।
4. ब्रह्माण्डे पूर्णनियमः। सृष्टिः ब्रह्माधारिता। ईशावास्यमिदं सर्वं। जगत् मिथ्या कदापि न।
5. जगत्-मिथ्या-निरूपणं कारणं पलायनस्य।

अरविन्दमतमेतत् तिलकस्यापि तथैव।
परोक्षरूपेण प्रोक्तं जगत्-हित-शिक्षयापि॥

6. ममैवांशो जीवलोके जीवभूत: सनातन:।
अयमात्मा ब्रह्म। अहं ब्रह्मास्मि। तत्त्वमसि।
अमृतस्य पुत्रा: सर्वे मानवा: इति संदेश: विवेकानन्दस्य।

7. ब्रह्मरूपा: विशुद्धात्मा: पातकीभावो नोचित:।
न हि स्वर्गप्रलोभनं तथा न नरकभयम्॥

8. मयाध्यक्षेण प्रकृति: सूयते सचराचरम्।
ब्रह्म मूलं जगत् वृक्षो जीव उभयसेवक:।
मानवसेवा हि माधवसेवा।

9. मुख्यमुख्यमंत्राणां तु चयनं बुद्धियोगेन।
देशकालपात्रोचितं जनकल्याणकारकम्॥

10. केवलं ह्यात्मोद्धारस्तु न हि पर्याप्तं सर्वेभ्य:।
अभ्युदयस्य संदेश: वांछित: लोकयात्रायै॥

10.6. II पुरुषार्थानां परिभाषायां किंचित् परिवर्तनम्?

11. अधुना पुरुषार्थयो: नवीना भाषा वांछिता।
धर्म: सर्वहितकर: जीवन्मुक्ति: चतुर्थश्च॥

12. मोक्षप्राप्ति: संशयिता विदेहमुक्तिरूपेण।
मृत्युपरान्तमोक्षस्तु न हि विज्ञानसम्मत:॥

13. आर्षवाक्यमिव मतमेतद् जनकभार्याया:।
वर्णितं ह्यनुगीतायां श्रीवैशम्पायनमुखात्॥

14. जीवन्मुक्त्या: महिमा च प्रोक्ता श्रीगीतायामपि।
इहैव तैर्जित: सर्गो येषां साम्ये स्थितं मन:।
निर्दोषं हि समं ब्रह्म तस्माद् ब्रह्मणि ते स्थिता:॥

10.7. III ज्ञानस्य का परिभाषा?

15. अधुना संज्ञितं ज्ञानं येन भेदभावनाश:।

आचारो यस्य तद्रूपः स हि ज्ञानी सुनिश्चितः॥

16. संलग्नाः भेदनाशार्थे ज्ञानिनः रूढिमुक्ताः ये।
पण्डिताः समदर्शिनः सम्मानिताः श्रीगीतासु॥

17. ज्ञानस्य परिभाषार्थं रूढिभावस्तु नोचितः।
नेतिभावो नवभावो वांछितो हि वर्तमाने।
शिक्षाप्रदः ह्यरविन्दः राधाकृष्णन् तिलकश्च॥

18. नवीनज्ञानेन मुक्तिः रूढिग्रस्तकुशासनात्।
जनानां हृदये कांक्षा जनतंत्रशासनाय।

10.8. IV सात्त्विककर्मणः का परिभाषा?

19. सात्त्विककर्मणो भाषा कथिता ह्यनुगीतायाम्।
सर्वभूतहितं प्रोक्तं सात्त्विककर्मलक्षणम्॥

20. नवीना भाषा कर्मणः सद्गुणसम्पान्निता हि।
दैवीसम्पत्-मिश्रितापि वर्णिता ह्यनुगीतायाम्॥

10.9. V जीवनलक्ष्यस्य का परिभाषा?

21. लक्ष्यं सर्वभूतहितं ह्याध्यात्मिकं लौकिकं च।
सर्वहितं समानार्थी लोकसंग्रहशब्दस्य।
लोकसंग्रहकर्माणि कर्तव्यानि यथाशक्ति॥

22. कर्मणा लोकसंग्रहः शिक्षा भगवद्गीतायाः।
आप्नोति स जीवन्मुक्तिं निःस्पृहः कर्मयोगी यः।
जीवन्मुक्तो योगारूढः सर्वभूतहिते रतः॥

23. जीवन्मुक्त्याः परिभाषा लोकसंग्रहाधारिता।
कार्यभावात् परं गतः ह्याचारः स्वतःप्रेरितः।
महात्मागांधिनापि च ह्युच्चादर्शः प्रस्थापितः॥

24. भक्तानपि ह्याश्वासनमुद्घोषितं श्रीकृष्णेन।
ते प्राप्नुवन्ति मामेव सर्वभूतहिते रताः॥

10.10. VI भिन्न-भिन्नयोगात् का उपलब्धिः?

25. कर्मभक्तिज्ञानयोगाः समन्विताः श्रीगीतासु।
तथापि जगद्-हिताय कर्मयोगो विशिष्यते॥

26. समन्वयः कथं कृतः ज्ञानकर्मसमुच्चयात्।
भक्तिकर्मसमुच्चयात् ध्यानकर्मसमुच्चयात्।
व्यावहारिके वेदान्ते तु न हि कर्मसंन्यासः॥

27. ईशा-उपनिषदि कर्मयोगः प्रतिष्ठितः—
ईशावास्यमिदं सर्वं यत्किंच जगत्यां जगत्।
तेन त्यक्तेन भुंजीथा मा गृधः कस्यस्विद्धनम्॥1॥
कुर्वन्नेवेह कर्माणि जिजीविषेत् शतं समाः।
एवं त्वयि नान्यथेतोऽस्ति न कर्म लिप्यते नरे॥2॥

28. छांदोग्य-उपनिषद्यपि कर्मयोगः सम्मानितः—
आचार्यकुलाद्वेदमधीत्य यथाविधानं गुरोः
कर्मातिशेषेणाभिसमावृत्य कुटुम्बे शुचौ देशे
स्वाध्यायमधीयानो धार्मिकान्विदधदात्मनि
सर्वेन्द्रियाणि सम्प्रतिष्ठाप्य अहिंसन् सर्वभूतानि
स खल्वेवं वर्तयन्यावदायुषं ब्रह्मलोकमभिसम्पद्यते
न च पुनरावर्तते॥8.15॥

29. संन्यासशब्दप्रयोगात् कर्मत्यागो न संज्ञितः।
अनाश्रितः कर्मफलं कार्यं कर्म करोति यः।
स संन्यासी च योगी च न निरग्निर्न चाक्रियः॥

30. कर्मयोगसमानार्थी गीतानुरूपः स्वधर्मः।
स्वधर्मपालनं ज्ञेयं निश्चितं सात्त्विकं कर्म॥

31. कर्मणैव हि संसिद्धिं आस्थिता जनकादयः।
स्थितप्रज्ञो जीवन्मुक्तः कर्मयोगी न संन्यासी॥

10.11. VII दीनानां हिताय का विधिः ?

32. अधुना कर्मयोगस्य समानार्थी सेवायोगः।

ऋणवन्तः सदा मर्त्याः संदेशो ह्यनुगीतायाः।
मतं विवेकानन्दस्य गांधीमहात्मनश्चापि॥

33. न सेवा दैन्यभावेन नाहंकारमानेच्छया।
हरिरूपदरिद्राय मत्वैवं ज्ञानप्रेरिता॥

10.12. VIII मानवाधिकारं प्रति का दृष्टिः ?

34. अधिकारः सुकर्मणि श्रीगीतायां सम्मानितः।
देशकालपात्रोचिताः ह्यधिकाराः नवरूपाः।
साफल्यं हि प्रयासस्य संविधानसंशोधनात्॥

35. जातिभेदाः रंगभेदाः वर्तमाने वर्जनीयाः।
आचारः साम्यभावात् हि समानाधिकाराश्रितः॥

36. अधुना गीताधर्मोऽपि ज्ञेयो वर्णभेदमुक्तः।
अस्पृश्यवर्गस्योन्नतिः ह्यधिकाराः विशेषतः॥

37. अधिकाराश्रिता सेवा क्रान्त्यनुरूपः संदेशः।
दानं देयं दीनेभ्यस्तु शिक्षा ह्यंधरूढिग्रस्ता॥

38. तथैवादिवासीनां हि शिक्षास्वास्थ्योपलब्धिश्च।
आर्थिके क्षेत्रेऽपि सेवा समानाधिकाराश्रिता॥

39. अहिंसाप्रेरिता यदि ह्यधिकारप्राप्तिकांक्षा।
पराधीनदेशानां च स्वतंत्रताप्राप्तिकांक्षा।
पूर्णतः समर्थनीया नवरूपवेदान्तेन॥

40. परिस्थितिः सामाजिकी बाहुल्येन कुरीतीनाम्।
अंधशिक्षाप्रचारात् च धर्मध्वजसमावृतैः॥

41. विषमा ह्यतिदुःखदा नारीभ्यस्तु विशेषतः।
महिलाधिकारप्राप्तिः समर्थनीया सर्वत्र॥

42. तथैव बालबालानां शिक्षाविकासाधिकाराः।
सुरक्षितव्याः सर्वत्र सर्वैश्च हितकामिभिः।
सेवाधिकाराः वृद्धानां विकलांगानां पात्राणाम्॥

43. पशूनां प्रत्यपि न्यायो वेदान्तेन समर्थित:।
पशुहत्याविरोध्स्तु प्रयासो जटिलतम:॥

10.13. IX विश्वशान्तिं प्रति का दृष्टि: ?

44. विश्वशान्त्यै परा चेष्टा कर्तव्या भेदनाशार्थं।
शान्तिपर्वाधारितै: वा वेदान्तिकै: ग्रन्थै: चापि।
विश्वशान्तिप्रदा नीति: श्रीगीताया: ध्रुवा नीति:॥

45. परस्परसंवादेन कुर्यात् निर्वैरस्थापनम्।
सर्वधर्मसमत्वेन ह्यन्त:राष्ट्रमैत्रभाव:॥

46. विश्वशान्तिस्थापनाय ह्यहिंसायोगो वांछित:।
पशूनां प्रत्यप्यहिंसा विश्वशान्तिप्रयासश्च॥

47. वेदान्तज्ञानप्रचार: भिन्नभिन्नभाषायां हि।
शान्तिभाववर्धनाय विद्यालयेषु कर्तव्य:॥

48. विश्वशान्तिस्थापनाय ह्यातंकशासनाद् मुक्ति:।
जनतंत्रशासनं हि राष्ट्रसंघसमर्थितम्॥

49. पर्यावरणस्य शुद्धि: विश्वशान्त्यै हि वांछिता।
फलमूलभोजनस्य प्रचार: शुद्धिकारक:।
फलमूलभोजनमित्यनुगीताया: सन्देश:॥

10.14. X के के आधाररूपा: ग्रन्था: ?

50. प्रस्थानत्रयस्तवाधार: शंकराचार्यशिक्षाया:।
वर्तमाने वांछनीया शान्तिपर्वानुगीतापि।
पंचशास्त्रोपयोगो ह्याधाररूपेण संज्ञित:॥

10.15 Suggested Formulation of Practical Vedanta for the 21st Century: Ten-point Presentation

Second Variant—Formulation in detail

I What are the main mantras?

There are ten sub-groups of mantras. For purposes of explaining them in English, it is convenient to present them in five instalments (viz. 1-4, 5, 6-7, 8, 9-10).

10.16 Sub-groups 1-4

Aurobindo's explanation is given below—

(a) The Divine being does not create the universe out of nothingness or a void. Out of Himself He creates, therefore all forms are essentially Brahman.[1]

(b) The perfect orderliness in the universe is because of its Divine origin.[2]

(c) According to the Gita, jagat is real (not mithya), a creation of the Supreme.[3]

(d) Shankaracharya ignored Isha-upanishad when he declared jagat as mithya.

10.17 Sub-group 5

(a) Aurobindo wrote in "Essays on the Gita"—
If you accept the jagat-mithya doctrine, then you get the wrong message of escapism.[4]

(b) Tilak blamed Shankaracharya for supporting Samnyasa — the society suffered because the number of Karmayogins contributing to socio-economic development went down.

(c) Vivekananda implicity rejected the jagat-mithya doctrine when he emphasized jagad-hitam—if people were to believe that jagat is mithya, then they would not attach much importance to jagad-hitam.

10.18 Sub-groups 6-7

(a) While addressing the Parliament of World Religions, Vivekananda gave the message of fearlessness—Listen to the confidence-building message of Vedanta—human beings are not sinners—all of them have the Atman, and are therefore divine.

(b) Vedanta declares that all people have their

origin in Brahman, and in Brahman they will merge after death—therefore, there is no need to be afraid of hell.

10.19 Sub-group 8

Practical Vedanta puts forward a modified doctrine in Sanskrit, which can be translated as—

Brahman is the root of the world-tree, and the role of individuals is to serve both—particularly serve the poor, seeing God in them. Serving God means serving the poor.

10.20 Sub-groups 9-10

(a) Shankaracharya wrote in his "Introduction to Gita-commentary" that the message of the Gita is two-fold—

(i) nihsreyasa i.e. attainment of perfection by the individual.

(ii) abhyudaya i.e. social upliftment.

But in the "commentary" itself, he ignored abhyudaya. Thus there is inconsistency between the "Introduction" and the "Commentary".

(b) Practical Vedanta removes this inconsistency by picking up those mantras which emphasize abhyudaya.

10.21 II Is there a need for any change in the definition of Purusharthas?

(a) Yes, two Purusharthas are redefined—

(i) Dharma is redefined as service to the world, following the example of Gandhi.

(ii) Moksa is re-defined as jivan-mukti, as recommended by Anu-Gita shloka 7.12 which says—

Aiming at moksa is an irrational idea of doubtful veracity. Jivan-mukti by helping others is rational, because that is while living and therefore verifiable. But moksa after death is non-verifiable (because no one knows what will happen after death).[5]

(b) Bhagavad-Gita shloka 5.19 glorifies jivan-mukti.

10.22 II What is the definition of jnana?

(a) Shankaracharya defined jnana as atma-jnana, that is, knowledge of the identity of Atman and Brahman. He used Bhagavad-Gita chapter 4, but ignored chapter 13.

(b) Radhakrishnan says that chapter 13 can not be ignored, particularly shlokas 13.7-11, which declare that jnana includes the practice of the moral virtues. Mere theoretical knowledge will not do. Therefore, jnana is redefined as discrimination-free-behavior.

(c) Gita shloka 5.18 declares that a man of knowledge is Samadarshi i.e. his behavior is discrimination-free.

(d) Tagore says that we must view jnana as infinite knowledge which has no end-point.[6]

(e) An important purpose of jnana is to update old commentaries on the Gita and to ensure their relevance today.

(f) Practical Vedanta incoporates new ideas which are consistent with the philosophy of one-ness of all beings. Concepts of "democracy, and liberty-equality-fraternity" are included in Practical Vedanta.

10.23 IV What is the definition of Sattvika karma?

Sattvika karma is redefined as karma for jagad-hitam. This is the teaching of Anu-Gita, shloka 12.1.

10.24 V What is the goal of human life?

(a) The goal of human life is to serve the society, covering both spiritual and secular aspects.

(b) Vivekananda included secular aspects when he specified the role of Ramakrishna Mission in 1897.

(c) Gandhi said, "For me, the road to salvation lies through incessant toil in the service of my country and humanity"

(d) Common people need not feel any pressure, because Gita shloka 18.25 clarifies that service activities should be yatha-shakti i.e. consistent with one's capacity.

10.25 VI What is the role of different yogas?

(a) Although Karma-Bhakti-Jnana-Yogas are harmonized in the Gita, still, for purposes of jagad-hitam, Karma-yoga receives top priority.

(b) Tilak's Gita-Rahasya is called "Karma-Yoga-Shastra".

(c) Gita Shloka 3.19 explicitly declares that Karma-yoga leads to Perfection. So Shankaracharya's statement that Karmayoga leads to Chitta-shuddhi, can not be accepted.

(d) Shankaracharya says that, after Perfection, a state of Karma-samnyasa is reached. He says that Gita shloka 6.3 gives this message. But Radhakrishnan has explained that the message of shloka 6.3 is— Lokasamgraha leads to Perfection, and then a Perfect person performs Lokasamgraha spontaneously. He has pointed out methodological errors in Shankaracharya's commentary on shloka 6.3.

(e) Shankaracharya's statement, that all the upanisads support Karma-samnyasa, is not acceptable, because we have quoted Isha-upanisad (mantras 1-2) and Chandogya upanisad (mantra 8.15), which reject Shankaracharya's statement.

(f) Shankaracharya says that Sthitaprajna is a monk. He ignored Janaka who was a Karmayogi Sthitaprajna.

10.26 VII How to help the poor?

(a) By seva, seeing God in the poor.

(b) Vivekananda coined the expression Daridra-Narayana' to give this message.

(c) Gandhi also used the expression 'Daridra-Narayana'.

(d) Shankaracharya advised people to give 'Danam' (charity) to the poor. This is an out dated concept.

10.27 VIII What about human rights?

(a) Practical Vedanta supports human rights, but the demand for rights must be made non-violently.

(b) Human Rights Commission of the United Nations is trying to obtain support for human rights in all the countries. Practical Vedanta extends its support to this effort.

10.28 IX What about World Peace?

(a) Practical Vedanta recognizes that World Peace is an integral part of jagad-hitam.

(b) United Nations has sought help, not only from governments, but also from religious leaders. Inter-faith dialogues are being held, and Vedantins can make a very useful contribution.

(c) Shanti-Parva of the Mahabharata contains useful suggestions.[7] They should be made available to United Nations.

(d) Will Tuttle has recently come forward with the pioneering idea of 'World Peace Diet'. This is summarized in Chapter Nine of this book.

10.29 X What are the basic texts?

Shankaracharya used three basic texts, called Prasthanatraya (Upanisads, Brahmasutras, and Bhagavad-Gita). Practical Vedanta expands its coverage to new areas like Human Rights and World Peace. We therefore add two more texts, viz Shanti Parva, and Anu-Gita (both from the Mahabharata). Prasthanatraya are thus widened to Pancha-Shastra (i.e. five basic texts).

10.30 **Concluding Remarks**

While concluding this chapter and this book, we would like to say that a ten-point modification in Vedanta-formulation can be viewed as an inevitable outcome of big changes that have occurred in 1200 years (as predicted in the desh-kala-patra message of the Gita). In fact, periodical modification may be needed in future also, to keep Vedanta up-to-date at all times, so that Practical Vedanta is rightfully honored by scholars all over the world as Universal Vedanta.

Notes

1. Aurobindo, Essays on the Gita, op. cit., p. 333.
2. Ibid., p. 331.
3. Ibid., p. 426.
4. Ibid., p. 558.
5. Satya P. Agarwal and Urmila Agarwal, Anu-Gita in the Mahabharata. Motilal Banarsidass, Delhi, 2014, p. 56.
6. Ramachandra Guha (ed.) Makers of Modern India. The Belknap Press of Harvard University Press, 2011, p. 173.
7. Satya P. Agarwal, The World Peace Agenda. Based on Shanti-Parva of the Mahabharata. Motilal Banarsidass, Delhi, 2007.

Books by the Authors

ANU-GITA IN THE MAHABHARATA
ISBN: 978-81-7822-4688

APAD-DHARMA IN THE MAHABHARATA
ISBN: 978-81-7822-3612

GITA AND TULASI-RAMAYANA
ISBN: 978-81-208-1752-4

GITA FOR THE TWENTY-FIRST CENTURY
ISBN: 978-81-7822-1535

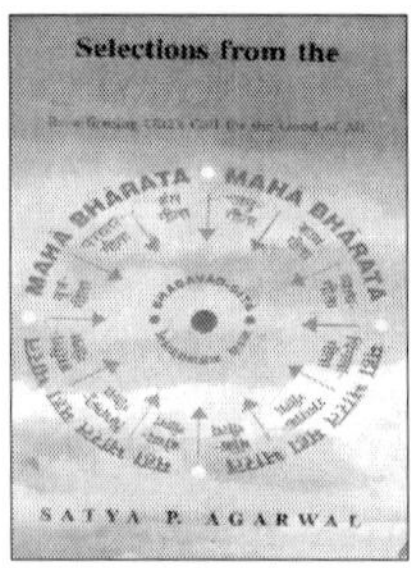

SELECTION FROM THE MAHABHARATA
ISBN: 978-81-208-1874-3

SOCIAL MESSAGE OF THE GITA
ISBN: 978-81-208-1319-9

SOCIAL MESSAGE OF MAHAYANA BUDDHISM
ISBN: 978-81-7822-3841

SOCIAL ROLE OF THE GITA HOW & WHY
ISBN: 978-81-208-1524-7

WORLD PEACE AGENDA
ISBN: 978-81-7822-3087